The Re-Imagined Text

The Re-Imagined Text

Shakespeare, Adaptation,
& Eighteenth-Century
Literary Theory

Jean I. Marsden

THE UNIVERSITY PRESS OF KENTUCKY

Copyright © 1995 by The University Press of Kentucky

Scholarly publisher for the Commonwealth,
serving Bellarmine College, Berea College, Centre
College of Kentucky, Eastern Kentucky University,
The Filson Club, Georgetown College, Kentucky
Historical Society, Kentucky State University,
Morehead State University, Murray State University,
Northern Kentucky University, Transylvania University,
University of Kentucky, University of Louisville,
and Western Kentucky University.

Editorial and Sales Offices: Lexington, Kentucky 40508-4008

Library of Congress Cataloging-in-Publication Data
Marsden, Jean I.
  The re-imagined text : Shakespeare, adaptation, and eighteenth-century literary theory / Jean I. Marsden.
    p. cm.
  Includes bibliographical references (p.   ) and index.
  1. Shakespeare, William, 1564-1616—Criticism and interpretation—History—18th century. 2. Shakespeare, William, 1564-1616—Adaptations—History and criticism. 3. English drama—18th century—History and criticism—Theory, etc. 4. English drama—Adaptations—History and criticism. 5. Criticism—Great Britain—History—18th century. 6. Theater—Great Britain—History—18th century. 7. Literary form. I. Title.
PR2968.M37   1995
822.3'3—dc20   94-3399

This book is printed on acid-free recycled paper meeting
the requirements of the American National Standard
for Permanence of Paper for Printed Library Materials. ∞

For my MOTHER
and in loving memory of
my FATHER

Contents

Acknowledgments ix

Introduction 1

Part I: The Re-Imagined Text

1 Radical Adaptation 13

2 The Beginnings of Shakespeare Criticism 47

Part II: Refined from the Dross

3 Adaptation in Decline 75

4 Criticism at Mid-Century 103

5 The Search for a Genuine Text 127

Conclusion 150

Appendix 155

Notes 157

Index 187

Acknowledgments

I would like to thank a variety of people and institutions who helped make this book possible. First, the research for this book was supported by a Danforth Award from the Harvard English Department and by grants from the University of Connecticut Research Foundation and the American Philosophical Society. The project began under the guidance of Walter Jackson Bate and of Gywnne Blakemore Evans, for whose encouragement over the years I am deeply grateful. My readers for the University Press of Kentucky also deserve special recognition for their detailed and constructive comments on the manuscript. In particular, I would like to thank my editor, Nancy Grayson Holmes, for her friendship and for her faith in this project.

Fellow reception scholars Margreta de Grazia and Howard Felperin both read earlier versions of this book, as did Lennard Davis. Michael Dobson, who more than anyone else shares my enthusiasm for obscure bits of Shakespeariana, deserves a special note; over the course of several years he has shared his work and assisted with mine. I would also like to thank Noelle Arrangoiz, Anne Goldgar, and Susan Stacey for their intellectual support and unfailing patience. At the University of Connecticut, I have been fortunate in the support of my colleagues; Raymond Anselment and Margaret Higonnet read the entire book and generously gave me advice and encouragement while John Abbott, Patrick Colm Hogan, and Thomas Recchio cheerfully read portions of the manuscript. In addition, I am grateful for the efforts of my research assistants Dennis Lazor, Patricia Pallis, Julie Pfeiffer, Monica Hatzberger, and Hilary Hodgkins.

My greatest debt is and always will be to Lane Barrow, who has lived with this project since its inception and not only read every page (and commented rigorously upon it) but provided me with the moral support that in the end enabled me to finish.

Portions of this book have appeared in earlier publications. Part of chapter 1 appeared as "Rewritten Women: Shakespeare Heroines in the Restoration" in *The Appropriation of Shakespeare: Post-Renaissance Recon-*

structions of the Works and the Myth (Harvester Wheatsheaf, 1991), and a segment of chapter 5 appeared as "The Individual Reader and the Canonized Text: Shakespeare Criticism after Johnson" in *Eighteenth-Century Life* 17 (1993):1. I am grateful to these publications for permission to reprint this material.

The Re-Imagined Text

Introduction

The Restoration and eighteenth century produced one of the most subversive acts in literary history—the rewriting and restructuring of Shakespeare's plays. We have all heard of Nahum Tate's "audacious" adaptation of *King Lear* with its resoundingly happy ending, but Tate was only one of a score of playwrights who adapted Shakespeare's plays. Between 1660 and 1777, more than fifty adaptations appeared in print and on the stage, works in which playwrights augmented, substantially cut, or completely rewrote the original plays. The plays were staged with new characters, new scenes, new endings, and, underlying all this novelty, new words.[1]

Early playwrights and critics, it seemed, saw Shakespeare's plays as plastic material which could be remolded at will, but this attitude changed in the course of the eighteenth century. Fewer playwrights wrote or produced adaptations and the text itself changed less and less.[2] Adaptations which made substantial changes were not written after the 1780s, and by the end of the eighteenth century, only a few adaptations were still being performed: Tate's *King Lear* appeared until 1836, Garrick's *Catherine and Petruchio* until 1887, and elements of his *Romeo and Juliet* until 1884.[3] Cibber's *Richard III* endured into the twentieth century, and its ghost still haunts us each time Olivier's Richard III cries, "Off with his head. So much for Buckingham."[4]

Why did this happen? Were Restoration and eighteenth century audiences really deaf to Shakespeare's genius and did true taste only appear with the romantic poets? Obviously not. But the adaptations are more than an embarrassing group of obscure plays symbolizing the Enlightenment's poetic bad taste. Not only are they the Shakespeare that most theater-goers in the Restoration and eighteenth century saw on the stage, more importantly, they are also a manifestation of the period's perception of Shakespeare, and as such they demonstrate an important evolution both in the definition of poetic language and of the idea of what constitutes a literary work.

Today the idea of changing Shakespeare's words seems blasphemous; not only do we revere Shakespeare, with our reverence centering on his text, but twentieth-century theory in general has focused almost exclusively on the printed word. Modern theorists have pronounced the death of the author, disclaiming the restrictions of authorial intention and leaving us with only the text.[5] The sanctity of the text has become so firmly established in our consciousness that we shudder at the thought of altering a writer's words. Criticism under these assumptions has consisted of a series of varying interpretations of an unchanging literary work. In contrast, the later seventeenth century, though it held Shakespeare in high regard, did not defer to his text. As Dryden wrote in the "Preface" to *Fables*, "words are not like landmarks, so sacred as never to be removed."[6] Yet, although our performances of Shakespeare reflect our reverence for the written word, even without changing the text twentieth-century stagings alter Shakespeare as substantially as did the Restoration playwrights.[7] What differentiates us from the Restoration is that while we feel free to alter Shakespeare's context, we do not change his text.

Our sense of textual sanctity and its antithesis as exemplified by the adaptations form the basis of this study. We clearly find genius within the words of Shakespeare's text, hence our horror at these attempts to rewrite or remove his words. Equally clearly, the playwrights and critics of the Restoration and eighteenth century, while they revered the poet, did not revere his language *per se*. In the intervening two hundred and fifty years, attitudes toward Shakespeare and his text have been inverted. This shift is not simply an attempt to canonize an author, as argued by R.W. Babcock but an attempt to canonize words, a crucial distinction.[8] Shakespeare as author also becomes Shakespeare as document. He was not the only Renaissance author whose texts, now treated with reverence, were adapted during the later seventeenth and eighteenth centuries; revisions of Beaumont and Fletcher, Massinger, even Jonson appeared regularly on the Restoration stage.[9] Shakespeare, however, remained the principal object of adaptation as well as the favorite focus of literary theory, and thus the fate of his work was symptomatic of larger philosophical issues.

Hans Robert Jauss writes that a literary work is not a "monument that monologically reveals its timeless essence." The Shakespeare adaptations, as well as the response to these adaptations, provide such a dialogue between the Shakespearean play and its interpreters. This dialogue tells us more about those who reacted to Shakespeare, their culture and their values, both social and literary, than about Shakespeare or the Shakespearean text. Jauss continues: "[a] literary event can continue to have an effect only if those who come after it still or once again respond to it—if there are readers who again appropriate the past work or authors who want to imitate, outdo, or refute it."[10] The Restoration and eighteenth century provide a history both of readers appropriating Shakespeare's works and of writers, in an ever increasing stream, attempting to imitate if not outdo them. This is the time when Shakespeare's works became public property and an intrinsic, even defining, part of English national culture. Adaptors and critics are both a part of this dialectic, each writer imprinting his or her own image on the works. The original work is perpetuated at the same time that it becomes itself almost irrelevant to the finished adaptation or critical essay.

No example of literary reception is as well known or as well publicized as that of Shakespeare. For more than three centuries his name has been appropriated to support a myriad of causes, literary and otherwise, while his words have been used to sell a vast quantity of un-Shakespearean goods. No other English writer is so thoroughly canonized both inside and outside of the academic community. (A quick glimpse of the crowds today outside "The Birthplace" in Stratford-upon-Avon provides a vivid example of the contemporary adoration of Shakespeare.) It has become commonplace to state that this canonization began in the last half of the eighteenth century. The reality is not quite so simple.

Certainly, the eighteenth century saw the beginning of what has been termed the Shakespeare industry. Scholarly editing of Shakespeare got its start with Pope and Theobald, reaching its apex in Edmond Malone's monumental 1790 edition with its complex scholarly apparatus of notes, emendations, and explanations.[11] In addition, Shakespeare's plays had become an essential part of eighteenth-century theater repertoire, copies of his works were read by a large and varied audience, and critics in the last half of the century anticipated the romantic poets in their praise of all things Shakespearean. But it cannot be forgotten that these events did not spring fully formed out of some pre-Romantic consciousness. Critics in the later seventeenth century also praised Shakespeare above all other English writers and Restoration audiences flocked to see his plays—albeit the performances they saw were frequently altered versions of his works. To attribute the canonization of Shakespeare solely to the age of Garrick and the Shakespeare Jubilee is to misread the history of Shakespeare reception after the Restoration.

At the center of this history are the seventeenth- and eighteenth-century adaptations of Shakespeare, and their appearance—and disappearance—pose questions which go beyond the simple act of adaptation:
1. Why were the adaptations written? What perception of Shakespeare and of literature in general encouraged such radical revision of his works?
2. Why, in the later eighteenth century, did playwrights stop adapting

Shakespeare? What new conception of the literary work prohibited rewriting the playwright's words? These questions have serious implications regarding both the aesthetics of the literary text and its treatment. The decision of playwrights and theater managers to revise Shakespeare, and the popularity of the resulting adaptations, shows that the concept of adaptation was widely accepted from the late seventeenth century on and that it was not considered taboo to tamper with the work of a literary genius. As the second question implies, assumptions concerning the sanctity of a literary text underwent a radical change during the course of the eighteenth century. By mid-century, adaptation, in its guise of rewriting, had become an object of contempt and a symbol of an earlier age's literary failings. This contempt, focused on the previous age's insertion of non-Shakespearean language or "dross"[12] into Shakespeare's golden words, depends upon a changed vision of literature in which the text is fixed and cannot, or should not, be changed. Surprisingly little attention has been paid to these questions and to the adaptations themselves,[13] and until recently it was common to look back to the Restoration as a time when the public taste was so debased that the genius of Shakespeare's plays was unappreciated unless it was "improved."[14]

Michel Foucault's postulation of an "author-function," the assumption that a literary work was written by and belongs to a specific and privileged individual, the author, provides a useful framework for my discussion of Shakespeare and adaptation. The evolution of such an "author-function" corresponds both to the establishment of certain authors as sacred figures, conveying privilege or sanctity to their texts, as well as to the development of a "system of ownership for texts," or copyright. Foucault notes that "the coming into being of the notion of the 'author' constitutes the privileged moment of *individualization* in the history of ideas,"[15] a development he locates generally in the seventeenth or eighteenth century. The adaptations of Shakespeare present a specific history of the period's most revered writer and his establishment as "author." This notion was clearly absent in the late seventeenth and early eighteenth century when the most radically revised adaptations were written. At the time, a writer did not own his works (that privilege belonged to his publisher) nor did the name of the author sanctify his written work. Altering an author's works was not only possible but popular.

Foucault's theory is limited, however, in considering only the concept of the author, not the phenomenon of the author *as text*. By the end of the eighteenth century, literary works had become recognizable printed texts, private property protected by their creators, or, posthumously, by the now exalted status of their author/owner. Only the writer himself could authorize change, a sentiment reflected in the adulation which eventually surrounded Shakespeare's name and his "genuine text."

The individualization of the author is only one aspect of the larger emphasis on the individual subject which developed during the eighteenth century and which profoundly influenced the history of Shakespeare adaptation and reception. Raymond Williams writes that "we can trace our concept of the 'individual' to that complex of change which we analyze in its separable aspects as the Renaissance, the Reformation, the beginnings of capitalist economy. In essence it is the abstraction of the individual from the complex of relationships by which he had hitherto been normally defined."[16] Such changes can be tied to the final breaking up of the feudal system and the emergence of a new class system, in which individualism is intrinsically linked to the growth of the bourgeoisie.[17] This newly emerged individual, separate from its larger group, possessed certain rights, an ideological development reflected in the emphasis on individual rights espoused by Paine and other late eighteenth-century radicals, and deeply distrusted by conservatives such as Burke. Williams notes elsewhere that "it is not until [the late eighteenth century] that a crucial shift in attitudes can be seen."[18]

The literary world reflected these changes in the establishment of copyright,[19] the individual author's right to claim what he or she had written as property, and in the individual reader's right to interpret a text as he or she chooses. The growing emphasis on individual "rights" most affects this study of Shakespeare and reception in the emphasis on the individual reader and the validation of individual response rather than the earlier emphasis on consensus. This displacement of authority is vividly illustrated in the differences between early literary criticism such as Dryden's *Essay of Dramatick Poesy* with its quartet of reasonable gentlemen who discuss world drama in search of a civilized accord, and the emphasis on subjective readings which dominates criticism by the end of the eighteenth century.

A second, more specific issue involves the evolution of print culture throughout the eighteenth century. In the first decades after the Restoration, publishing grew slowly.[20] Plays such as the Shakespeare adaptations were published and sold at theaters, as a corollary to the performance rather than an incitement to private reading. Critics addressed their essays to a small and often specialized audience which consisted largely of other writers and their patrons. By the mid-eighteenth century, the literary marketplace shifted from this small, educated elite, to a broad-based reading public. Fueled by growing literacy and the expanding market for the printed word, literary production grew exponentially. Concurrently, the emerging middle class relied on literature and literary culture as a sign of status, creating new market pressures. Vast quantities of books, essays, pamphlets, and novels were needed to fill the demand. Periodicals appeared and multiplied. A new breed of professional writers proliferated to fill the demand for print (their prominence reflected in the stock figure of the Grub Street hack who replaces Bayes the hack playwright as literary stereotype—the setting is the publishing house not the stage). Shakespeare and his works were an important part of this industry; the eighteenth century witnessed not only the remarkable proliferation of new editions of Shakespeare but a phenomenal growth in the number of books and essays written about Shakespeare.[21]

These two issues interlock at the text, bringing together the individual reader and the printed page. In contrast to the public and communal experience of theater, the act of reading is individual and private. The effect of this shift from public to private, from theater to book, on the study and understanding of Shakespeare's works was immense. In the later seventeenth century, when the percentage of the population owning a copy of Shakespeare's works was relatively small, Shakespeare was understood and discussed primarily as performance, as visual and audible action designed to provoke audience response. As his works became readily available, and as a larger percentage of population was able to read them, the emphasis shifted to subjective interpretation. In place of adaptations, writers produced criticism, a newly popular genre dependent upon reading other texts. Also enabling the explosion of the Shakespeare industry was the increasing idolization of Shakespeare and his works—the canonization of England's first literary saint.

As the subject of this study is reception rather than production, it is not my intention to provide a detailed history of the Restoration and eighteenth-century stage. Theater history, a register of continual changes in taste, can only suggest possible reasons for specific aspects of adaptation; it can offer no explanation of why playwrights stopped adapting Shakespeare. The playwrights themselves rarely comment specifically on their reasons for changing Shakespeare; in fact, in their prefaces and epilogues they often claim to be "restoring" Shakespeare to the stage.[22] The network of criticism surrounding the adaptations, a much neglected subject, provides more explicit treatment of the subject of adaptation as well as presenting the view of literature which allowed such changes to take place.[23] The relationship I draw here between drama and literary theory is one of conjunction, not cause and effect. This point must be stressed; otherwise we run the risk of making the same errors as those who attributed the adaptations' existence to the "rules of drama." The relation between theory and practice is never that simple. Rather, the criticism of Shakespeare written during the Restoration and eighteenth century arises out of the same literary consciousness as the adaptations; it provides a part of the context rather than a cause. Along with current theatrical practices, an age's perception of what literature is and how it should be treated determines the form adaptation will take and can itself be tied to larger, nonliterary issues.

Because the adaptations have been treated as a symptom of a diseased popular taste (hence the insistence on examining the adaptations solely in the context of dramatic tradition), they have been kept separate from the world of eighteenth-century criticism. By focusing on the literary context rather than stage history, I hope to bridge the perceived gap between one form of popular culture, as represented by the adaptations, and critical theory. This relationship brings up the complex question of what differentiates popular taste and theory, or, to invert the proposition, at what point theory becomes popular taste. Here Shakespeare is an ideal subject because in his perceived status as the English Homer, the finest of all English writers, he was used by seventeenth- and eighteenth-century critics as the exemplar of many of their literary theories. The critical prominence of Shakespeare in the eighteenth century was boosted by the acceptance of English literature as a legitimate focus of study and the rise of literary criticism as a popular genre—as well as the enshrinement of Shakespeare as the genius of English poetry.

For the purposes of this study, I define adaptation in its strictest sense as significant changes made to a pre-existing literary work. Within this definition, the first criterion is publication; in order to examine the nature of the changes made to Shakespeare's text, it will be necessary to deal only with those adaptations which were actually published. Rumors of unpublished adaptations are intriguing, but these lost plays can only be speculated about, not scrutinized.

The next step is to determine which plays can be classified as adaptations. For the purposes of this study, I consider only published plays which change Shakespeare more substantively than by making cuts to reduce the playing time (changes made frequently even today), or adding a few scattered new lines or phrases. Under these criteria, actual acting versions of Shakespeare, such as Bell's Shakespeare (*Bell's Edition of Shakespeare's Plays, as they are now performed at the Theatres Royal in London. Regulated from the Prompt Books of each House*, 1774),[24] or Kemble's revisions in the last decades of the eighteenth century, do not fall under the heading of adaptations. On the other hand, a play which has Shakespeare as its source but which itself represents a totally different work must also be omitted, works such as Dryden's *All for Love* (1678, a work which Dryden explicitly labels an "Imitation" rather than an alteration of Shakespeare) or Thomson's *Coriolanus* (1749) which simply use the events in Shakespeare's plays as a general framework. The study focuses on those adaptations which were performed successfully to prevent undue emphasis from being placed on those adaptations which were limited in their influence. Certainly other forms of altering Shakespeare existed and do still exist, such as Bowdler's notorious *Family Shakespeare* as well as the numerous operas, ballets, and films popular in the nineteenth and twentieth centuries. These forms, however, are outside the compass of this study.

The book covers the period usually described as the Restoration and eighteenth century. It begins in 1660 with the restoration of the monarchy and the reopening of the theaters when Shakespeare was first adapted and performed on a new stage and under new theatrical conditions; this period also saw the beginnings of critical discussions of Shakespeare as dramatist. The book concludes on the eve of a literary event which would alter the study of Shakespeare, the publication of Edmond Malone's edition of Shakespeare.[25] I make one exception to this final demarcation in concluding the book with Walter Whiter and *A Specimen of Shakespeare Commentary* (1794) as, by conflating the author and the text so that the text becomes the mind of the poet, his work sums up the ongoing process of textualization discussed throughout this study. I recognize the dangers inherent in a chronological study, where the temptation to make an overly coherent whole of disparate pieces is always present. But in a case such as this, where change unfolds over time, running that risk is necessary.

The book falls into two parts, which I have titled "The Re-Imagined Text" and "Refined from the Dross," in reference to the change in attitude toward the Shakespearean text. The first section examines the late seventeenth and early eighteenth centuries, when Shakespeare's text was perceived as fluid and capable of change, and the second section the gradual loss of that fluidity as Shakespeare's works become fixed and inviolate. Chapter 1 examines the adaptations of Shakespeare which appeared in the theaters between the reopening of the theaters in 1660 and the Licensing Act of 1737. Chapter 2 links these changes to the critical discussions of Shakespeare which began to appear in the same period. Chapter 3 begins the second half of the book by examining a later group of adaptations and the ways in which these plays attempted to restore Shakespeare's words to the stage, refining them from the "dross" of previous adaptations. Chapter 4 is the first of two chapters examining the proliferation of critical studies of Shakespeare (far outweighing in volume the actual adaptations of Shakespeare attempted during this period). Its focus is criticism at mid-eighteenth century when neoclassical formalism and attempted objectivity were being replaced by more individualized *readings* of the plays. Chapter 5 concludes the book with an examination of criticism at the end of the century, when new stage adaptations ceased, and critics located meaning within Shakespearean words, not in the larger dramatic action, and sought to protect this sacred text.

The rise and fall of the adaptations thus represents a pivotal moment in literary and cultural history, testifying to the new focus on language which would soon infiltrate all aspects of eighteenth-century thought. When concern for Shakespeare as text replaces emphasis on Shakespeare as performance, even the words once deemed "barbaric" become precious. For the later eighteenth century, Shakespeare becomes an author to be read, a change of status indicated by the increasingly numerous editions of his works. Not simply the canonization of a single author, this growing fascination with specific words heralds the adoration of the text and, ultimately, when carried to its logical extreme, the "death" of the author in the twentieth century. Put in this context, the redefinition of Shakespeare's genius in terms of his words represents a general down-grading of the element of performance in literature. Shakespeare's works, and English literature in general, were to be defined by their words rather than by the plots and morality on which the older aesthetic theory focused—a clear step toward our modern concern for the word and its varying levels of signification.

Part I
The Re-Imagined Text

1.
Radical Adaptation

In 1660, theaters opened in London after an eighteen-year hiatus. The repertoire of these fledgling companies depended heavily on available Renaissance drama, in particular on Shakespeare and Beaumont and Fletcher.[1] Their plays, written at least two generations before, were readily at hand, although somewhat out of date for the new audiences which soon flocked to the theaters. No one denied that these plays had merit,[2] but they were decidedly old-fashioned, lacking, for example, the female roles made popular by the introduction of actresses. Not surprisingly, the elements which made Restoration plays successful began to appear in the adaptations of Shakespeare, as managers of the new theaters felt that many of Shakespeare's plays had to be altered in order to make them marketable. Many of these changes are easily discernable attempts to fit Shakespeare into the conventions of Restoration staging, such as the addition of elaborate scenery and special effects,[3] or the revision of characters so that they conformed to popular dramatic types.[4]

Moreover, the plays were linguistically out of date. Restoration audiences found their old-fashioned, even "barbaric," fondness for wordplay distasteful, and playwrights sought to modernize this aspect of Shakespeare as well. Dramatic literature in particular was envisioned as performance, and the treatment of Shakespeare keyed to the effect upon a specifically Restoration audience. Authors such as Shakespeare and Milton might be revered, but their genius was situated not in the words they wrote but in larger issues such as character, plot, and even ideas—and these elements needed a bit of refurbishing so that the overall performance would be more effective.

For Restoration theater managers, Shakespeare's works presented substantial problems. In the plays, the forces of good appear muddled: a princess uses harsh words to tell her father she loves him; a king behaves in a notably unkinglike fashion; the good and the vicious suffer alike. Bothered by these problems (as we are still today), the adapters used what we see as a radical approach to the problem—they rewrote the plays, reshaped the characters, and, thus, resolved the problems.

Just as subplots and minor characters were cut away to simplify the plot and focus attention on the main action (or what the adapter wanted to present as the main action), the nature of this action and the characters who perform it were also simplified. In this way, characters are clearly identified as either good or bad while the principle of poetic justice informs the outcome of each play. Questions of motivation or of the fine line between good and evil vanish, and, as a result, moral dilemmas disappear. Simple causes motivate these characters; the evil characters scheme because they are evil by nature, while the good characters follow the dictates of love or honor, favorite themes in Restoration heroic drama. The scope of the plays narrows to these two topics as the adaptations become a series of variations on the standard melodramatic theme of good versus evil, where the nature of these two absolutes is never questioned. Consequently, the adaptations devolve into a polarized struggle with no loose ends left untied.

On a larger scale, the distrust of ambiguity during this period can be tied both to an overwhelming concern with drama's effect on the audience and to a fear of disorder outside of literature, in the public mind and in the body politic. Not surprisingly, the polarization of good and evil within the plays parallels the political polarization which resulted in the formation of political parties. Good defines itself in opposition to evil just as the Tories defined themselves in opposition to the Whigs, who were themselves the party of the opposition. In each case, lines are drawn and ambiguities dissolved.

The scope of these developments is particularly noticeable when the adaptations are compared not only with Shakespeare but with a larger range of Renaissance literature. Writers of the late sixteenth and early seventeenth centuries delighted in enigmas and conundrums; as such verbal games indicate, puzzling, mystifying, even tricking the reader was part of the pleasure. In the Renaissance, the assumption that ambiguity was a readily acceptable literary tool permeated writing on all levels. In contrast to the adaptations, with their painstaking linguistic simplicity, Renaissance literature abounds with puns and sometimes elaborate conceits, literary figures which by their very nature promote ambiguity by adding an additional layer of meaning.[5] By the time of the Restoration, these literary attitudes had changed as the radical instability of the recent civil war, coupled with political struggles and social upheavals, made permanence a desired virtue. Creating hierarchies helped establish a sense of order, and classifying literature and people, and thus controlling any incipient disorder or anarchy, became crucial.[6] The social class system developed along with theories concerning hierarchies of genre which established qualities that should separate comedy from tragedy. The popularity of neoclassical theory, with its rigid definitions of genre and its focus on the psychological underpinnings of audience response, indicates a suspicion of social and literary uncertainty. Writers, and subsequently critics, questioned the audience's ability to decipher ambiguity, fearing the possible confusion it might foster and the moral as well as political problems such confusion could create. Questions such as these, which might seem to narrow the scope of literature, are paradoxically tied to belief in its affective power, based as they are on the assumption that literature can sway a reader or auditor to action. Theater became a subject of particular concern because its emotional power could impact large groups of people.

The belief that the enticing power of literature can lead an audience astray necessitates resolution of the threat of ambiguity; thus improper lessons are neither learned nor acted upon. The conservative politics of most of the adaptations, where instability becomes an ideological evil, intensifies this tendency. These changes are particularly striking when we consider that the reconfiguration of Shakespeare occurred at the same time that the most "immoral" of the Restoration comedies appeared on the stage. While libertinism and morally questionable motives might go unpunished within the confines of comedy and the social world familiar to the audience, similar qualities could not be tolerated in the more precarious and politically charged climate of Shakespeare's plays, where the moral stakes loomed larger. It is not surprising that one exception to this pattern of adaptation appears in the D'Avenant/Dryden *Tempest* in its guise as a Restoration sex comedy. Thus, while the Horners and Dorimants of contemporary comedy could prosper, the characters in Shakespearean drama had to be carefully corralled within the controlled environment of poetic justice.

The group of plays I have termed "radical adaptations" were written between 1660 and 1737, from the reopening of the theaters to the enactment of the Licensing Act. The broadness of this time frame is deceptive—almost half of the twenty-three adaptations written during this time appeared between 1678 and 1682, between the Popish Plot and the union of the King's and the Duke's companies (see appendix). Only six were written after 1703, and of these only one was performed more than ten times.[7] Most appeared during the last decades of the seventeenth century. During the time these plays were written, Shakespeare's works were found more often in the theater than on the printed page, and thus the Restoration audience's emphasis was on Shakespeare as performance rather than as text. This conception of Shakespeare shaped the form adaptation took as the revisions were necessarily tied to visual representation.

In addition to the simplification of Shakespeare's complex linguistic and moral ambiguities, issues of gender and politics also played a role in the Restoration adaptations as playwrights restructured Shakespeare's plays in order to adapt them to topical events, such as the new practice of actresses on the stage, or political upheaval (particularly true of the plays written between 1678 and 1682). My discussion of the adaptations focuses on these three topics. Representations of gender and politics provide a paradigm of the ways in which the adaptation of Shakespeare was affected by two very different issues: the portrayal of women shows the ways in which Shakespeare's works were altered in order to survive in a theater which had adapted to a changed social climate; the repoliticization of the plays reflects the direct influence of changes in the world outside the theater.[8] The changes to Shakespeare's language, at once the simplest and the most fundamental of all alterations, begin the process of alteration which culminates in the widespread application of poetic justice to the plays, emphasizing the didactic and providing a comforting sense of closure in an unstable world. As the scope of these alterations suggests, theater-goers may have venerated the idea of Shakespeare—but not his text.

LINGUISTIC AND MORAL SIMPLIFICATION

On the most basic level, the Restoration adapters changed the words of Shakespeare's text as they refitted his plays for the new theaters. This act of rewriting was the foundation for all other changes made to Shakespeare's text. The adaptations of the Restoration and early eighteenth century rarely used the original language of Shakespeare's plays, replacing it instead with a more "refined" and modern English. Some playwrights made relatively few changes, updating expressions, removing archaic words, and cutting out long stretches of figurative language. Others completely rewrote the plays, substituting their own words for Shakespeare's. Though playwrights and audiences were perfectly capable of appreciating Shakespeare's poetry, they did not see his language as an essential part of his genius which they regarded as moral or mimetic. Unlike readers in the twentieth century, playwrights and audiences in the late seventeenth and early eighteenth centuries felt that Shakespeare's diction was often flawed, a by-product of the barbaric age in which he lived rather than a foundation on which all his other beauties rested.

With the exception of Thomas Rymer, playwrights and critics were eager to assert Shakespeare's genius; they did not, however, believe it resided in the words he used to express his ideas—hence the rewriting. Because playwrights did not see Shakespeare's language as an intrinsic element of his genius, they were able to treat his works as a plastic material which could be reshaped at will. As the adaptations prove, when a literary text is not seen as fixed, any number of changes can be made. Revered though Shakespeare was, his *works* were not yet canonized—changes could and would be made. The industry of publishing Shakespeare's works (made profitable by the growing reading public) had not yet taken hold,[9] and his genius was perceived in general terms more compatible with theater performance than reading.

This disregard for the Shakespearean text appears particularly strongly in the earliest adaptations. These plays, written between 1660 and 1682, translate Shakespeare's Elizabethan English into the language considered proper for a self-professedly more sophisticated and literate age. Like most adapters of this time, Sir William D'Avenant (author of the two earliest published adaptations) substantially rewrote the plays he adapted, providing a model for subsequent playwrights to follow. His plays, especially *Macbeth* (1664), often appropriate whole scenes from the original, including soliloquies, dialogues, even brief snippets of conversation, but the words themselves are D'Avenant's own. At times he retains the Shakespearean end-rhymes—but rewrites every other part of the couplets. His most frequent changes involve removing words unfamiliar to the Restoration audience and making Shakespeare's figures of speech less obscure. Thus, Macbeth's:

>   Come seeling night,
> Scarf up the tender eye of pitiful day,
> With thy bloody and invisible hand
> Cancel and tear to pieces that great bond
> Which keeps me pale! Light thickens, and the crow
> Makes wing to th' rooky wood;
> Good things of day begin to droop and drowse,
> Whilse night's black agents to their preys do rouse.
> Thou marvel'st at my words, but hold thee still:
> Things bad begun make strong themselves by ill. [III.ii.46–55]

becomes:

>   Come dismal Night.
> Close up the Eye of the quick sighted Day
> With thy invisible and bloody hand.
> The Crow makes wing to the thick shady Grove,

Whilst Night's black Agent's to their Preys make hast,
Thou Wonder'st at my Language, wonder still,
Things ill begun strengthen themselves by ill. [III.iii.47–54]

Here D'Avenant modernizes Shakespeare's diction, getting rid of words such as "seeling" and "scarf." He also simplifies Shakespeare's personification of night by eliminating the second half of the image, "cancel and tear to pieces that great bond/Which keeps me pale!" Night puts out its hand to close Day's eyes—a simple metaphor. The passage cannot be misconstrued; no archaisms or subtleties such as the indirect reference to Banquo's life ("that great bond") are left to complicate the sense.[10] These linguistic simplifications have larger ramifications, acting to simplify the characters who speak the words, as well as the words themselves. This passage, for example, contributes to D'Avenant's more general goal of recasting Macbeth not as a tormented tragic hero, but as a villain.

Complex passages of figurative language were frequently omitted or reconstructed, containing, as they do, verbal ambiguities which in turn promote ambiguities in character or thought. Fifteen years after D'Avenant's *Macbeth*, Nahum Tate displays revisions similar in scope to those in D'Avenant's plays, particularly in *The Ingratitude of a Common-Wealth: Or, the Fall of Caius Martius Coriolanus* (1681). Shakespeare's Volumnia beseeches her son:

> I prithee now, my son,
> Go to them, with this bonnet in thy hand,
> And thus far having stretch'd it (here be with them),
> Thy knee bussing the stones (for in such business
> Action is eloquence, and the eyes of th' ignorant
> More learned than the ears), waving thy head,
> Which often thus correcting thy stout heart,
> Now humble as the ripest mulberry
> That will not hold the handling. [III.ii.72–80]

Tate's character takes a much simpler approach:

> I Pray go to 'em
> With mild Behaviour; for in such Business,
> Action is Eloquence; and the Eyes of the Vulgar,
> More Learned than their Ears. [p.32]

The examples which Shakespeare's Volumnia couches in figurative language ("thy knee bussing the stones," "thy head . . . humble as the ripest mulberry") are summed up as "mild behavior," a change which both simplifies the diction and complements the heroic picture of Coriolanus Tate carefully projects throughout his adaptation. Shakespeare's version, on the other hand, suggests that Coriolanus's behavior is no more than a calculated act.

Elsewhere, playwrights replace entire sections of Shakespeare's plays with new passages written in strictly Restoration idiom. Almost every adaptation is rife with late seventeenth-century phraseology: Thomas D'Urfey's Cloten swears "I Gad this damn'd Armour is plaguy troublesom" (21) while in *The Ingratitude of a Common-wealth*, Tate's Valerie complains of "my lady *Galatea*, such a fantastical, fulsome Figure, all Curls and Feathers!" (30). An example of Restoration figurative language, inserted by D'Urfey' into *The Injured Princess: Or, the Fatal Wager* (1682), a version of *Cymbeline*, illustrates a similar change in vernacular. Here Eugenia laments her pitiful state in distinctly non-Shakespearean terms:

> Ah some kind Silvian God,
> That rul'st these Groves, rise from thy mossie Couch,
> And with thy hoord of Summer wholesom Fruits,
> Preserve an innocent Lady from sharp Famine!
> I saw an Apple-tree in yonder Thicket,
> On which eager to feed, as I drew near it,
> A large grown Serpent from the hollow root,
> Oppos'd my raging hunger, and instead of pittying
> My pale and pining Looks, with flaming Eyes,
> And dreadful Hisses, like the *Hesperian* Dragon,
> Frighted me from the place. [34–5]

The imagery here is based on a series of simple oppositions: the innocent lady attacked first by sharp famine, and later by the hideous serpent. The description of this anti-Eden, although elaborate, is unambiguous, posited upon the binary opposition of good ("kind Silvian God" and "innocent Lady") and evil ("sharp famine," "large grown Serpent," and "*Hesperian* Dragon"). While the contrast between this passage and Shakespeare's less heavy-handed descriptions arises in part because D'Urfey's poetic talent is limited, the similarities in style between it and passages from the other adaptations suggest a common poetic taste which incorporates a suspicion of ambivalence, both verbal and moral.

Subtle changes in diction are even more widespread. As is often the case with Restoration drama, the adaptations simplify both thought and language, so that not only the sense of any given passage is made explicit, but the thoughts of the character who utters the words become equally unambiguous. Examples can be readily found in any adaptation, as in Tate's *King Lear* (1681) when Edmund ogles Cordelia, commenting in an aside:

> O charming Sorrow! how her Tears adorn her
> Like Dew on Flow'rs, but she is Virtuous,
> And I must quench this hopeless Fire in' th' Kindling.[11]

In a passage equally stocked with generalizations, Cordelia relates her intention to rescue her father:

> What have not Women dar'd for vicious Love,
> And we'll be shining Proofs that they can dare
> For Piety as much; blow Winds, and Lightnings fall,
> Bold in my Virgin Innocence, I'll flie
> My Royal Father to Relieve, or Die. [III.ii.107–11]

The first passage establishes Cordelia as an icon of virtue and indicates Edmund's (improper) desire for her—desire which will, in Tate's play, culminate in an attempted rape. While Edmund's speech hints at his own villainy, Cordelia's speech, with its references to "Piety" and "Virgin Innocence," reiterates her virtue. Both passages clearly outline the speakers' intentions using abstractions and simple figures to get the point across, resulting in simple language as well as characters with a correspondingly simple psychology.

By thus mapping out the meaning of each passage, adapters, like many of their contemporaries, hoped to reduce possible misconstructions and minimize subversive interpretations. This need to clarify Shakespeare's language bespeaks a profound distrust of language, a fear that unless carefully controlled, words both printed and spoken can undermine social and political order. Empiricist philosophers from Bacon onward warned of the perils of ungoverned discourse. In *The New Organon*, Bacon outlines the attributes of language and their dangerous ramifications:

> There are also Idols formed by the intercourse and association of men with each other, which I call Idols of the Marketplace on account of the commerce and consort of men there. For it is by discourse that men associate, and words are imposed according to the apprehension of the vulgar. And therefore the ill and unfit choice of words wonderfully obstructs the understanding. Nor do the definitions of explanations wherewith in somethings learned men are wont to guard and defend themselves by any means set the matter right. But words plainly force and overrule the understanding, and throw all into confusion, and lead men away into numberless empty controversies and idle fancies.[12]

Aimed at the lowest common denominator, "the apprehension of the vulgar," words are frequently used improperly, "obstruct[ing] the understanding," and, even under the best of circumstances, they can "force and overrule" it, throwing everything into confusion. Hobbes and Locke after him decry the dangers of "the Abuse of Words" and the corresponding need for careful definitions (*Leviathan*, I, iv; *Essay Concerning Human Understanding*, III, x).

Summing up these concerns, Thomas Sprat provides the explicit link between politics and language when he observes: "For the purity of Speech, and the greatness of Empire have in all Countries, still met together."[13] Refining impurities (many of which Sprat attributes to the recent civil war) not only prevents destabilizing misinterpretation but will help provide political "greatness" for England. The conquest of Shakespeare's language thus becomes a step toward the establishment of a British empire. Not surprisingly, rewriting Shakespeare was particularly prevalent in times of political strife, especially during the Exclusion crisis, and was a necessity for performance of those adaptations with a political argument.

As the seventeenth century drew to a close and political tensions eased, adapters became more cautious in their treatment of Shakespeare's language, at least in print. Rewriting of the Shakespearean text became less widespread, and adapters began to indicate where they had added new material. The practice of marking where the Shakespearean play had been altered had its start in the 1670s, in acting versions of Shakespeare sold in conjunction with productions of his plays; these editions printed the entire text of the play along with inverted commas to indicate the passages which had been cut in performance. Both *Hamlet* and *Henry IV* appeared in this form, with an explanatory note prefacing each play:

To the Reader

This play being too long to be conveniently Acted, such places as might be least prejudicial to the Plot or Sense, are left out upon the Stage: but that we may no way wrong the incomparable Author, are here inserted according to the Original copy with this Mark ".[14]

By the beginning of the eighteenth century, the use of inverted commas to identify Shakespeare's language also began to appear in published adaptations. In *Richard III* (1700), Colley Cibber makes an attempt to distinguish between Shakespearean and non-Shakespearean versions to "satisfy the curious." His symbols are complicated, as he makes note of not only those lines which Shakespeare wrote, but also the lines containing Shakespearean ideas. He explains this system in the "Preface" to the first (1700) edition:

> I have caus'd those that are intirely *Shakespeare's* to be printed in this *Italick Character,* and those lines with this mark (') before 'em, are generally his thoghts, in the best I could afford 'em: What is not so mark'd, or in a different Character is intirely my own.[15]

Like the explanatory note which accompanied the acting versions, Cibber's "Preface" expresses a need to identify the Shakespearean text. Where the acting versions differentiate between text and performance, Cibber, however, struggles to identify not only Shakespeare's words but Shakespeare's ideas as distinguished from his language. He assumes that readers and perhaps even spectators would want to know where Shakespeare left off and Cibber began.

While Cibber's additions are usually easily distinguishable from Shakespeare's own words, he avoids the Restoration diction which marks so many earlier adaptations. He scrupulously attempts to isolate the various degrees of Shakespeare within his *Richard III*, making distinctions almost within a line, as seen in this excerpt:

> So—I've secur'd my Cousin here: These Moveables
> Will never let his Brains have rest till I am King:
> Catesby, *go thou with speed to Doctor* Shaw *and thence*
> 'To Fryar *Beuker.* Haste, and bid 'em both
> 'Attend me here, within an hour at farthest:
> Mean while my private orders shall be given
> To lock out all admittance to the Princes. [III.i.149–55]

According to Cibber's notation, *Richard III* consists of slightly more than half Shakespeare, mostly in italics; the remainder is Cibber's work.[16] Despite his elaborate system, Cibber is not always accurate, often attributing his own lines to Shakespeare, such as the notorious "Conscience Avant. Richard's himself again" (V.v.85). In spite of the introduction of printed symbols such as inverted commas, the concern for authenticity which was to mark later eighteenth-century attitudes to Shakespeare was not present. Cibber's inverted commas represent the embryonic need to differentiate Shakespeare from non-Shakespeare, but clear lines had not yet been drawn, nor was it necessary to draw them.

Other playwrights, though not all, followed Cibber's lead. What represented Shakespeare's words to these adapters, however, was not always what we, today, would accept as the unaltered text. For example, *The Jew of Venice* (1701), George Granville's adaptation of *The Merchant of Venice*, claims to mark all those lines which are not Shakespeare's, so that "nothing may be imputed to *Shakespear* which may seem unworthy of him."[17] An excerpt illustrates Granville's representation of the "original." Portia's speech on mercy:

> The quality of mercy is not strain'd,
> It droppeth as the gentle rain from heaven
> Upon the place beneath. It is twice blest:
> It blesseth him that gives and him that takes.
> 'Tis mightiest in the mightiest, it becomes
> The throned monarch better than his crown.
> His sceptre shows the force of temporal power,
> The attitude to awe and majesty,
> Wherein doth sit the dread and fear of kings;
> But mercy is above this sceptred sway,
> It is enthroned in the hearts of kings,
> It is an attribute to God himself;
> And earthly power doth then show likest God's
> When mercy seasons justice. [IV.i.184–97]

appears unmarked as:

> The Quality of Mercy is not strain'd;
> It drops as does the gentle Dew from Heav'n
> Upon the Place beneath: It is twice blest,
> It blesses him that gives, and him that takes:
> 'Tis mightiest, in the mightiest: It becomes
> The crown'd Monarch, better than his Crown;
> 'It is the first of Sacred Attributes,
> And Earthly Power does then seem most Divine,
> When Mercy seasons Justice. [IV.i.107–15]

As this passage indicates, even playwrights who claim to be concerned with preserving Shakespearean language are less than exact in their distinctions. While Granville marks only the seventh line as new, the rest of the passage also makes changes to Shakespeare's text. Granville modernizes the diction and simplifies the phraseology; his changes are minor compared to the sweeping alterations D'Avenant made forty years earlier, but they indicate a certain lack of interest in textual accuracy which was to change by mid-century.

In general, adaptations in the early eighteenth century followed Cibber and Granville and gradually moved closer to Shakespeare's original language.[18] The advent of printed symbols such as the inverted commas indicate that Shakespeare was beginning to be perceived as a printed text, but even by the 1730s this perception was not universal. Not surprisingly, the period of the greatest textual changes occurred when Shakespeare's plays were available to the reading public only in acting versions or in the textually corrupt Third and Fourth Folios. (Indeed, the most radical adaptations were written many years before Nicholas Rowe's 1709 edition.) Tonson's popular and inexpensive volumes, which would make Shakespeare's works available to a large reading audience, would not appear until the mid-1730s. The inverted commas used by Granville and Cibber were the precursors of quotation marks, the device now used to separate one author's words from another, in essence to distinguish the property of one author from that of another.[19] As the numerous rewritings of Shakespeare demonstrate, this form of authorial attribution was not yet a compelling need.

As the examples cited above indicate, simplification of Shakespeare's language goes beyond mere changes in diction, and by eliminating verbal ambiguity, adapters participate in a more extensive process of clarification. When speeches are rewritten to clarify thought and intent, the figures who make the speeches change as well. The general distrust of ambiguity demonstrated in revisions of Shakespeare's diction manifests itself in exaggerated characterization as adapters resolve complex characters into easily comprehensible types. Apart from the comedies, where character types are less absolute, playwrights rarely mingle vice and virtue. Unsympathetic characters slip into utter depravity; there are no redeeming features in the adapters' villains.

The portrayal of Macbeth and Shylock in their respective adaptations (D'Avenant's *Macbeth* and Granville's *The Jew of Venice*) provide vivid examples of this new vision of villainy. Where Shakespeare's Macbeth is a basically good man goaded into evil, D'Avenant's is a greatly simplified character who, as the example cited above indicates, lacks the conflicts and doubts which rack the original. His intentions are clear from the very beginning: having carried through his plot to kill Duncan, he outlines a plan to kill Banquo and Fleance, and, in a revision of the sleepwalking scene with Lady Macbeth, declares his design to kill Malcolm. Similar changes appear thirty years later in the character of Shylock. In spite of the changed title, Granville's *The Jew of Venice* (1701) reduces both Shylock's lines and his stature within the play. Under Granville's hands, Shylock shrinks from a major figure to a minor one characterized simply by a love of money. Shylock's only new lines appear in a banquet scene (II.ii) where he follows Antonio's toast to friendship and Bassanio's toast to love with a toast to money: "I Have a Mistress, that out-shines 'em all . . . My Money is my Mistress! here's to/ Interest upon Interest" [II.ii.27–31].

Inevitably, virtuous characters become equally conventionalized as adapters balanced their pictures of evil with representatives of good (even the besieged royalty in the history plays is unerringly virtuous). In *The Jew of Venice*, the combined forces of Portia, Bassanio, and Antonio stand opposed to Shylock, overcoming his threatened ill. To offset the perfidy of his Macbeth, D'Avenant increased the importance of Macduff and reinvented the minor character of Lady Macduff as a type of female virtue: modest, moral, and eventually destroyed by the forces of evil. While Lady Macbeth urges Macbeth to murder, Lady Macduff counsels forbearance:

> If the Design should prosper, the Event
> May make us safe, but not you Innocent;
> For whilst to set your fellow Subjects free
> From present Death, or future Slavery,
> You wear a Crown, not by your Title due,
> Defence of them, is an Offense in you;
> That Deed's unlawful though it cost no Blood,
> In which you'l be at best unjustly Good.
> You, by your Pitty which for us you plead,
> Weave but Ambition of a finer thread. [III.ii.29–38]

The moral dilemma is clearly laid out for the audience—and the proper answer indicated. D'Avenant's shift to heroic couplets emphasizes Lady Macduff's elevated thoughts. The orderly progression of the couplets underlines the reason and order of her words, in stark contrast to the irrational and immoral sentiments spoken in blank verse by Lady Macbeth.

Simplifying Shakespeare also involved clearing up shady questions of motivation by rewriting scenes, adding new characters, or omitting offending passages in order to provide reasons for a character's behavior. Because these characters are either inherently good or inherently bad, their actions are revised to conform to these expectations, and as a result their motives are never in question. Good characters may act badly—but always with a good reason which the adapters carefully explain, while villains behave badly because of their inherent ill nature. Ridding the plays of ambiguous and morally complex characters marks the boundaries of good and evil and clarifies the moral action of each play still further. In the political adaptations, the moral action becomes the political action as good characters represent the political goals of the adapter. The moral polarization makes the political message unambiguous in the same way that the redefinition of Shakespearean heroines such as Lady Macduff as types of female virtue made them unambiguous—although flat—pictures of morality.

Tate's *King Lear* presents a vivid example of the urge to rationalize motivation. In Shakespeare's play, the tragic action stems from the moment when Cordelia not only refuses to follow her sisters' example and flatter her father, but seemingly goes out of her way to anger him by saying "nothing" to his request for love. To Tate, and to some subsequent critics,[20] her behavior appeared unduly harsh; in attempting to explain the possible reasons for such behavior, he invented Cordelia's love for Edgar, thus justifying her words in I.i and linking the main plot and the subplot structurally as well as thematically. Before Lear divides the kingdom, Edgar and Cordelia have a brief exchange establishing their secret love:

> *Edg. Cordelia*, royal Fair, turn yet once more,
> And e're sucessfull *Burgundy* receive
> The treasure of they Beauties from the King,
> E're happy *Burgundy* for ever fold Thee,
> Cast back one pitying Look on wretched *Edgar*.
> *Cord.* Alas what wou'd the wretched *Edgar* with
> The more Unfortunate *Cordelia*;
> Who in obedience to a Father's will
> Flys from *Edgar's* Arms to *Burgundy's*? [I.i.56–64]

The inclusion of this thwarted romance creates a new struggle for Cordelia between love for her father and for her lover. She refuses to flatter Lear, not because she thinks it wrong, but because to do so would force her into a loveless marriage. As her turn to speak arises, she laments:

> Now comes my Trial, how am I distrest,
> That must with cold speech tempt the chol'rick King
> Rather to leave me Dowerless, than condemn me
> To loath'd Embraces! [i.i.92–95]

Through asides such as this, Tate presents a simple explanation for her conduct; in order to avoid a loathsome marriage to a man she cannot love, she must oppose her father.[21] With Cordelia's mysterious conduct placed in the context of romantic love and the plot altered to include a focus on the lovers,[22] *King Lear* becomes a conventionally structured pathetic play: evil characters are punished; the two fathers, Lear and Gloucester, learn the error of their ways; and, despite many travails, their offspring are ultimately united in love.

Love acts to rationalize action in numerous other adaptations; in Thomas Shadwell's alteration of *Timon of Athens* (1678), for example, it becomes the foundation of the entire plot. Shakespeare's Timon alters swiftly, plummeting from an extreme love of man to an extremity of hatred.[23] Shadwell uses the addition of two new female characters, Melissa, a conventional Restoration coquette, and Evandra, a model of feminine virtue to explain this sudden change; it is rejection by Melissa which sparks his misanthropy and selfless fidelity from Evandra which redeems him.[24] As in Tate's *Lear*, seemingly inexplicable behavior is provided with a conventional explanatory motive, although at the cost of the characterization, as romantic betrayal provides an uncomplicated motive for his change of temperament. Mutual affection softens Timon's misanthropy, an effect which Shadwell strengthens by cutting some of Timon's most vituperative lines to make room for affecting scenes with the noble Evandra. As in Tate's *Lear*, love is the ultimate motivating force for good characters. Properly administered, it provides convenient and decorous explanation for otherwise inexplicable conduct. Thus simplified, most virtuous characters in the adaptations become variations on the type of the star-crossed lover.

Such explicit moral simplification and flat characterization result in a group of plays which progress in an orderly manner; as the characters become more predictable, the action itself becomes more predictable. The audience is never allowed to doubt a character's moral status because playwrights clearly identify each figure as either righteous or corrupt. With the battlelines so clearly delineated, the plot of each play becomes a variation on the struggle of Good against Evil where even if virtue does not win in the end, the clash at least makes a point. Such ideological conflict, while less prominent in the comedies, is inescapable in tragedy or tragicomedy. These plays depend on the interplay of heroes and villains for their impact, and by limiting the characterization, playwrights are able to present a clearly visible iconography of virtue and vice. In this way, the play's physical form becomes its moral form.

Nowhere is this moral conflict and its inevitable outcome seen more strongly than in the concluding scenes of the adaptations, where the action in each play becomes overtly moral. While Shakespeare's plays frequently end with ambiguity and anticlimax, the adaptations present conclusions in which everything could be said to be concluded. Plot lines are neatly wrapped up, characters married or killed off, and through these strategies of closure, the plays' moral messages are relayed. As a result, the sense of closure is complete. In these plays death and marriage provide an ending; conclusions focus on who kills whom or, alternatively, who marries whom. The struggle between Good and Evil comes to a climax in these final scenes. Even if virtue suffers, as in many tragedies, it suffers nobly, and villainy is inevitably punished. Commonly known as poetic justice, this system of allotting just deserts ensured that virtue was rewarded and vice punished. By working in these simple terms, playwrights provided the audience with a comfortable sense of cosmic order as well as a neatly packaged moral message. While poetic justice as a theoretical term was not to come into common use until after most of the Restoration adaptations had been written,[25] the concept is practiced even in the earliest adaptations.

In cases where poetic justice could not be strictly observed, such as plays with historical subjects, adapters mete out justice as best they can. In general, playwrights arrange conclusions so that, if possible, the injured parties avenge themselves by killing their oppressors; in these plays ethics dictate both how a character dies and by whose hand. Tate's Coriolanus, for example, is slain by his enemy Aufidius rather than a mob of conspirators, and he himself manages to dispose of Aufidius before he dies. By killing the man who has destroyed him and his family, he avenges his own honor and thus distills the conclusion into a battle between hero and villain.

This need for moral closure was not restricted to tragedies, as seen in *The Injured Princess* where D'Urfey punishes the iniquity of Shattillion (Jachimo) by inventing a scene in which Ursaces (Posthumus), meeting the villain in the woods, slays him for his misdeeds. Such insistence on equity sometimes instills a harshness alien to the original play, as in this incident, where the forgiveness initiated by Shakespeare's Posthumus is transformed into a scheme of retributive justice. In each case the sense of closure depends on the representation of moral order, of good vanquishing evil, thus giving the illusion that a benevolent deity and not chance presides over these fictional worlds. In the political and social turmoil which characterized the Restoration, the desire to control chaos by writing over it was overwhelming; in the adaptations playwrights are able to impress their own desire for order on a chaotic world.

The notorious ending of Tate's *King Lear* presents a vivid example of poetic justice at work. In startling contrast to Shakespeare's play,[26] Tate's *Lear* ends happily with the restoration of Lear to the throne (which he abdicates in favor of Cordelia) as well as the marriage of Edgar and Cordelia. The restoration of virtue begins in V.v where, unlike the equivalent scene in Shakespeare, Edgar challenges Edmund undisguised in a carefully orchestrated struggle. Tate's Edmund dies as entrenched in evil as he lived;

unlike Shakespeare's villain who gasps out "some good I mean to do,/ Despite of mine own nature" (V.iii.244–5), he dies unrepentant, attended by the adulterous Regan and Goneril, crying triumphantly: "Who wou'd not choose, like me, to yield his Breath/T'have Rival Queens contend for him in Death?" (V.v.112–14). Meanwhile, a similar battle occurs within the prison as Lear successfully fights off Edmund's murderous guards, aided by the timely entrance of Edgar and Albany, who arrive a few minutes earlier than their Shakespearean counterparts. The chance which governs the end of Shakespeare's tragedy and makes its ending so horrifying vanishes. In the world of Tate's play, the Gods protect the virtuous and punish the wicked, leaving nothing to accident or impersonal fate. Edgar kills Edmund because "the Gods confirm'd his Charge by Conquest" (V.vi.75), a point Tate reiterates in the play's concluding lines while placing the event in a specifically political contest:

> Our drooping Country now erects her Head,
> Peace spreads her balmy Wings, and Plenty Blooms.
> Divine *Cordelia*, all the Gods can witness
> How much thy Love to Empire I prefer!
> Thy bright Example shall convince the World
> (Whatever Storms of Fortune are decreed)
> That Truth and Vertue shall at last succeed. [V.vi.155–161]

Despite Edgar's claims to love Cordelia over "Empire," the rest of the passage stresses Britain's growing power, spurred by this fictional scene of restoration. With truth and virtue thus ascending the throne in the form of Edgar and Cordelia, England no longer "droops," but stands erect, confident of her own success (an important consideration at a time of bitter political debate). Poetic justice here becomes more than a simple depiction of virtue rewarded and vice punished—it constitutes political strength by bringing peace and prosperity as well as moral certainty.[27]

While no published play follows Tate in transforming a tragic ending into a comic one,[28] almost every adapter makes sure that in his play "Truth and Vertue" do "at last succeed." As Tate suggests, these pictures of moral stability carry with them overtones of political stability which link the representation of successful virtue on the stage to success in the state. Thus Restoration playwrights tie clarity of moral action to national triumph just as Thomas Sprat had linked purity of speech to greatness of empire. In the process, the adaptations exude an almost desperate need for reassurance as Shakespeare's adapters present his plays as emblems of social and political security.

Rewritten Women

After 1660, actresses appeared on the public stage consistently for the first time in English history.[29] Consequently, the number of female characters increased, but the nature of these roles was constricted, an outgrowth of social as well as theatrical change. Drama devoted new attention to the subjects of family, love and marriage, a development closely linked to the definition of women as inhabitants of the private or domestic sphere[30] and their exclusion from the public world of politics and commerce. Restoration playwrights were quick to rework Shakespeare's plots in order to take advantage of the new dramatic possibilities the actresses offered. On the most basic level, there was the simple titillation of seeing women on the stage, and many of the adaptations exploit this voyeuristic impulse by creating breeches roles for their new female characters. In addition to the successful adaptations of *Cymbeline* (1682) and *The Merchant of Venice* (1701) (and the later, less popular adaptations of *As You Like It* and *Twelfth Night*[31]), breeches roles were created for the character of Lady Elinor Butler in *The Misery of Civil War* (1680) and, several decades later, for Harriet in *Henry V* (1723), both deserted mistresses who rush off to war to seek out their unfaithful lovers. While the numerous breeches roles in Shakespeare's original plays may have allowed boy actors to play more realistic parts, the popularity of these roles in the Restoration and eighteenth century is clearly due to the opportunity they gave of showing off a well-turned feminine ankle.

A less obvious form of titillation developed out of the popularity of pathetic drama in the late seventeenth century. The pathetic plays strive to provoke the sympathy of their audience and depend for their effect on the sufferings of oppressed and helpless virtue. The object of this pathos is almost inevitably a woman. Pathos as a dramatic device appears in almost all forms of drama after the Restoration, consistently absent only in the cynical sex comedies. This widespread introduction of pathos exposes deeper social and philosophical issues, depending as it does on the sufferings of women.

The change in women's roles within society after the Restoration has become a critical and historical commonplace.[32] While not a simple causal relationship, as Laura Brown has shown, the changes in women's social roles correspond to changes in literary representation, particularly in the drama.[33] A brief survey of the attitude toward women expressed by contemporary courtesy books provides a useful backdrop for the portrayal of women in the adaptations. By their exemplary nature, conduct books define proper female behavior and thus present an idealized picture of femininity—a function filled also by the virtuous paragons in the adaptations of the late seventeenth and early eighteenth century. Conduct books most frequently describe proper feminine behavior in terms of studious passivity, stressing the necessary role of "meekness" in virtuous behavior. Meekness appeared near the head of any list of a woman's virtues, identified as both a woman's Christian duty and as a physiological necessity. In *The Ladies Calling* (1673), the most widely read of the courtesy books, Richard Allestree cites meekness as "particularly enjoin'd to Women," a virtue which "even Nature seems to teach, which abhors monstrosities and disproportions, and therefore having alloted to women a more smooth and soft composition of body, infers thereby her intention, that the mind should correspond with it."[34] In the eyes of Allestree and his contemporaries, passivity was part of a woman's physical as well as emotional nature. To act against its biological imperative could label the woman a "monstrosity."

In addition to discussing a woman's physiological nature, courtesy books stress that she inhabits a world which is distinctly different from that of her male contemporaries. As Allestree observes in his "Preface," the temptations men are subject to are "out of [women's] road," for while men "converse in the world," women do not.[35] A woman's "world" is of limited compass, comprising her home and family, a constricted setting for which, Allestree adds, she should be grateful as it makes the path to virtue so much smoother. In contrast, men, the stronger and more resilient sex, were suited for "converse" outside this world. In *The Lady's New-Years Gift* (1688), the Marquis of Halifax explained such differentiation to his daughter as the law of nature: "You must first lay it down for a Foundation in general, that there is *Inequality* in *Sexes*, and that for the better Oeconomy of the World; the *Men* who were to be the Lawgivers, and the larger share of *Reason* bestowed upon them; by which means your sex is the better prepar'd for the *Compliance* that is necessary for the performance of those *Duties* which seem'd to be most properly assign'd to it."[36] Compliance, a passive virtue like meekness, becomes a necessary part of the female character, and a woman's "duties," presumably marriage and motherhood, are dependent on this passivity. As Halifax explains, feminine submission is part of God's greater plan; to behave differently would be to go against nature.

The ideal woman could be said to be characterized by "piety and devotion, meekness, modesty, submission," as in *The Vertuous Wife is the Glory of her Husband* (1667).[37] Paradoxically, these passive virtues are said to constitute her strengths as well as define her emotive nature. As Allestree reminds his readers: "the Female Sex, which being of softer mold, is more pliant and yielding to the impressions of pitty."[38] Such feminine softness makes women particularly sensitive to the two "most sensible passions," namely "Fear and Love."[39] This perception of women, prevalent throughout the later seventeenth and eighteenth centuries, corresponds to alterations made to Shakespeare's plays as, in keeping with the nature of the pathetic play, adapters add scenes featuring helpless female virtue, ennobled by love and fraught by fear.

With the possible exception of Desdemona and Ophelia, both of whom appeared virtually unaltered on the Restoration stage, Shakespeare's women are rarely meek and seldom passive. Though many could qualify as monstrosities under Allestree's definition, the same is not true of female characters in the adaptations. Instead, the plays recreate a patriarchal system in which women have no power beyond the masochistic ability to arouse sympathy by their suffering,[40] an ability mirrored in the audience response to pathos. This suffering is rarely caused by the heroine's own wrongdoing; it instead results from her selfless love or from her passive attempts to defend her virtue against malefactors. In effect, virtuous women in these plays, as in pathetic drama, prove their virtue by their ability to suffer, and the adaptations abound with pictures of helpless women, suffering under the oppression of villains. Aside from a few of the female characters in the romantic comedies (rarely performed in the late seventeenth century), women—such as Regan, Goneril, and Lady Macbeth—who display impatient or aggressive tendencies are uniformly represented as villainesses.

Because the women of the adaptations inhabit a world different from that of their Shakespearean counterparts, a world in which women have been defined by their emotive qualities, they are excluded from the public world of politics and government. Good women are detached from their political context, leaving adapters uncertain of how to treat women who are neither apolitical nor passive. Even (or perhaps especially) Shakespeare's strongest and least domestic women are rewritten to fit into this category. Dryden's *All for Love* (1678), although not strictly an adaptation, provides a succinct expression of the new Shakespearean heroine when Cleopatra, according to Dryden a "pattern of unlawful love," laments her failure to conform to the feminine ideal and comments wistfully:

> Nature meant me
> A Wife, a silly harmless houshold Dove,
> Fond without art; and kind without deceit;
> But Fortune, that has made a Mistress of me,
> Has thrust me out to the wide World, unfurnish'd
> Of falshood to be happy.[41]

Cleopatra's words set up a dichotomy between the woman happy in her restricted domestic world and the woman who transgresses and moves beyond this realm into "the wide World." Cleopatra falls uncomfortably between these two extremes, wanting the "proper" role, but forced unwillingly into impropriety by "Fortune." Her definition echoes the views of women's place expressed by Allestree: by nature, good women cannot survive in the outside world; only those furnished with sufficient falseness can be happy. She has sinned because she has stepped outside the household into a realm where, as Allestree emphasized, the path to virtue is not so smooth. Other adapters adhere to this vision of women, and rewritten characters like D'Urfey's Eugenia or Tate's Virgilia are just the domestic doves Cleopatra would like to be. Dryden's Cleopatra is still a queen, but her disclaimer suggests that, in the Restoration at least, uneasy lies the female head that wears a crown.

Ironically, one of the strongest statements regarding a woman's proper realm comes from the mouth of Lady Macbeth when, maddened by guilt, she faults her husband for listening to her advice:

> You were a Man.
> And by the Charter of your Sex you shou'd
> Have govern'd me, there was more crime in you
> When you obey'd my Councels, then I contracted
> By my giving it.[IV.iv.54–57]

This explanation negates the power of Shakespeare's Lady Macbeth by recasting her strength as Macbeth's weakness. The passage's legal language ("charter," "Govern'd," "crime," "contracted") emphasizes the natural law ("Charter of Sex") which makes it a "crime" to step outside of approved sexual roles; women should not dabble in the public realm as does Lady Macbeth. Lady Macbeth is further marginalized by the increased focus on Lady Macduff, a harbinger of the passive heroines in the pathetic drama whose suffering brought vicarious pleasure to eighteenth-century audiences. While Shakespeare's Lady Macduff appears only once, the thumbnail sketch Shakespeare gives of a wife and mother develops into a picture of wifely devotion—the great love interest of the play. She provides the play with a sympathetic moral voice as D'Avenant exploits the opposition between the Macbeths and the Macduffs, creating parallel scenes between the two couples; every scene in which Lady Macbeth entices her husband into crime is juxtaposed with one in which Lady Macduff warns hers of ambition's evils and urges him to resist its temptation.

With few exceptions, the women in these plays are governed by love, either marital or maternal, while those women who do not display this feminine attribute are invariably villains, such as Lady Macbeth, the evil sisters in *Lear*, or Tamara in *Titus Andronicus*. Such a recasting of feminine nature requires major revisions to Shakespeare's works in general, for, while love is an important element in the romantic comedies and in some tragedies, it does not play a central role in many other plays, such as the political plays and the histories. By contrast, in the adaptations a focus on love is no longer restricted by genre. Almost every play focuses on a love story; where no love story is present in the original plays, new plots are created; where a love interest seems understated, adapters re-emphasize its importance, focusing attention more strongly on the domestic realm—marriage, love, and family. Even the political adaptations with their strong didactic messages move closer to the domestic realm than their Shakespearean originals. Virtuous kings and princes, like the ladies and gentlemen of other plays, are motivated by love above all else. Like the plays which both preceded and followed them, they too include a non-Shakespearean emphasis on love.[42]

Where love interests could already be said to exist, adapters generally took one of two paths. Some, like D'Avenant, simply multiplied the number of couples in the plays. Faced with the lackluster romances of *Measure for Measure*, D'Avenant added Beatrice and Benedict from *Much Ado about Nothing* and created a somewhat unconvincing attachment between Isabel and Angelo for good measure. In other plays he augmented the role of Lady Macduff to provide a loving, domestic counterpart to Lady Macbeth, and, with Dryden's help, scattered couples throughout *The Tempest*; even Ariel has a helpmeet. Few playwrights had D'Avenant's fascination with balance; most chose to augment relationships which were present, if understated, in the original plays. Both Nahum Tate and John Dennis stress the sentimental in their revisions of *Coriolanus*, and even the ill-fated adaptations of *Richard II* are careful to accentuate the affection between the doomed monarch and his queen.[43]

The emphasis on love necessitates a wholesale revision of most Shakespearean heroines in order to accommodate their new romantic function. Dryden, a consummate adapter himself, articulated what many other playwrights clearly saw as a weakness in Shakespearean drama: "Let us applaud his Scenes of Love; but, let us confess that he understood not either greatness or perfect honour in the parts of any of his women."[44] Shakespeare's women lack what *The Ladies Dictionary* (1694) defines as that "pliant and yielding nature"[45] conducive to self-abnegating love, the quality which provides the fount for female "greatness" in Restoration pathetic drama. The desire to elevate Shakespeare's earthbound women dovetails with the generally acclaimed heightening effect of love, and as a result, love becomes the ruling characteristic for virtuous women. It motivates all proper female action, and can only be checked by proper filial duty.

To preserve the impression of feminine meekness and modesty, a woman should display initiative only if motivated by love, so that Portia in Granville's *The Jew of Venice* (1701) explains that she disguised herself as the learned doctor in order to increase Bassanio's love for her. These changes have the cumulative effect of "elevating" Shakespeare's women by flattening them into one-dimensional icons of virtue who, not surprisingly, share many characteristics with the idealized women described in conduct books. The emphasis on love as a defining characteristic erases many more active qualities and, because love acts as the general cause of female suffering, its prominence stresses the heroines' ability to suffer passively, once again evoking pathos. Moreover, emphasizing a woman's role as loving and beloved defines her in relation to a man and de-emphasizes her autonomy as well as her political significance. Thus Tate's Cordelia gives up her dowry and the political power it represents to remain true to her heart, and by the same token, D'Urfey's Imogen (significantly rebaptised Eugenia, a name which emphasizes her noble birth rather than her link to a British Queen) loses her position as heir to the throne of Britain and, like Tate's Cordelia, sins by loving against her father's wishes rather than by creating a possible political misalliance. These rewritten women are Cleopatra's doves, paragons of a purely domestic realm where home and family are the only honorable concerns.

The most notorious of the superadded love interests appears in Tate's *King Lear*, where Tate creates a long-standing attachment between Cordelia and Edgar, two characters who, as Tate himself notes, never speak to each other in Shakespeare's play. Tate congratulates himself on the discovery of this structural and emotional bonus: " 'Twas my good Fortune to light on one Expedient to rectifie what was wanting in the Regularity and probability of the Tale, which was to run through the whole, a *Love* betwixt *Edgar* and *Cordelia*, that never chang'd word with each other in the Original. This renders *Cordelia*'s Indifference and her Father's Passion in the first scene probable. It likewise gives Countenance to *Edgar*'s Disguise, making that a generous Design that was before a poor Shift to save his Life. The Distress of the Story is evidently heightned by it."[46] Tate's goal, to "rectifie" a wrong and make what was improbable probable, hinges on the characterization of Cordelia who represents the major source of *King Lear*'s improbability. By furnishing her with a love interest, Tate provides a motive for her seeming lack of filial tenderness which thus becomes more "probable"; lack of filial duty is unnatural, but romantic love is not. Cordelia's elevation into a pattern of virtuous love brings a corresponding change in Edgar, and the result is more "distress" or pathos for the audience to savor. Tate here makes explicit not only the link between suffering and dramatic pleasure, but also the role love plays in inducing such suffering.

Revised to fit in with Tate's rubric of probability, Cordelia's comments in the opening scene are motivated entirely by her love for Edgar and her desire to avoid the political marriage sanctioned by her father. Torn by her duty to her father and her selfless love for the noble Edgar, she explains her plight to the audience; she must speak coldly to her father in order to avoid being "condemned" to the "loath'd Embraces" of a man she does not love.

What could be seen as the dross of Cordelia's character, her seemingly harsh answer to her father, is refined into an act of maiden purity. This Cordelia's character is defined by her affection for her father and for Edgar, and she rarely ventures beyond the limits of these familial and romantic concerns. Unlike her Shakespearean original, she does not appear at the head of an army avenging her father's wrongs. Instead, Edgar leads the army while Cordelia's only weapons are her beauty and her tears. Tears are unavailing when she is faced with danger; unable to help herself, she must await the assistance of Edgar or her father. (Ironically, conduct books such as *The Lady's New-Years Gift* frequently cite tears as one of the most powerful weapons in a woman's arsenal.[47])

In other plays, adapters kept the pre-existing love interests, but through careful cutting and rewriting made these love interests the central focus of the plays. Adapters of *Cymbeline* and *Troilus and Cressida*, two plays in which love is only one aspect of a multi-plotted drama, foreground the romantic stories while discarding other characters and subplots which they found irrelevant. In *Troilus and Cressida* (1678), Dryden's energies are directed toward reshaping Shakespeare's portrayal of two flawed lovers into a tragic story of star-crossed love—hence the subtitle "Truth Found Too Late." Carrying out this interpretation requires considerable pruning and reshaping, and Dryden trims away many of the scenes depicting the Greek camp in order to focus attention on the story of Troilus and Cressida.[48] His portrayal of virtuous and faithful lovers causes radical alterations to Shakespeare's play. Dryden's Cressida is a virtuous maid who only agrees to spend the night with her lover when Troilus promises to marry her, and whose constancy never wavers.

This premise necessitates major changes once Cressida arrives in the Greek camp; while Dryden follows the general outline of Shakespeare's play, he carefully explains the reasons behind the conduct of his characters. A faithful daughter as well as a faithful lover, Dryden's Cressida feigns love to Diomede only as a means to help her father escape back to Troy. As Calchas explains:

> You must dissemble love to *Diomede* still:
> False *Diomede*, bred in *Ulysses* School,
> Can never be deceiv'd,
> But by strong Arts and blandishments of love:
> Put 'em in practice all; seem lost and won,
> And draw him on, and give him line again.
> This *Argus* then may close his hundred eyes
> And leave our flight more easy.[49]

When Cressida asks, "How can I answer this to love and *Troilus*?" her father replies, "Why 'tis for him you do it" (IV.ii.262–263). Dryden's adaptation stresses the fact of Cressida's innocence, the "truth" which was found too late. This emphasis forces a conclusion rife with the sense of tragic romantic closure which Shakespeare's play so carefully avoids. Troilus accuses Cressida of infidelity but refuses to listen to her pleas of innocence. To prove her point, she stabs herself, and the play ends in a blood bath. When the "truth" which has defined Cressida's character is questioned, self-destruction becomes her only means of expressing herself and reinstating her virtue. She is not allowed to exist as a cipher, virtuous but dishonored. Death removes that ambiguity, and allows her to remain an exemplary pathetic heroine, chaste and silent forever.

By stressing the pathos of the defenseless woman, such alterations better fitted Shakespeare to the dramatic climate of the Restoration and to the eighteenth century. A generation later, an anonymous critic praises both Tate's *Lear* and Aaron Hill's *Henry V* (1723) for their skillful interpolation of love interests. In a pamphlet letter to Colley Cibber he advises Cibber to follow their example: "An Instance of improving or heightening a Character we have in *Edgar*, (in *King Lear*) as well as in *Cordelia*, between whom a Love Episode is not ill woven.—Another yet stronger is in *Catherine* (in *Henry* the fifth) whose Character in *Shakespear* is abominably low and obscene—The Improvement of her's has naturally rais'd that of *Harry*—Other Instances might be produced to shew, where *Shakespear* might admit, with great Beauty and Propriety, of strong Alterations, nay Amendments."[50] Echoing Dryden's sense of the "lowness" of many Shakespearean heroines, the author advocates love as the great ennobler, attesting to the success of the early adaptations. As with Tate's own comments on *Lear*, the author associates a "heightened" or "improved" female character with love, once again reiterating the views found in conduct book descriptions of the female character.[51] The motif of height, used repeatedly in discussions of Shakespeare's women, suggests a hierarchical conception of drama which corresponds to the role played by women. Laura Brown claims correctly that the "development of English tragedy is bound to the ideology of the defenseless woman,"[52] but this statement should be expanded to include the pathetic play and its precursors. These "higher" forms of serious drama depend for their emotional impact on the sufferings of a helpless but virtuous woman, her character "elevated" by love and self-denial.

Because of the essential connection between the suffering woman and serious drama, the issue of genre becomes key to the fate of Shakespeare's heroines. Shakespearean tragedies and histories were popular throughout the late seventeenth century, but, with the exception of the D'Avenant/Dryden *Tempest*, Shakespeare's comedies were rarely performed before 1700.[53] Restoration theater depended instead on a variety of different modes of comedy,[54] most notably the so-called comedy of manners in which ladies and gentlemen of polite society engage in witty banter and which frequently contains an underlying current of contemporary social satire.

Comparing the portrayal of women in drama to those in fiction, Jane Spencer is only partially correct when she describes women in Restoration drama as "passionate, sexual being[s]" in contrast to "the innocent, passionless, easily deceived creature gaining ascendancy in [the fiction of] the early eighteenth century."[55] Those characters which Spencer describes as passionate and sexual are, however, the heroines of Restoration comedies, plays built around the issue of marriage and frequently dependent on marriage to establish a sense of comic closure. Women can be portrayed as more active and outspoken because their power is once again limited to the domestic realm. Despite their wit and passion, they are still to some extent harmless household doves. More common in the tragedies, pathetic plays, and later so-called sentimental comedies are characters who act as exemplary figures, suffering patiently at the hands of a villain and thus not only proving their own innocence by their inability to react aggressively, but also providing concrete evidence of the villainy of their oppressors.[56]

The pathos of passive female virtue appears in its most extreme form in the adapters' fondness for scenes of attempted rape. While the threat of rape is uncommon in Shakespeare's plays,[57] it appears repeatedly in the adaptations. In *The Injured Princess*, D'Urfey creates a new character, Pisanio's virtuous daughter Clarinda, to share the role of innocent victim with Imogen/Eugenia. In a series of new scenes heavily laden with sensationalistic melodrama, the Queen accuses Clarinda of foiling her plans by helping Eugenia escape. Cloten and his drunken companion Jachimo (the Shakespearean Jachimo has been rebaptized Shattillion) promise to provide "punishment" and prepare to rape her. Pisanio arrives in the nick of time and kills Jachimo just as he is about to carry out his evil designs.

Likewise, in Tate's *Lear*, Edmund, not content with Regan and Goneril, compounds his villainy by resolving to kidnap Cordelia:

> Where like the vig'rous *Jove* I will enjoy
> This *Semele* in a Storm, 'twill deaf her Cries
> Like Drums in Battle, lest her Groans shou'd pierce
> My pittying Ear, and make the amorous Fight less fierce.[III.ii.122–25]

Fortunately, Edgar appears just in time to save Cordelia, and she is able to beseech him piteously to "befriend a wretched Virgin" (III.iv.33). Tate uses the titillation of attempted rape yet again in *The Ingratitude of a Common-Wealth*, his adaptation of *Coriolanus*, where Aufidius plans to "glut" his last minutes by raping Virgilia (who has come to find her husband), taunting Coriolanus that "to thy Face I'll Force her . . . And in Revenges Sweets and Loves, Expire."[58] Once again this evil is thwarted, but tragically, for Virgilia has chosen to die rather than meet a fate worse than death. She explains her suicide in terms of preserving a commodity as rape becomes a theft rather than a violation:

> My Noble *Martius*, 'tis a *Roman* Wound,
> Giv'n by *Virgilia*'s Hand, that rather chose
> To sink this Vessel in a Sea of Blood,
> Than to suffer its chast Treasure, to become
> Th' unhallowed *Pyrates* Prize.[59]

Virgilia here follows the example of Lucrece, another Roman matron, and preserves her honor by destroying herself. She acts to protect her virtue, but can do so only in a negative way; she sinks the vessel rather than saves it. Dryden's Cressida reacts similarly when her virtue is called into question. For the virtuous women in the adaptations, suicide is an acceptable alternative action. It reaffirms both virtue and femininity while completing the picture of pathetic suffering.

In each case the attempted rape functions to establish moral distinctions. It represents an assault on innocent virtue and provides clear evidence of villainy, making the distance between good and evil characters more obvious. The scenes present an obvious exposition of masculine evil. By being set in opposition to this evil, female virtue is made to appear more absolute—particularly virtue in the form of chastity. Only pure, virtuous women are the victims of would-be rapists (who are attracted by their very innocence) as the plays suggest that only true chastity can be threatened by rape. Thus, in these scenes, an attempted rape becomes perverse proof that such chastity exists. If the character is not virtuous, then rape cannot be a threat. Such chastity, and by extension feminine virtue in general, is a valuable commodity which becomes useless if marred, hence the suicide of characters such as Virgilia and Cressida. Chaste virtue must be destroyed if damaged because it has become a contradiction in terms.[60]

The depiction of women as icons of virtue leaves them defenseless against the world, seemingly glorifying them while actually camouflaging their ultimate victimization. Perversely, it is a woman's purity which attracts her ravisher, and her passivity which prevents her from repelling his attack. Passive rather than active, meek rather than aggressive, these paragons of virtue cannot survive outside their narrowly defined sphere. The presence of women on the stage as well as the idealization of the passive female has a profound effect on the larger structure of drama, creating a need for new generic forms to accommodate these rewritten women. Focusing on woman as denizens of the private sphere results in the transmutation of Shakespearean genres—romantic comedy, history, romance, and even tragedy are transformed into Restoration modes such as the pathetic play.

Politicizing Shakespeare

Stirring up emotion through powerful visual representation, theater is by its very nature a political act, and adapters were quick to exploit the political potential of Shakespeare's drama. The Restoration provided a new political climate, and the treatment of Shakespeare's plays was highly politicized as playwrights found new dangers and new opportunities in the Shakespearean plot. Tensions peaked between the years 1678 and 1682 when England was in a state of turmoil; not only was the memory of civil war still fresh, but these years also saw the furor over the supposed Popish Plot, spurred by Titus Oates's lurid testimony of Catholic conspiracy, and the increasing struggles of Charles II with the Parliament over the Exclusion Act. During these same years the number of adaptations written and produced increased dramatically; ten new adaptations appeared on the stage, almost all of them dealing directly or indirectly with the problem of factions and rebellions.[61]

Many depended for their effect on the audience's ability to recognize resemblances between what appeared on the stage and contemporary politics. The playwrights of this period used adaptation as a potentially safe way to express political views, and to attract spectators into the theaters. In a politically charged era political drama was a good business proposition, and these adaptations generally enjoyed good runs, making money for both their creators and the theaters which produced them. Although censorship was less organized than in earlier and later eras, government forces effectively shut down most opposition drama with the result that most adaptations contained a distinctly pro-Charles flavor.

Shakespeare's histories and Roman plays were ripe for political reinterpretation, representing as they did the struggles for power during the War of the Roses or in the Roman Empire. Many playwrights saw parallels between their troubled times and the turmoil Shakespeare portrayed. As Nahum Tate observes in the "Epistle Dedicatory" of *The Ingratitude of a Common-Wealth*, "Upon a close view of this Story, there appear'd in some Passages, no small Resemblance with the busie *Faction* of our own time." The adapters chose to emphasize this similarity, using their plays to comment upon the current situation, a didactic intent which they emphasize in dedications and prologues. Tate's title is itself an explicit political statement, and he elaborates on the message his audience should receive in the Epistle Dedicatory: "Where is the harm of letting the People see what Miseries *Common-Wealths* have been involv'd in, by a blind Compliance with their popular Misleaders: Nor may it be altogether amiss, to give these Projectors themselves, examples of how wretched their dependence is on the uncertain Crowd . . . The Moral therefore of these Scenes being to Recommend Submission and Adherence to Establisht Lawful Power, which in a word is LOYALTY." Tate both states his own position and distills drama's inherent political effect. It incites action by vivid visual representation, "letting the People see" the errors of their ways. In the case of *The Ingratitude of a Commonwealth*, theatrical representation should incite loyalty to the "establisht Lawful Power." Loyal subjects should submit to this authority, revering the government of Charles II rather than Parliament with its "projectors."

Like Tate, most Restoration playwrights insist that their adaptations be politically interpreted. In his letter "To The Reader," Edward Ravenscroft explains the genesis of his adaptation of *Titus Andronicus* as a reaction to contemporary politics:

It first appear'd on the Stage, at the beginning of the pretended Popish Plot, when neither Wit nor Honesty had Encouragement: Nor cou'd this expect favour since it shew'd the Treachery of Villains, and the Mischiefs carry'd on by Perjury, and False Evidence; and how Rogues may frame a Plot that shall deceive and destroy both the Honest and the Wise; which were the reasons why I did forward it at so unlucky a conjuncture, being content rather to lose the Profit, then not expose to the World the Picture of such Knaves and Rascals as then Reign'd in the Opinion of the Foolish and Malicious part of the Nation: but it bore up against the Faction, and it confirm'd a Stock-Play.[62]

Despite Ravenscroft's disclaimer, his *Titus* was indeed profitable, if not for the pious reasons he reiterates; it is more likely that the play thrived because of the *frisson* created by its parallels with Titus Oates and his accusations. The play alludes to the Popish Plot by dwelling on "the Mischiefs carry'd on by Perjury, and False Evidence," as well as bringing the "Knaves" who perpetrate these crimes to a particularly bloody and painful end. The final scene not only includes Shakespeare's cannibalistic feast and the deaths of Lavinia, Tamara, Titus, and the Emperor, but provides even more graphic horrors such as the bloody remains of Tamara's sons, Tamara stabbing her own child, and culminates with Aaron tortured on the rack and ultimately burned alive on stage—a vision of justice not imposed by the contemporary judicial system.

With the exception of Shadwell's *Timon of Athens, the Man-Hater*, the political adaptations of the late 1670s and early 1680s reshape Shakespeare to emphasize the horrors of civil war and the disasters that can result from the attacks of "busie factions." Ravenscroft's *Titus Andronicus* (1678) stays close to Shakespeare's plot, yet becomes topical by emphasizing the horrible end of plotting and perjury. John Crowne's two adaptations of the *Henry VI* plays, *The Misery of Civil War* (1680) and *Henry the Sixth, the First Part. With the Murder of Humphery Duke of Gloster* (1681), display the horrors of civil war brought on by rebellious factions and the dangers of a court filled with Catholic advisers (a feature which made *Henry VI, the First Part* unpopular at court where Catholic sympathies ran high). Thomas Otway's *The History and Fall of Caius Marius* (1680), a romanized version of *Romeo and Juliet*, portrays a republican Rome governed by warring factions; the Caius Marius of the title is the leader of one of the factions, not a lover, and his ambition, coupled with what Otway portrays as the inherent instability of a republic, destroys the star-crossed lovers.[63] Tate's *King Lear* (1681) portrays a civil war, not the invasion of England by France, and ends with the restoration of the true heirs to the throne (Edgar and Cordelia) while *The Ingratitude of a Common-Wealth* (1682), like *Caius Marius*, shows the dangers of a commonwealth where factions seduce the multitude resulting in bloodshed, suffering, and eventual destruction not of Rome (for Rome read England) but of the faction itself.[64]

With their emphasis on the evils of rebellion against rightful authority, these plays present staunchly conservative political statements. In each play, rebellious factions plot to overthrow authority with the result of civil war and general misery. Only Tate's *King Lear* ends happily with the Restoration of the king.[65] Scenes of destruction coupled with didactic speeches explaining the evils of rebellion abound, as in *The Misery of Civil War*, where Crowne graphically indicates the horrors of civil war:

> *The Scene is drawn, and there appears Houses and Towns burning, Men and Women hang'd upon Trees, and Children on the tops of Pikes.*
> 1 & 2 *Country Girls.* Oh Heaven! have mercy on us! have mercy on us!
> 1 *Souldier.* Now Rogues, how do you like Rebellion? [36]

This apocalyptic scene provides a visual icon of the results of rebellion as Crowne, along with other adapters, reminds his audience that rebellion spells the destruction of civilization. Agitation inevitably leads to misery, and in the end the instigators are punished, often regretting the blind ambition which led them to rebel. Thus, Otway's Marius Senior, having just witnessed the suicide of Lavinia (Juliet) laments his radical activities:

> Be warn'd by me, ye Great ones, how y' embroil
> Your Country's Peace, and dip your Hands in Slaughter.
> Ambition is a Lust that's never quencht,
> Grows more inflam'd and madder by Enjoyment. [V.477–80]

The moral here could with equal ease be applied to the other Tory adaptations.

Only in Thomas Shadwell's *Timon of Athens* (1678) do the political undertones run counter to this trend. Unlike Crowne, Tate, and Otway, Shadwell was a Whig, and his adaptation of *Timon* reveals these sympathies. While his play makes no overt references to contemporary politics (the subject never appears explicitly in his prologue or dedication), it stands alone as the only play in which a rebellious faction not only surges to victory but by doing so cleanses a corrupt system and brings liberty to the people, suggesting a parallel between Alcibiades' attacks on the Athenian Senate and the Duke of Buckingham's attacks on what Whigs saw as a corrupt government, an aim which Shadwell emphasizes by dedicating the play to Buckingham. To make his point, Shadwell increases the importance of Alcibiades, making him a foil to Timon. Thwarted in love like Shadwell's Timon and betrayed by those whom he had assisted, this Alcibiades chooses the path of moderation, rather than misanthropy. Like Shakespeare's character, he goes before the senate of Athens to argue for the life of a fellow soldier, but he then goes further and exclaims against the corruption of the Athenian government:

> Banish me! Banish your dotage! Your extortion!
> Banish your foul corruptions and self ends!
> On the base Spirit of a Common-wealth![66]

Alcibiades frees Athens from its corrupt rulers, and, in a speech unlike any found in Tory adaptations, lauds the benefits of rebellion against corrupt authority, here embodied in a republic which sounds remarkably like the monarchy of England:

> Thus when a few shall Lord it o're the rest,
> They govern for themselves and not the People.
> They rob and pill from them, from thence t'increase
> Their private stores; but when the Government
> Is in the Body of the People, they
> Will do themselves no harm. [272]

In a time when Charles II was beginning his long struggle against the Whigs in Parliament, this speech represents an explicit political stand against the king and in favor of Parliament, which did, in part, represent the body of the people. Timon's death is briefly noted, but the play ends with a rosy look at the future:

> May Athens *flourish with a lasting Peace;*
> *And may its wealth and power ever increase.*
>   *All the People shout and cry,* Alcibiades! Alcibiades!
> *Liberty, Liberty, &c.* [273]

By following the action of Shakespeare's play, Shadwell cannot be accused of inventing the struggle within Athens. His representation of government by an elite versus the need for a governing body (Parliament), however, as well as his portrayal of a virtuous and bloodless uprising (in stark contrast to Crowne), set *Timon of Athens* apart from the Tory adaptations which were to follow.[67]

Occasionally a play's political message made it too inflammatory for the stage. Despite Nahum Tate's attempts to paint Richard II as a saintly hero and the usurping Bolingbrook as a villain, his adaptation of *Richard*

II was immediately banned. Tate tried unsuccessfully to sneak the play into production under the title of *The Sicilian Usurper* (1681), apparently believing that an Italian setting might make the crime of regicide more forgivable, but the play was banned once again. Not only was the portrayal of the successful deposition of a king a touchy subject in the troubled years of the early 1680s, but the censors feared it might suggest an uncomfortable parallel between Charles II and his unfortunate father as well as presenting an unflattering portrait of a king "*Dissolute, Unadviseable [and] devoted to Ease and Luxury.*"[68] Twenty years later the first act of Colley Cibber's *Richard III* (1700), where Richard's murder of Henry VI presents another picture of deposition and regicide, was also suppressed.[69]

As politics moved off the stage and into the pamphlet wars of the mid-eighteenth century, political adaptations became rare, especially in the aftermath of the censorship imposed by the Licensing Act of 1737. In 1723, Aaron Hill's revision of *Henry V* moves Shakespeare's play resolutely away from politics and into the domestic realm. Rather than portraying Henry's conquest of France, the play focuses on Henry's courtship of Katherine; the battle scenes function only as a backdrop for a plot against Henry's life and for the reuniting of the lovers.[70] Political adaptation did not disappear in the eighteenth century, but, with the exception of Colley Cibber's virulently anti-Catholic *Papal Tyranny in the Reign of King John* (1745), the *modis operandi* of infusing a play with political significance changed.[71] Rewriting plays was no longer a ready option both because of censorship and because of the growing reluctance to tamper with the text. In general, the Restoration adaptations represent the malleability of Shakespeare's plays in the late seventeenth-century theater. The political slant is given by changing the text, not simply by innuendo or superadded appendages such as prologues, epilogues or Epistles Dedicatory. Playwrights appropriate Shakespeare's works for their own cause, usurping his text in order to make use of his authority. By "letting the People see," they use Shakespeare as theater, creating an effect by means of a physical representation dependent on the modification of Shakespeare's text.

The emphasis on contemporary political themes, as with the rewriting of Shakespeare's heroines, controls the Shakespearean text by limiting it and thus rendering it less dangerous, just as the omission of Shakespeare's language reduces the danger of misinterpretation. Like the labeling of female characters as "good" or "bad," the attempt to convey an unmistakable political message necessarily involved the eradication of any ambiguity which could lead to misinterpretation. Whether the message being promulgated was Tory or, in the case of Shadwell, Whig, it required considerable simplification of the complex issues raised in

Shakespeare's plays in order to avoid misinterpretation. Political mottos had to be clearly expressed, carefully avoiding figurative language which could confuse the point being made, and the political heroes and villains made suitably distinct. Such didactism negates ambiguity as it attempts to guide (if not control) choice.

The widespread nature of these changes underscores the impact of the drama and the potential danger which the performance of a play represented. Only with the disturbing qualities of his language and action explained and thus controlled could Shakespeare become a mainstay of Restoration theater. In the guise of Restoration drama these adapted works lost the danger they possessed in their original form and fit more neatly into the world of Restoration and early eighteenth-century theater. They represent the history of a literary text before it was subsumed beneath the weight of an author, before the canonization of Shakespeare included a canonization of his words. The lack of textual sanctity, which allowed playwrights to consider his plays remoldable, sanctioned the very changes which reshaped his drama into a formal dance of rigid stereotypes. This paradox of simultaneous fluidity of text and rigidity of form typifies a world before the growth of the print industry had made drama a product of the page as well as the stage; consequently plays were perceived as works to be performed, not read.[72] Poised between the world of Renaissance theater and the deification of all things Shakespearean, the radical adaptations reflect a vision of literature as moral action rather than text.

2
The Beginnings of Shakespeare Criticism

Literary criticism focused upon Shakespeare appeared during the same period in which the most radical adaptations flourished. Occasional critical commentary of Shakespeare had existed during the first half of the seventeenth century, but discussion of native English literature was rare before the Restoration.[1] Loosely defined as "neoclassicism," this early period of literary criticism includes the decades between the Restoration and the Licensing Act and ends with the rush of new editions of Shakespeare in the 1730s and 1740s. During the later seventeenth century, literary criticism was infrequent and occasional, generally taking the form of dedicatory essays or prefaces. Critics directed their essays toward a specific patron, and thus the intended audience almost invariably consisted of the aristocratic and well-educated. The advent of Addison and Steele and the periodical essay in the second decade of the century marked a change in both the form of criticism and its audience. The patronage system which had supported earlier critics such as Dryden slowly fell out of use, and by 1730 most critics wrote periodical essays at least occasionally. Addressed to a broader audience, this new form consisted of shorter, less erudite essays and generally appealed to more bourgeois interests.

While the form of criticism changed during this time and writers placed more emphasis on the inculcation of culture and manners, the critical vocabulary and approach to literature remained essentially constant. Despite the changes, critics retained their goal of rational, balanced critical assessments, and within this framework their attitude toward Shakespeare remained unaltered. Critics from Dryden to Addison, Pope, and Theobald regarded Shakespeare as England's greatest natural genius but tempered their praise with judicious references to his flaws. While political affiliation may have affected a critic's choice of texts, it did not affect his attitude toward Shakespeare—nor his assessment of Shakespeare's beauties and faults. Critics touted Shakespeare as a noble but flawed exemplar of the English national character, and his status as the national poet created a tension with the interest in French-influenced neoclassic theory. Looking back to classical critics such as Horace and Aristotle and reading (if not always agreeing with) French critics such as Boileau, Shakespeare's early critics assume that literature's function is both to please and to instruct, with the emphasis generally falling upon instruction. By the first decades of the eighteenth century, the concept of instruction broadens from the purely moral to include topics such as the development of taste popular with the more bourgeois audience of the periodical essayists. But in the end, most discussions of Shakespeare incorporate the question of moral instruction.

Early criticism of Shakespeare has long been consigned to neglect and misrepresentation. These works have often been blamed for inciting the Shakespeare revisions through their attacks on Shakespeare and their endorsement of the neoclassic "rules."[2] Such cause and effect arguments have little relevance; rather than drama being affected by criticism or vice versa, they share a common set of literary goals, ideals, and authors. Most of these early critics were themselves playwrights, and many major critical works were originally prefaced to plays. This dual role of playwright/critic was particularly characteristic of the adapters of Shakespeare. Tate, Shadwell, Cibber, and Gildon all wrote critical essays, while the two greatest critics of the period, John Dryden and John Dennis, both experimented with adaptation. Almost every playwright wrote on Shakespeare and almost every critic was himself a playwright. The notable exception to this rule was Thomas Rymer, a scholar (and for many years Historiographer Royal) with few connections to the world of theater. Where the critic/playwrights of necessity were familiar with audience reaction and could appreciate Shakespeare's ability to elicit emotion, Rymer could not. During this period, criticism became a viable literary form; although few critics other than Dryden and Howard wrote during the decade after Charles's restoration, soon every literary figure of any note was printing his views on literature. Few, however, created a structured critical system; most wrote out of the heat of the moment, influenced strongly by particular circumstances and many, not infrequently, later changed their minds.[3]

Theory and Nationalism

The great link between early and late critics in this period is their adulation of Shakespeare. They lavish praise upon him in terms as extravagant as any used by the Romantic poets, finding him "incomparable," "immortal," and even "divine." Effusive praise prefaces each piece, even when a discussion of faults is necessary in order to prevent charges of blind partiality, as John Dennis explains in "On the Genius and Writings of Shakespeare" (1712):

Who shews most Veneration for the Memory of *Shakespeare*, he who loves and admires his charms and makes them one of his chief Delights, who sees him over and over and still remains unsatiated, and who mentions his Faults for no other Reason but to make his Excellency the more conspicuous, or he who pretending to be his blind Admirer, shews in Effect the utmost contempt for him, preferring empty effeminate Sound to his solid Beauties and manly Graces, and deserting him every Night for an execrable *Italian* ballad, so vile that a Boy who should write such lamentable Dogrel, would be turn'd out of *Westminster*-School for a desperate Blockhead, too stupid to be corrected and amended by the harshest Discipline of the Place.[4]

Enumerating a writer's faults, in this case those of Shakespeare, represents an important rhetorical ploy. It acts as a foil "to make his Excellency the more conspicuous" and also proves the critic's objectivity—he can be believed because he is no "blind Admirer." Unadulterated praise, on the other hand, is linked to effeminacy, foreignness ("*Italian* ballad") and stupidity—qualities in direct opposition to Shakespeare's manly and English virtues. Writings on Shakespeare followed one of the two patterns Dennis describes: a general panegyric, or an essay beginning with general homage, moving to a discussion of Shakespeare's faults and concluding with a final burst of praise. Commentary quickly becomes conventional, a series of almost formulaic tributes in which critic after critic lauds Shakespeare for his fire, variety, soul, natural genius, and ability to move.

The fundamental contention of these early critics is that Shakespeare is the greatest English poet, perhaps the greatest poet of all time.[5] Dennis writes that "there is nothing perhaps more accomplish'd in our *English* Poetry" (II, 4), while Dryden, in the encomium in the *Essay of Dramatic Poesy*, commends him as "the man who of all modern, and perhaps ancient poets had the largest and most comprehensive soul"—"soul" being the seat of inspiration and thus of poetic greatness. Such eulogizing presents Shakespeare as the epitome of all that is great in English drama—the poet of fire and master of variety who excelled in moving his audience. These two qualities, fire or liveliness and variety, were seen by many as the defining characteristics of English drama, the qualities that raised it above the French and even, in the eyes of many critics, above the Greek and Roman stage. The praise of Shakespeare thus defines the qualities of an emerging national literature—and indirectly establishes the virtues of the British national character. In his plays, fire and variety work together to move the emotions, even those of the discerning English audiences. "He had so truly fine a Talent for touching the Passions, and they are so lively in him, and so truly in Nature," writes Dennis, "that they often touch us more without their due Preparations, than those of other Tragick Poets, who have all the Beauty of Design and all the Advantages of Incident" (II, 4). In more colloquial terms, Robert Gould, a minor Restoration satirist, expresses a similar idea:

> When e'er I *Hamlet* or *Othello* read,
> My Hair starts up, and my Nerves shrink with Dread!
> *Pity* and *Terror* raise my Wonder high'r
> 'Till betwixt both I'm ready to expire![6]

Here nonclassical (i.e., English) drama produces the supreme classical emotions of pity and fear, proving that Shakespeare's talent was more than merely provincial, making him a classic in his own right. Whatever he might lack of "Mechanick Beauties," he excelled at the essentials of dramatic poetry.

Stressing Shakespeare's virtues as an English poet, the Restoration and early eighteenth-century critics implicitly and often explicitly contrasted his plays, and through them the English stage in general, to contemporary French drama. Despite the neoclassic label frequently applied to this period, few critics could bring themselves to exalt the rigid orthodoxy of French drama with its rules and propriety, over the wild irregularity of English drama. Where theory opposed national pride, national pride won easily. The late seventeenth century was marked by political distrust of the French and, for the two decades after 1690, almost continual war with France (War of the Grand Alliance, War of the Spanish Succession). Striving to remain patriotic Englishmen, critics defined themselves in opposition to their political and literary enemies, the French. With his unregulated vigor, Shakespeare represented a distinctly English mode that could be appropriated for the patriotic cause, and critics touted him as a national hero—the native genius who could outshine the insipid French. In the critics' hands, Shakespeare becomes a powerful ideological tool, the representative of English virtue and a focus for patriotic emotion. In adaptations, playwrights used Shakespeare's works to validate a variety of political positions. Critics went one step further and created a mythological figure who could be easily appropriated, establishing Shakespeare, both the man and his works, as a national emblem.

Both Dryden and Dennis at times approved of many elements of French neoclassic theory; nonetheless both scathingly condemned French vapidness. Dryden in particular attributes literary flaws to defects in national character; the French excel at "nicety of manners," a quality that, though polished, is superficial and deeply boring:

Their heroes are the most civil people breathing; but their good breeding seldom extends to a word of sense; all their wit is in their ceremony; they want the genius which animates our stage; and therefore 'tis but necessary, when they cannot please, that they should take care not to offend. But as the civilest man in the company is commonly the dullest, so these authors, while they are afraid to make you laugh and cry, out of pure good manners make you sleep. They are so careful not to exasperate a critic that they never leave him any work; so busy with the broom, and make so clean a riddance, that there is little left either for censure or for praise: for no part of a poem is worth our discommending where the whole is insipid; as when we have once tasted of palled wine, we stay not to examine it glass by glass.[7]

The English, on the other hand, are untidy but animated, keeping the critics busy and theater audiences awake.

A generation later, Joseph Addison (himself the author a strictly regular play) outlined the limitations of the French mode:

Among great Genius's, those few draw the Admiration of all the World upon them, and stand up as the Prodigies of Mankind, who by the meer Strength of natural Parts, and without any Assistance of Art or Learning, have produced Works that were the Delight of their own Times and the Wonder of Posterity. There appears something nobly wild and extravagant in these great natural Genius's, that is infinitely more beautiful than all the Turn and Polishing of what the *French* call a *Bel Esprit*, by which they would express a Genius refined by Conversation, Reflection, and the Reading of the most polite Authors. The greatest Genius which runs through the Arts and Sciences, takes a kind of Tincture from them, and falls unavoidably into limitation.[8]

Despite the early eighteenth century's interest in refinement and Addison's own extensive writings regarding literary and social taste, he rejects such tasteful productions as limited. Not only do the French lack true Genius, but if they had it, their rules and "refinement" would taint it irrevocably. In contrast, Shakespeare is, of course, Addison's example of England's great natural genius. With Addison, as with Dryden and with critics throughout the Restoration and eighteenth century, Shakespeare becomes the literary marker that distinguishes the English from their political and cultural enemies. His symbolic role in this battle made it necessary for critics to reconcile his works with contemporary literary theory, and the potent myth of Shakespeare as national genius establishes the literary figure as a new kind of hero, vanquishing the French in a war of wit while leading the English to victory. This political undercurrent is seen most directly in Dryden's *Essay of Dramatick Poesy* where Dryden's praise of Shakespeare is embedded within a dialogue spoken during the English defeat of the Dutch fleet.

The superiority of England's native genius over (foreign) artificiality informs the widespread praise of Shakespeare as the poet of nature. The favorite approach to Shakespeare during this period was to portray him as natural genius, unlearned in the ways of art. The comparison with Homer, another great spirit of nature, is inevitable, and Shakespeare quickly becomes the English Homer. Both poets embodied natural genius and were seen as the starting points of a national body of literature. "Art" developed later and, though an admirable quality, should not replace nature (the mistake made by French neoclassicism). Critical commonplaces comparing the virtues of Nature and Art abound, as in Gould's "The Play-House" (1689): "*Homer* was Blind, yet cou'd all Nature see; / THOU wert unlearn'd, yet knew as much as He!" (p. 177); or in the Preface to Nicholas Rowe's edition of Shakespeare where Rowe claims that "Art had so little, and Nature so large a Share in what he did."[9] Comparisons with the "artful" Jonson arise so frequently that they too become conventional. Even with all the benefits of his learning and craft, "faultless Jonson" cannot please as well as Shakespeare. The critics concur with Dryden: "I admire Jonson, but I love Shakespeare."

In the eyes of Restoration writers, Shakespeare's lack of art could be easily explained by the "barbaric age" during which he wrote. As seen by seventeenth- and eighteenth-century writers anxious to vindicate their own talents, poetry in previous centuries was as yet undeveloped, and the English language rough and unrefined. The taste of the people was equally crude. Because he wrote to please an untutored audience whose lack of discernment was most apparent in its vulgar love of puns, Shakespeare could be easily forgiven. To many critics, these disadvantages only made his genius shine the brighter, for, as Dennis observes, they prove that "his beauties were entirely his own, and owing to the Force of his own Nature" (II, 4). Although some critics, such as Dennis and occasionally Dryden, reiterated Shakespeare's lack of art and sighed over what might have been, others (such as Nicholas Rowe) even saw these liabilities as advantages, for too much learning might have tamed Shakespeare's great "fire" or restrained his luxurious "fancy." The unspoken fear that their own age lacks the genius of Shakespeare, Jonson, and Beaumont and Fletcher adds a certain poignancy to the words of these critics. Despite their refined language and education, as Dryden laments, they cannot match the original genius of their predecessors:

"Not only we shall never equal them, but they could never equal themselves, were they to rise and write again. We acknowledge them our fathers in wit; but they have ruined their estates themselves, before they came to their children's hands. There is scarce a humour, a character, or any kind or plot, which they have not used" (Monk, 72–3). Dryden and his fellow critics present an early example of what W. Jackson Bate has termed "the burden of the past" and Harold Bloom the "anxiety of influence" in their sense that all the good plots and ideas have already been used. All that is left for the Restoration poets, continues Dryden, is to perfect the language and write in rhyme. His observation provides a melancholy gloss on the practice of adapting Shakespeare's plays where playwrights borrowed plots and characters from their "fathers in wit," contributing the garnish of a "more perfect" idiom.

The greatest single misconception attached to this period is its fondness for the so-called rules, the dramatic unities and the standard of decorum. Scholars in the nineteenth and twentieth centuries have been too willing to attribute early disapproval of Shakespeare to his failure to follow these neoclassical strictures—and many leave their examination of Shakespeare criticism at that. Showing little if any correspondence to the rules, the Shakespeare adaptations of the Restoration are themselves evidence of the inadequacy of this generalization. When looking at contemporary criticism, we see that the conflict between Shakespeare and the rules is a point glossed over by most writers. During this period, only three critics, Dryden, Rymer, and Dennis, examined Shakespeare in terms of the rules. Most of their contemporaries were interested in the rules and found them important assets to tragedy—but only in contemporary drama. Much twentieth-century abuse of the early critics of Shakespeare can be attributed to a misunderstanding of the rationale of objectivity that underlies the beauties-and-faults mode of criticism, as outlined in the passage from Dennis quoted above. In our own idolatrous age it is often difficult to remember that in the early eighteenth century, Shakespeare, although revered, was not yet beyond reproach. Praise of his works was expected to be balanced by an acknowledgment of his faults; within this context, his lack of "art" as embodied in the mechanical rules was his most obvious flaw—and one which could easily be overturned by a defense of natural genius.

When discussing Shakespeare, most critics rejected the rules in terms as conventional as their praise. In general, any mention of Shakespeare and the "mechanical" rules came either in a catalogue of beauties and faults (where his failure to follow the rules was a fault overweighed by his multitude of beauties), or at the beginning of any essay devoted to his praise. As Rowe observes, all agree that his plays are consistently irregular, and "it is without controversie, that he had no Knowledge of the Writings of the Ancient Poets, not only from this Reason, but from his Works themselves, where we find no traces of anything that looks like an Imitation of 'em" (p. iii). However, Rowe goes on to argue that these standards are not applicable because Shakespeare had no knowledge of the ancients and thus cannot be expected to conform to their guidelines; unacquainted with the regularity of classical precepts, he "lived under a kind of mere Light of Nature" and thus "it would be hard to judge him by a Law he knew nothing about" (p. xxvii). By this logic, reproaching Shakespeare with his failure to follow the rules is not only irrelevant but improper critical practice. As Lewis Theobald was to write twenty years later, such an attack is outside the realm of the critic: "As to the General Absurdities of *Shakespeare* in this and all his other Tragedies, I have nothing to say. They were owing to his Ignorance of the *Mechanical* Rules and the Constitution of his Story, so cannot come under the Lash of Criticism."[10] He adds later that even if they could be held against Shakespeare, "I could without Regret pardon a Number of them for being so admirably lost in Excellencies."[11] In essence, the issue of rules versus brilliant irregularity is nothing more than an example of the conflict between art and nature where, once again, nature is elevated over art. Nor should it be forgotten that the rules were seen as French influenced and thus politically suspect, so that denigrating them presented once again the triumph of British nature over French art.

Too little has been said about the negative reactions to the rules; disclaimers appeared as early as 1664 in Richard Flecknoe's *A Short Discourse of the English Stage* (and, in 1668, in Sir Robert Howard's "Preface" to *The Great Favourite, or The Duke of Lerma*), and such attacks continued throughout the first half of the eighteenth century, culminating in Samuel Johnson's "Preface to Shakespeare" (1765). Important not only as a footnote in the history of criticism, these assaults align critics with broader political concerns. English drama is irregular, these critics argue, but better it should be so than to degenerate into insipidity like the drama of the French. If the French have fewer faults, says Richard Flecknoe in his *Short Discourse*, it is because they confine themselves to narrower limits.[12] They have regularity, but they lack genius. In contrast, the English stage is a large canvas on which major actions can take place: "Our *Genius* of Stage-poetry can no more reach the Heights that can please our Audience under [Corneille's] unity Shackles than an Eagle can soar in a Hen-coop. If the *French* can content themselves with the sweets of a single Rose-bed, nothing less than the whole Garden, and the Field round it, will satisfie the English."[13] In the eyes of these critics, the rules are destructive and even unpatriotic, "shackles" that hinder the flight of genius. They destroy the delight drama should bring by curtailing its variety, and by opposing variety, the rules deny the defining characteristic of the English stage. If English playwrights follow the rules too closely, they will produce plays as limited and spiritless as the French. The implicit equation of regularity with the superficial and the inane appears even in conservative critical works, as in Thomas Purney's "Preface" to *Pastorals* (1717) where Purney concludes, "yet give me a dozen faults if there's half as many noble Graces blended with 'em, before a Poem that's as regular as insipid."[14] Shakespeare may have his faults, but in the eyes of these critics he is never insipid, a sentiment tangibly supported by the adapters' refusal to reduce Shakespeare to regularity.

Only John Dennis seriously argues that Shakespeare should have adhered to these French "unity shackles." While praising Shakespeare's power to move (a quality Dennis found essential to good drama), he stresses that had Shakespeare followed the rules, practiced "poetic art," he would have moved "ten times more" (II, 5). However, like Dryden, his interest in the rules fluctuates with the object of his essays. The appraisal of Shakespeare's genius in "On the Genius and Writings of Shakespeare" (1712) incorporates a discussion of Shakespeare's irregularity into the traditional beauties-and-faults framework. As usual, Shakespeare's genius far outweighs his artistic faults. In Dennis's defenses of the stage, such as his attacks on Jeremy Collier (1698) and on Mr. Law (1726), the topic of dramatic rules disappears.[15] They become an issue only in the works that attack the modern stage or which attempt to codify contemporary taste (such as "The Advancement and Reformation of Modern Poetry" [1701], which discusses the regression of dramatic poetry since Shakespeare's time, or "The Decay and Defects of Dramatic Poetry, and of the Degeneracy of the Publick Tast" [1725], which laments the disappearance of Restoration drama). Dennis subscribes to a vision of a national drama slowly becoming more correct, moving from unregulated glories to a more regular, if less inspired, future. The rules are important to him only in terms of this future; he regrets their absence in Shakespeare but freely admits that the preceding age got along well enough without them. Where he does differ from his own age is in his adaptations, *The Comical Gallant*, 1702 (*The Merry Wives of Windsor*), and *The Invader of His Country*, 1719 (*Coriolanus*), which attempt to regularize Shakespeare's less "artistic" works. The fate of Dennis's adaptations reveals the extent to which he was atypical of his age; both failed miserably and were never revived, proving that a critic's ideal of drama does not always make a good play.

The Defeat of Rymer

The praise of Shakespeare over any critical system was not entirely universal, and one critic, the "infamous" Thomas Rymer, was unrelenting in his disparagement of Shakespeare and of English drama in general. Rymer has received attention disproportionate to his actual contribution to late seventeenth-century criticism. His name frequently appears as an example of the stupidity of Restoration and eighteenth-century attitudes toward Shakespeare (or, more recently, as "the first would-be rebel against Shakespeare's aesthetic sovereignty").[16] Neither approach is adequate. Although known today chiefly for his two books on tragedy, Rymer's occupation was historiography; he practiced criticism only occasionally. His first book of criticism, *The Tragedies of the Last Age Consider'd and Examined by the Practice of the Ancients, and by the Common Sense of All Ages*, appeared in 1677, not long after the publication (and failure) of Rymer's one attempt at playwriting, his highly regular tragedy, *Edgar* (1677). The work emphasizes rationality and common sense, as Rymer passes over the unities, focusing his argument on decorum, which he terms common sense, but, as editor Curt A. Zimansky notes, "by easy steps this use of common sense leads to rules and rules to a system."[17] Rymer's "system" decrees that poetry should imitate ideals, or types. Thus, kings should always be portrayed as behaving nobly, because to do otherwise would not be in the character of a king. Under the same criterion, "in Poetry no woman is to kill a man except her quality gives her the advantage above him; nor is a Servant to kill the Master, nor a Private Man, much less a Subject to kill a King, nor on the contrary" (65). The occasion which prompted these strictures was an attack on three plays by Beaumont and Fletcher, with a promise to move next to Shakespeare.

Perhaps the most interesting aspect of *The Tragedies of the Last Age* is the *lack* of critical response it received. Despite the maligning of Beaumont and Fletcher, no critic felt called upon to defend them in print. Rymer's book was largely ignored when it first appeared, although Dryden commended it to Charles, Earl of Dorset as "the best entertainment" he had had in a long while (Watson, I, 209). He admired the essay's wit, although he disagreed with many of Rymer's statements and jotted down notes for a response. Never published in Dryden's lifetime,[18] "Heads of an Answer to Rymer" has become the most famous, although not necessarily the most effective, refutation of Rymer. Complaining that *Tragedies* "is extreamly Learned; but that the Author of it is better Read in the *Greek* than in the *English Poets*," Dryden opposes Rymer's demand that English drama follow the form of ancient drama. The two traditions, he argues, are too different to be judged by the same criteria. While he does not mention the "mechanical" rules, the separation of English and Ancient drama implies that these rules are not necessarily relevant to English drama; the English have qualities the Greeks lacked. "It is not enough that *Aristotle* has said so," he adds, "for *Aristotle* drew his Models of Tragedy from *Sophocles* and *Euripides*; and if he had seen ours, he might have changed his Mind" (Monk, 191).

Rymer's second book, *A Short View of Tragedy; Its Original, Excellency, and Corruption. With Some Reflections on Shakespear, and other Practitioners for the Stage* (1693), was not so calmly received. Rymer begins by devoting six chapters to a brief history of tragedy until the Elizabethan period. Then, in his seventh chapter, he launches into his controversial study of *Othello*. Unlike the conversational wittiness of *Tragedies of the Last Age*, the tone of *A Short View* is bitter and rancorous. Rymer makes no attempt to be judicious, focusing his energies on an all-out assault: "In the *Neighing* of a Horse, or in the *growling* of a Mastiff, there is a meaning, there is a lively expression, and, may I say, more humanity, than many times in the Tragical flights of *Shakespear*" (136). As in *Tragedies of the Last Age*, Rymer passes over the unities and focuses his attention on the rules of decorum, or, as he terms it, probability. Othello, Iago, and Desdemona all come under attack because they do not conform to proper stereotypes: Moors cannot become generals, soldiers should be "open-hearted, frank, and plain-dealing," not deceitful and wicked, and Venetian ladies do not marry blackamoors. Having disposed of the characters, thought, and expression, Rymer moves on to the plot, hoping to show, he remarks sardonically, "how probable, how natural, how reasonable the Conduct is, all along" (143). He defines probability more rigidly than in his earlier critical work; every event, he argues, must be absolutely realistic, and thus he can find no virtue in *Othello*'s plot. Othello's jealousy is impossible, the loss of the handkerchief improbable, and, in general, the characters do not speak or act as they should in real life. Thus, "instead of moving pity, or any passion Tragical and Reasonable, [*Othello*] can produce nothing but horror and aversion, and what is odious and grievous to an Audience" (150). Applying strict logic to the plot, Rymer presents his famous "Morals": "First, This may be a caution to all Maidens of Quality how, without their Parents consent, they run away with Blackamoors . . . Secondly, This may be a warning to all good

Wives, that they look well to their Linnen. Thirdly, This may be a lesson to Husbands, that before their Jealousie be Tragical, the proofs may be Mathematical" (p. 132). For Rymer, *Othello* has no redeeming features unless read as a "bloody Farce."

The immediate and universal rejection of this attack (unlike the lack of response to Rymer's disparagement of Beaumont and Fletcher) shows how much English critics had invested in their national poet—and belies their impartial stance. Dryden, who had respected Rymer's first appraisal of tragedy, responded angrily to Rymer's slurs against his own plays, and even more strongly to his review of Shakespeare. In the "Epistle to Lord Radcliff" (1693), Dryden lashes out against Rymer's style of criticism: "But there is another sort of insect, more venomous than the former; those who manifestly aim at the destruction of our poetical church and state; who allow nothing to their countrymen, either of this age or the former age. These attack the living by raking up the ashes of the dead; well knowing that if they can subvert their original title to the stage, we who claim under them must fall of course. Peace be to the venerable shades of Shakespeare and Ben Jonson!" (Watson, II, 159–60). In contrast to his previous notes, *Tragedies of the Last Age*, Dryden rails at Rymer, finding him not only personally repugnant but even dangerous in his attack on England's poetical forefathers—namely Shakespeare. Rymer's commentary is not merely wrongheaded, it "aims at the destruction of our poetical church and state" and thus constitutes a national threat. Dryden himself feels vulnerable, for if Rymer "subverts" Shakespeare's genius, all poets who follow will be undone as well. He uses equally strong language in a letter to the young critic John Dennis, the only letter published during Dryden's lifetime:

I cannot but conclude with Rym[er] that our English comedy is far beyond any thing of the Ancients. And notwithstanding our irregularities, so is our tragedy. Shakespeare had a genius for it; and we know, in spite of Mr. R——, that genius alone is a greater virtue (if I may so call it) than all other qualifications put together. You see what success this learned critic has found in the world after his blaspheming Shakespeare. Almost all the faults which he has discovered are truly there; yet who will read Mr. Rym[er] or not read Shakespeare? For my part, I reverence Mr. Rym[er]'s learning, but I detest his ill nature and arrogance. I indeed, and such as I, have reason to be afraid of him, but Shakespeare has not. [Watson, II, 178]

As with his reference to the destruction of England's poetical church and state, Dryden's use of "blaspheming" implies that Shakespeare is in some way sacred so that attacks of this sort are akin to heresy, whereas his rhetoric sets up a source for this sanctity—genius. In Shakespeare, this genius is so great that it cancels out any faults that might weaken its creations. Dryden dismisses Rymer's argument by pointing out the simple truth that, despite Rymer's virulence, people will still read Shakespeare and be moved by his works. He admits the "faults" that Rymer lists but reminds his reader that Rymer did not balance this argument by considering genius, the most important aspect of Shakespeare's work. Left so unbalanced, Rymer's argument is nothing but empty sound.

Although a sense of outrage united Dryden's fellow critics, they nonetheless had difficulty articulating their indignation. Dryden promised a defense of Shakespeare in answer to Rymer, but never completed the project. Dennis, however, did write a rebuttal, *The Impartial Critic* (1693). Billed as a refutation of Rymer, the work, written as a series of dialogues between two urbane gentlemen, focuses on tangential issues, Rymer's call for a chorus in tragedy and his praise of Edmund Waller, but never manages to discuss Shakespeare. While Dennis shares Dryden's sense of outrage, he makes no dent in Rymer's argument. Confounded by Rymer's logic, but determined to defend Shakespeare if only by presenting an *ad hominem* assault, other critics quickly stepped in to take up the attack. Most focused on the discrepancies between Shakespeare's plays and Rymer's ill-fated *Edgar*.[19] Charles Gildon, however, avoided this temptation and attacked Rymer by defending Shakespeare. In "Some Reflections on Mr. Rymer's *Short View of Tragedy*" (1694), Gildon, after a discreet bow to Dennis, points out the inaccuracies of Rymer's analysis of character by using Rymerian logic: Othello is a Christian, which explains his high position; Desdemona's love for Othello is not unusual—Shakespeare was simply following a precedent set by the ancients such as Virgil's Dido who falls in love with Aeneas, a stranger; Iago's character also remains consistent with poetic decorum because on one hand many soldiers are not open-hearted and frank but bloody and vicious, while on the other, he is Italian which should make him "by Nature *Selfish, Jealous, Reserv'd, Revengeful, and Proud.*"[20]

But Gildon is most successful when he shows the flaws of Rymer's methods by turning them on the ancients Rymer so revered. Viewed through Gildon's witty impersonation of Rymer, the ancients become a collection of highly indecorous writers. Homer fails dismally; his Juno is nothing more than a scolding fishwife, far "too low for an *Heroic* Poem," who nags her husband so that all he can do is to "threaten to Thrash her *Divine Jacket.*"[21] In a brilliant parody of Rymer's "morals," Gildon mockingly denigrates classical tragedy by pointing out the improbabilities of one of its greatest triumphs, Sophocles' *Oedipus*: "First, then, let all Men before they defend themselves on the Highway think well of what they do, lest, not being Mathematically sure he's at home, he kill his own Father... Next, let e[v]'ry Younger Brother that ventures to ride in another Man's Boots be very circumspect, lest he marries his own Mother. Thirdly and Lastly, this may be a caution to the few Fools that doat on Virtue, that they trust to a rotten Reed that will be of little use to 'em, since all is whirl'd about by an unavoidable necessity."[22] The point of Gildon's mockery is clear; the flaws Rymer finds in *Othello* lie not in the play itself but in the methods used to examine it. No tragedy, not even those of the ancients, can succeed when subjected to such a rigorous dissection of probability.

The response to Rymer, like the attacks on "frenchified" rules, suggests that classical precedents were ultimately expendable and, conversely, that Shakespeare, with all his irregularities, was not. Even by the end of the seventeenth century, Shakespeare's stature as "poetical church and state" was well established as a source of national pride. No one denied that he failed to observe the "mechanic beauties" of plot (i.e., the unities and decorum), but they also agreed that this was a minor flaw. There is a melancholy implication behind these discussions of the rules, a sense that they are important to the contemporary playwrights because their age lacks the genius of Shakespeare and must fall back on the rules to support its literature. The outrage occasioned by Rymer's *A Short View of Tragedy* provides the most conclusive proof of the Restoration's ambivalence toward neoclassical theory. In Rymer's work, Shakespeare and the rules meet head to head, and in the angry attacks on Rymer, Shakespeare wins hands down. Perhaps the strongest evidence of Rymer's lack of influence appears when we consider that, despite his lengthy examination of *Othello*'s weaknesses, no adaptation of *Othello* was attempted.

Linguistic and Moral Chaos

Despite the ardor with which critics defended Shakespeare against Rymer, they were still able to see flaws in his works, and in their inventory of his failings we find the strongest connection between critical works and the adaptations. Though revered as the English Homer, Shakespeare had not yet become so sacred that any word which did not praise him was blasphemy (all-out attacks, however, were a different matter). It has been later generations of scholars who view Shakespeare and his works as sacrosanct and who, looking back, have seen this attempted objectivity as a desecration. This willingness to be critical, in conjunction with the desire to present a seemingly impartial judgment, leads to the frequent reiteration of a catalogue of Shakespearean faults. In general, Restoration critics focus on two subjects of censure: Shakespeare's language and the moral attitude represented by his plays. And, not surprisingly, these are the aspects of the plays most commonly revised by adapters. Many critics found Shakespeare's plays sadly lacking on both counts; his genius still greatly outweighed these flaws, but his works would have been almost beyond reproach had he only worked a bit harder to refine his language and define his morals. With the same set of writers involved in both criticism and playwriting, similar assumptions concerning the goals of drama (particularly tragedy) appear in both genres. In drama, the morals are expressed through action, particularly the denouement, while in criticism these values are set out as precepts, clarified and codified.

Characterized by double entendre, word play, and oratorical excess, Shakespeare's language attracted a variety of different responses. On its most basic level, his language was criticized for its "natural rudeness" (as in Shaftsbury's *Characteristics*, 1711).[23] Commentary of this sort echoes the discussion of Shakespeare's failure to follow the rules; critics agreed that, like Chaucer, Shakespeare lived in an age that spoke a ruder, less polished English, and thus he cannot be held responsible for his "unpolished Stile." It was commonly accepted, as Dryden argued in "The Defense of the Epilogue" (1673), that the English language had been greatly refined in the generations succeeding Shakespeare.[24] "Our thoughts are better dressed," he asserts, and then seeks to "prove" that language has progressed. While many critics supported this view of the evolution of language, some claimed that Shakespeare's English was clear and comprehensible, a view which became more prominent by the end of the seventeenth century. Even Dryden admitted in the "Preface" to *All for Love* that "it is almost a miracle that his language remains so pure."[25]

More specific objections arose from the discussion of whether Shakespeare's diction, use of metaphor, and love of puns was appropriate to the theater. This argument rested on a theory of decorum in language similar to Rymer's laws of probability. As Dryden states repeatedly, drama is mimetic, a "picture of nature," and as such its language must reflect that of the world. Characters must speak in ways appropriate to their station, their emotions and their dramatic genre, or the play will lose its sense of reality. On a basic level, this theory is straightforward and easily followed: kings do not speak like guttersnipes, a character in the throes of anger should speak so as to reflect his turmoil (a favorite example was Othello's speeches in Act IV), colloquial language should be reserved for comedy. Critics agreed that Shakespeare observed the first criterion but had problems with his representation of the second two, finding a disturbing element of "fustian" and "bombast" among the brilliance. While some, such as Charles Gildon, perceived Shakespeare's blank verse as "brought to such a Perfection, that the highest Praise is to imitate his Stile,"[26] most had problems reconciling their theories and Shakespeare's use of language.

Theories regarding the kinds of language suitable to poetry had multiplied by the latter part of the seventeenth century. Changes in dramatic practice were widely recognized and commented on, as in the prologue to a 1667 performance of Shirley's *Love Tricks*: "That which the World call'd Wit in *Shakespeare's* Age, / Is laught at, as improper for our Stage."[27] Shakespeare's "wit" attracted if not ridicule at least censure because it did not adhere consistently to post-Renaissance ideas of wit, which, as Dryden defines it, was "a propriety of thoughts and words; or, in other terms, thoughts and words elegantly adapted to the subject" (Watson, I, 207). A poet should not use words or expressions that are not appropriate to the subject or situation, a rule of thumb extending to the use of figurative language. Dryden writes,

The composition of all poems is, or ought to be, of wit, and wit in the poet, or wit writing (if you will give me leave to use a school-distinction) is no other than the faculty of imagination in the writer, which, like a nimble spaniel, beats over and ranges through the field of memory, till it springs the quarry it hunted after; or, without metaphor, which searches over all the memory for the species or ideas of those things which it designs to represent. *Wit Written* is that which is well defined, the happy result of thought or product of the imagination.[28]

Wit is recognized by its ability to define, to use imagery and diction to clarify a subject or situation. Letting the imagination run wild without the restraints (or "clogs") of judgment leads to overinflated diction or inappropriate imagery and confuses both the language and the sense. Critics labeled these excesses "bombast" or "fustian," "thoughts and words ill-sorted, and without the least relation to each other" (Dryden, Watson, I, 277).

Fustian was the Restoration's most common charge against Shakespeare, and the critics who praise his purity of expression are easily outnumbered by those who lament his lack of restraint. Once again, Dryden sets the tone, finding Shakespeare both the most brilliant and the dullest of poets: "He is many times flat, insipid; his comic wit degenerating into clenches, his serious swelling into bombast" (Monk, 55). This objection appears throughout Dryden's essays, particularly in "The Grounds of

Criticism in Tragedy" (1679), an essay published with Dryden's own adaptation of *Troilus and Cressida*, where he cites *Macbeth*, *Richard II*, and *Hamlet* as bombastic culprits. In these works Shakespeare gives "an extravagant thought, instead of a sublime one, a roaring madness, instead of vehemence; and a sound of words, instead of sense" (Watson, I, 259). Dryden's complaint would be echoed by Addison in a discussion of puns which he described as "a Sound and nothing but a Sound" and thus an example of false Wit.[29] Shakespeare's figurative language was also a point of contention in an age where metaphor in drama was often suspect because of its improbability: "The proper wit of dialogue or discourse, and consequently of the Drama, where all that is said is supposed to be the effect of sudden thought; which, though it excludes not the quickness of wit in repartees, yet admits not a too curious election of words, too frequent allusions, or use of tropes, or, in fine, anything that shows remoteness of thought or labour in the writer" (Dryden, Watson, I, 99). Extensive use of metaphor is inappropriate to drama because it is unlifelike; people do not use elaborate tropes extemporaneously, especially not in times of stress. As drama was perceived as a picture of nature, such figures were usually avoided.

The issue took on philosophical and psychological implications as writers pondered the mind's ability to form and comprehend metaphor. Hobbes cites the use of metaphor as second of his four "Abuses of Speech" (*Leviathan*, Part I, chapter 4).[30] John Locke addressed the problem in *An Essay Concerning Human Understanding*:

> He that applies the Words of any Language to *Ideas*, different from those, to which the common use of that Country applies them, however his own Understanding may be fill'd with Truth and Light, will not by such Words be able to convey much of it to others, without defining his Terms. For however, the Sounds are such as are familiarly known, and easily enter the Ears of those who are accustomed to them; yet standing for other *Ideas* than those they are usually annexed to, and are wont to excite in the Mind of the Hearers, they cannot make known the Thoughts of him who thus uses them.[31]

For Locke, the issue of metaphor is more one of psychology than decorum. By attaching unexpected words or expressions to an idea, or creating a metaphor, a poet makes himself and his thought incomprehensible to his readers who cannot bridge the void separating signifier and signified. Until such comparisons become familiar conventions, they remain "gibberish." Locke's predilection for empiricist logic here leads him away from actual human experience, for not even the strictest critic would argue that men cannot comprehend metaphors; nonetheless, he merely articulated more definitively the assumptions that prompted the widespread distaste for Shakespeare's imagery.

Shakespeare's frequent use of extended metaphor directly countered these theories. Dryden regretfully remarks moments when his "fancy" transports him "beyond the bounds of judgment" into an improper, even artificial use of language: "Racking words which were in use into the violence of a catachresis. It is not that I would explode the use of metaphors from passion, for Longinus thinks 'em necessary to raise it: but to use 'em at every word, to say nothing without a metaphor, a simile, an image, or description, is, I doubt, to smell a little too strongly of the buskin" (Watson, I, 257). Unwilling to attack Shakespeare directly, he picks an example from *Hamlet*'s play-within-the-play which he attributes to "some other poet," and decries its many faults of language.[32] Forty years later, Addison repeats these sentiments, finding Shakespeare "very Faulty" in his use of "hard Metaphors" and "forced Expressions."[33] As seen earlier, Shakespeare's adapters act on the general distrust of his diction and imagery and the ambiguity they embody; in each play rewritten during this period, the playwright refines Shakespeare's "barbaric" language. Archaisms are replaced by the Restoration's smoother tongue; puns are omitted; extravagant passages are pared down and their diction simplified; and, inevitably, the metaphors are literalized, eliminated, or conflated into simple similes.

While the disputes over the unities and Rymer's acerbic attack on Shakespeare had little or no effect on the adaptations, considerations of language clearly did. But critics assigned less importance to Shakespeare's language in the scale of literary merit. Following Aristotle,[34] critics such as Dryden and Dennis listed language third among drama's component parts. Shakespeare's faults of language, judged by this hierarchy, are a venial sin, easily forgiven by a seemingly more refined age. This ranking also contributes to adapters' lack of regard for Shakespeare's text; because language played a relatively minor role in literature, the plays could be reworded and still remain "Shakespeare." Separating Shakespeare's "thoughts" from his "language" was a commonplace idea. Dryden writes: "If Shakespeare were stripped of all the bombasts in his passions, and dressed in the most vulgar words, we should find the beauties of his thoughts remaining; if his embroideries were burnt down, there would still be silver at the bottom of the melting pot: but I fear (at least let me fear it for myself) that we, who ape his sounding words, have nothing of his thoughts, but are all outside; there is not so much as a dwarf within our giant's clothes" (Watson, I, 259–60). Like the dwarf in the ill-fitting clothes, thought and its cloak of words are easily separated. Shakespeare's genius, then, does not reside in these external trappings but in the core of thought—in his greatness of invention. In this way, an adapter can discard the cloak or refurbish it without damaging the genius beneath. Or, as Edward Ravenscroft remarked of his adaptation of *Titus Andronicus*, he was but restoring Shakespeare from the "heap of Rubbish" under which it lay hidden.[35]

Critics found Shakespeare's other "flaw," his suspect morality, harder to extenuate precisely because it could not be seen as superficial. A play's moral, according to the critics, resided in its plot or fable, in the actions committed by the characters and the consequences of these actions. Looking back to Aristotle's ranking of the parts of tragedy, Rowe remarks that the "fable" is generally ranked first among the constituent parts of serious drama, "not, perhaps as it is the most difficult or beautiful; but as it is the first properly to be thought of" (p. xxvii). When properly constructed, this fable would both move and instruct the audience; for most critics, the fable was the source of both effects. No one quibbled with Shakespeare's ability to move the passions of his audience, but most had some criticism of his plots and the moral message they conveyed. Some, like John Dennis in a particularly dyspeptic moment, even denied Shakespeare's ability to instruct. "Is there anything like a Fable in the celebrated Tragedies of Shakespeare," asks Dennis, "and consequently is there any instruction in them?" (II, 286).

The main focus of the debate over Shakespeare's morality was his failure to represent poetic justice. By rewarding the good and punishing the evil, a play should remind the audience that they too are subject to the same divine justice; failure to follow these guidelines could cause the playwright to be labeled as antireligious and even politically subversive. The phrase originated with Rymer in *Tragedies of the Last Age* (1677), but most critics employed the concept if not the term itself when discussing drama. Dennis, the most vocal advocate of poetic justice, explains the lesson it should present: "Those events are most entertaining, the most surprizing, and the most wonderful, in which Providence most plainly appears. And 'tis for the Reason that the Author of a just Fable must please more than the Writer of a Historical Relation. The Good must never fail to prosper, and the Bad must be always punished: Otherwise the Incidents, and particularly the Catastrophe which is the grand Incident, are liable to be imputed to Chance, than to Almighty Conduct and to Sovereign Justice" (II, 6). Poetic Justice, then, gives evidence that the world is guided by a just deity rather than the anarchy of chance; it provided writers like Dennis, and audiences like those that made Tate's *Lear* a success, the sense of security that they sought so desperately. Dennis elevates the theory, presenting it as the *raison d'etre* of tragedy: "I conceive that every Tragedy ought to be a very solemn Lecture, inculcating a particular Providence and showing it plainly protecting the good and chastizing the bad, or at least the violent; and that if it is otherwise, it is either an empty amusement or a scandalous and pernicious Libel upon the government of the World" (I, 200).[36] In addition to suggesting reasons for Dennis's failure as a playwright, this comment points to the supreme significance playwrights and critics attached to the fable. Characters and thought were important, but real instruction regarding "the government of the World" came from the plot and its outcome. (It is worth noting that Addison's famous attack on poetic justice defends the absence of such justice in drama on neoclassical grounds that can be traced back to the plot and its effect on the audience: the vicissitudes of virtue cause both "Terrour and Commiseration" and result in pleasure and an educational "serious Composure of Thought."[37])

Critics were quick to point out Shakespeare's failure to observe poetic justice. The list of offending plays is long, most of them tragedies. *King Lear* heads this list, where the death of Lear and especially Cordelia upset expectations, prompting a widespread outcry against the nihilistic catastrophe. Lewis Theobald spoke for many when he complained that "*Cordelia* and *Lear* ought to have surviv'd, as Mr. *Tate* has made them in his Alteration of this Tragedy: Virtue ought to be rewarded as well as Vice punish'd; but in their Death this Moral is broke through."[38] A wide array of tragedies were censured along with *King Lear*. Dryden questions the moral of *Troilus and Cressida* where "the chief persons, who give name to the tragedy, are left alive; Cressida is false, and is not punished" (Watson, I, 240).[39] Dennis, the most rigorous of critics in this regard, finds most of the tragedies at fault, particularly *Julius Caesar* and *Coriolanus*, "in which the Guilty and the Innocent perish promiscuously" (II, 7). He regards these tragedies as not only amoral but dangerous. In *Coriolanus*, the "promiscuous Events call the Government of Providence into Question, and by Skeptics and Libertines are resolv'd into Chance" (II, 7), while *Julius Caesar* suffers because it shows noble Romans committing a murder, "which Proceeding gives an Occasion to the People, to draw a dangerous Inference from it, which may be destructive to Government and to Human Society" (I, 200).[40] Dennis's comments link the "Government of Providence" with the Government of England. The absence of poetic justice is equally destabilizing to both—and equally dangerous. It encourages the audience ("the People"), "to draw a dangerous Inference"—i.e., to question the ruling power, whether it be God in his heaven or the King. Poetic justice would defuse such tensions and would encourage "the People" to support the controlling powers by showing such powers justly triumphant, as at the conclusion of Tate's *King Lear*. This search for coherence inspired interpretations that we today find perverse, such as Dryden's assessment of *Antony and Cleopatra*'s "excellent moral": "The chief persons represented were famous patterns of unlawful love; and their end accordingly was unfortunate" (Watson, I, 222). Poetic justice provided what many saw as a necessary curb on interpretation, controlling it within a predetermined moral matrix for reasons of social security.

In these two issues, language and especially in the representation of moral certainty, we see the conjunction of critical theory and adaptation. Like the criticism, the Restoration adaptations reflect a fear of ambiguity and the consequent obsession with poetic justice; most, if not all, incorporate an almost Manichean struggle of good and evil, resoundingly resolved. With the conclusion of the fable stressed as a political or philosophical statement, anything less than the triumph of good or destruction of evil would be immoral, a radical attack on the workings of government or of a benign God. Thus, in the adaptations, Lear and Cordelia triumph and order is restored, while the evil threat of villains such as Macbeth, Edmund, and Richard III is emphatically stamped out. Where the "mechanical beauties" of the unities failed to move critics or adapters, questions of morality, with their dangerous implications, inspired a vigorous response. Shakespeare's ambiguities posed a threat to the precarious world view of an age stripped of philosophic and social assurance. In a land recovering from civil war, in the midst of social and political flux, with the certainties of an earlier age gone, uncertainty was precarious and ultimately explosive. If drama presented an opportunity for instruction, dramatists (and the government censors) had to make sure that the audience did not learn the wrong lesson, and critics voice the fear that the audience, "the People," may be unpredictable. If drama was to instruct them wrongly, they could upset the moral, political, and social order. As so often, the desire for order masks a deeper fear of impending chaos. Shakespeare and his works are still too contemporary for comfort; their troubling ambiguities cannot be dismissed as simply one aspect of what a later age would call high culture. Critics and adapters present two reactions to the dilemma—one to comment upon, the other to remedy, and by restructuring Shakespeare's morality, each attempts to capture a modicum of order in a chaotic world.

The Emergence of a Shakespearean Text

Not all of the early eighteenth century's concern with Shakespeare was directed toward criticism and adaptation, and the new interest in editing Shakespeare makes an appropriate coda to this chapter. The stream of editions began with Nicholas Rowe in 1709, followed by Alexander Pope (1723), and Lewis Theobald (1734). Six editions followed in the mid- to later eighteenth century (Sir Thomas Hanmer, 1744; William Warburton, 1747; Samuel Johnson, 1765; Edward Capell, 1768; Edmond Malone, 1790—and numerous revisions of previous editions by George Steevens and Isaac Reed).[41] This concern with producing a fixed text of Shakespeare diverges from the Restoration adapters' interest in rewriting Shakespeare, and it would provide the impetus for a critical re-evaluation of Shakespeare's language. In direct contrast to the adaptations, these editions indicate a growing concern for preserving the words of Shakespeare as they were written. By the time of the Restoration, publishing Shakespeare's works was no longer as simple as reprinting an easily comprehensible near contemporary. The Restoration solution to this problem was to rewrite his text rather than to emend or annotate it. The early eighteenth-century editions represent part of the transition from the Restoration's cheerful disregard for the text to the later adaptations that would claim to preserve Shakespeare. With the surge of editions, critics directed their attention to the editors and the new editions quickly became a critical focus. The prefaces attached to each edition sparked a widespread reaction, as editors attacked one another while the critics took sides. The literary world's interest in works that attempted to provide a "genuine text" of Shakespeare heralds a break away from earlier attitudes toward Shakespeare and adaptation, a movement toward a new form of revision and a new literary focus on language that still dominates critical discourse.

Although they attempted to present a fixed canon of Shakespeare's works, these earlier editors often changed his text as much as they preserved it. Interest in performance rather than text is evident in Tonson's choice of Nicholas Rowe, the foremost tragic dramatist of the time, as editor of the first edition of Shakespeare. As the 1709 edition indicates, Rowe's interests lay with presenting Shakespeare as good drama rather than in elucidating his text. The text of the edition is taken almost unchanged from the most recent reprinting of Shakespeare's works (the 1685 Fourth Folio), and, rather than textual emendations or commentary, Rowe's contributions focus on dramatic production: division of the plays into acts and scenes and the assignment of localities to many of these scenes. His preface, "Some Account of the Life, &c. of Mr. William Shakespeare," provides a biography and a brief critical assessment of the plays but, not surprisingly, makes no attempt to discuss editorial practice. The title alone indicates Rowe's lack of interest in textual editing.

The focus on editing began in earnest twelve years later with Alexander Pope's edition. In his "Preface," Pope gives a general critical discussion of Shakespeare, but, unlike Rowe, he moves on to discuss the problems of Shakespeare's text. He admits that the Folio texts are corrupt and claims that Shakespeare's perceived lack of learning is actually owing to "the many blunders and illiteracies of the first Publishers of his Works."[42] He attributes many other "errors" to the ignorant players who copied and published the plays. In Pope's eyes, Shakespeare could not be held responsible for "errors" of language, meter, or history; such flaws were the work of other hands. This assumption establishes the editor, not the text, as the ultimate source of authority, and it allowed Pope as editor to take great liberties with the text in order to weed out this non-Shakespearean mishmash:

Some suspected passages which are excessively bad, (and which seem Interpolations by being so inserted that one can intirely omit them without any chasm, or deficience in the context) are degraded to the bottom of the page; with an Asterick referring to the places of their insertion . . . [and] the more obsolete or unusual words are explained. Some of the most shining passages are distinguished by commas in the margin; and where the beauty lay not in particulars but in the whole, a star is prefix'd to the scene. This seems to me a shorter and less ostentatious method of performing the better half of Criticism (namely the pointing out an Author's excellencies) than to fill a whole paper with citations of fine passages, with *general Applauses,* or *empty Exclamations* at the tail of them.[43]

By means of this physical manipulation of the text, Pope attempted to correct the "corrupted sense of the Author."[44] Although he collected a variety of Quartos and earlier editions, using them to replace lost passages, his edition has become infamous for its system of stars, commas, and asterisks. Metrical irregularities were refined, 1,560 lines were "degraded" to the foot of the page, and anachronisms, such as the use of hats in *Julius Caesar* were quietly removed. The eccentricities of Pope's edition echo his contemporaries in their depiction of both beauties and faults: Pope illustrates Shakespeare's beauties physically within the text and eliminates the faults. With its seemingly cavalier attitude toward Shakespeare's words, the edition graphically represents the absence of a sense of textual sanctity—a feature that would change in subsequent editions.

Scholarly clarification of the text was left to Shakespeare's next editor, Lewis Theobald. Eight years before his edition appeared in 1733, he attacked Pope's lack of scholarship by publishing *Shakespeare Restored* (1726). The book's subtitle, "A Specimen of the Many Errors, as well committed, as Unamended, by Mr. Pope in his Late Edition of this Poet," indicates his disapproval of Pope's methods. Focusing largely on *Hamlet*, Theobald quotes passages from Pope's edition along with his own "corrections," supporting his changes with internal evidence, a technique he also used in his edition. In his hands, the formerly rejected text becomes the ultimate authority: "As every Author is best expounded and explain'd in *One* place by his own Usage and Manner of Expression in *Others*; wherever our Poet receives an Alteration in his Text from any of my *Corrections* or *Conjectures*, I have throughout endeavour'd to support what I offer by *parallel Passages*, and *Authorities* from himself."⁴⁵ For Theobald, only evidence from Shakespeare's text, not an editor's faulty judgment, can authorize corrections and amendments. This method of textual comparison not only implies acceptance of the text but, more important, elevates the status of the text—in direct contrast to Pope's editorial practice.⁴⁶ Pope reacted angrily to the book, attacking Theobald in his second edition (1728) and crowning him King of the Dunces in the first *Dunciad* (1728). But, while he fumed, he did not hesitate to incorporate many of Theobald's corrections into his second edition.

Although damned in its time by Pope's ridicule, Theobald's edition can be seen as the first serious attempt to "correct" the "mangled condition" of Shakespeare's text. Recognizing the problem he was faced with, he gathered all available Quartos and Folios, collating them when he could and striving to support his changes with the use of parallel passages, as in *Shakespeare Restored*. His search, as he expressed it, was for the "genuine text"—not what Shakespeare should have written, but what he did write: "His genuine text is for the most part, religiously adhered to, and the numerous faults and blemishes, purely his own, are left as they were found. Nothing is altered but what by the clearest reasoning can be proved a corruption of the true text; and the alteration, as restoration of the genuine reading."⁴⁷ In his search for the "true text" of Shakespeare's works, "religiously adhered to," Theobald evokes a sense of textual sanctity (and even religious fervor) absent in previous approaches to Shakespeare but soon to become commonplace. Unlike Pope, Theobald's attitude toward Shakespeare is nonjudgmental, and unlike Rowe he is deeply concerned with presenting the words Shakespeare himself penned. As an editor, he strives to present an authoritative text, complete with blemishes. With his attacks on Pope's "unhandy slaughter" and his insistence on authorial support for any textual changes, Theobald stands in contrast to the early adapters who changed Shakespeare's text without scruples. Where early critics bemoaned Shakespeare's vulgar language, he claims that the language itself was at fault, not the poet: " '*Our language sunk under him, and was unequal to that Greatness of Soul which furnish'd him with such glorious conceptions.*' He therefore frequently uses old Words to give his Diction an Air of Solemnity; as he coins others, to express the Novelty and Variety of his Ideas."[48] Language fails, not Shakespeare. His archaisms and odd usages are not barbarisms but a struggle to express his genius within the confines of the English language. These sometimes scorned words need the protection of a careful edition, not the dangerous, if well-meaning, pruning of an overzealous editor. Theobald's edition, with its praise for the genius embodied in Shakespeare's words and its determination to render this genius inviolate, marks the path to be taken by future editors, critics, and adapters.

Part II
Refined from the Dross

3

Adaptation in Decline

Several decades elapsed between the Restoration adaptations and the next major cluster of Shakespeare adaptations. In the first forty years of the eighteenth century, the adaptation of Shakespeare's plays lost popularity. After Cibber's *Richard III* (1700) and Granville's *Jew of Venice* (1701), new alterations of Shakespeare appeared only sporadically and rarely achieved any lasting success. It was not until after 1740 that the adaptation of Shakespeare's plays again became common in the theater. But this later group of adaptations, written largely during the course of David Garrick's career, took forms that reflected major changes in attitudes toward Shakespeare and the increasingly important role "Shakespeare" played in the definition of Britain's cultural identity. During this time, the demand for drama in print (as opposed to on the stage) increased, and the display of one's acquisition of literary culture became a sign of social status. As the most prominent example of English literary genius, Shakespeare and his works were an important part of this process, becoming indelibly linked with the establishment of a national literature and a national culture. His works were as frequently read as seen, a development facilitated by the numerous editions which appeared after mid-century.[1] As literacy grew and the costs of printed works decreased, the literary marketplace shifted from the theater to the bookseller. All these events affected the treatment of Shakespeare's plays, both inside and outside the theater. Shakespeare's works were now widely recognizable as printed text, and attitudes toward them were shaped by a process of canonization in which the words themselves were sanctified.

These attitudes would seem to imply a conflict between Shakespeare adaptation and a greater reverence for the unaltered text. To some extent, the history of Shakespeare's works after 1700 involves playwrights and managers searching for ways to accommodate both Shakespeare's text and moral sentiments that appealed to an audience very different from that of the past. Whereas earlier adaptations, particularly Cibber's *Richard III* and Tate's *Lear*, were staged throughout the early decades of the eighteenth century, new adaptations appeared only sporadically, and then often died early.[2] Scattered though these plays were, they shared a common goal, that of making Shakespeare more decorous, more suitable to the refined taste of polite society.[3] Audiences in the early decades of the eighteenth century included a larger percentage of middle-class patrons than the more aristocratic audiences of the Restoration. Moral decency was, therefore, clearly an important selling point, a consideration that would become crucial to a later group of adapters.

Although relatively few adaptations of Shakespeare were written during this period, Shakespeare's plays, adapted or not, were staged in increasing numbers. The popularity of Shakespeare's plays fluctuated, reaching its height during the Shakespeare revival of the late 1730s and early 1740s.[4] As contemporary records indicate, the frequent productions of Shakespeare's plays were a response to audience demand, most notably the requests of the so-called "Shakespeare Ladies Club." During the late 1730s, playbills and prologues allude to Shakespearean plays (adapted or otherwise) performed "at the Desire of several Ladies of Quality." The prologues and epilogues to these revivals frequently thank "the Ladies" for restoring not only Shakespeare, but decency and virtue to the stage as well. As these prologues suggest, Shakespeare was seen as the defender of decency and associated with the defining traits of the British national character; he represented the "manly genius" of an earlier, more purely British age.[5] Reviving his plays was thus a patriotic act as well as evidence of good taste. During these years, almost the entire Shakespearean canon was staged, much of it unaltered. Even Shakespeare's comedies, most of which had never achieved the same degree of popularity as the tragedies and histories, played to full houses.[6] At the height of the revival, in 1740–41, Shakespeare constituted almost one fourth of London's theatrical bill. In the years after this peak, Shakespearean drama was still popular enough to support competing productions of the same play, thus breaking what Theophilus Cibber described as an "advantageous Rule . . . Which was that no Play acted at one house should ever be attempted at the other: This prevented a Satiety of the same Plays, and kept up the Pleasure which might otherwise grow languid."[7] By the mid-1740s, the public taste for Shakespeare was seemingly insatiable, a tribute both to the durability and to the popularization of his works.

This reverence for things Shakespearean especially inspired David Garrick, the man who, throughout his career, associated himself resolutely with the adoration of Shakespeare. Garrick made his debut as Richard III, and went on to become the leading Shakespearean actor of his day, a move that culminated in his paean to Shakespeare, the Stratford Jubilee. During Garrick's career as actor and manager, Drury Lane would stage more than seven new adaptations of Shakespeare, most of them written or compiled by Garrick himself.[8] Not only did new versions of Shakespeare appear on the stage during these years, but the form of these adaptations was markedly different from their predecessors in the Restoration and early eighteenth century. Two basic patterns of alteration appear among these plays. One group, compiled primarily between the years 1754 and 1763, consists of portions of Shakespearean plays severely reduced to one, two, or three acts.[9] The second group is smaller but more varied: full-scale adaptations of Shakespeare which re-examine plays more radically revised during the Restoration and early eighteenth century, a group which includes Theophilus Cibber's *Romeo and Juliet* (1748), Garrick's and Colman's versions of *King Lear* (1756 and 1768), and Richard Cumberland's *Timon of Athens* (1771).[10]

Restoration is the great theme of both groups of adaptations. Their playwrights did not claim, like Tate, to be refurbishing a "Heap of Jewels, unstrung and unpolisht,"[11] but to be bringing "more of [Shakespeare's] rich Scenes to light."[12] They are even more outspoken in their search to put unadulterated Shakespeare on the stage, and George Colman boasts that "Romeo, Cymbeline, Every Man in his Humour, have long been refined from the dross that hindered them from being current with the Publick; and I have now endeavoured to purge the tragedy of Lear of the alloy of Tate, which has so long been suffered to debase it."[13]

The emphasis here is on placing scenes before the public as Shakespeare wrote them, unrevised, if not complete. Even when the plays were shortened to one or two acts, additions were made in large blocks, usually in the form of new scenes inserted between previously existing Shakespearean scenes. Shakespeare's diction was rarely changed, and in plays that had been previously adapted, large segments of the original play were restored. Garrick's plea for his *Romeo and Juliet* characterizes this new attitude; he claims that "the only merit that is claim'd from [the play] is, that it is done with as little Injury to the Original as possible."[14] In the Prologue to a double bill of *Florizel and Perdita* and *Catherine and Petruchio*, Garrick expressed this desire for preservation even more directly:

'Tis my chief Wish, my Joy, my only Plan,
To lose no Drop of this immortal man.[15]

Ironically, Garrick used these lines to introduce his own adaptation—which eliminated the first three acts of *The Winter's Tale*.

The number of new adaptations declined during the last decades of the century, and few were published after the brief appearance of

Colman's *The Sheep-Shearing* in 1777. Occasionally, abortive efforts appeared in the early nineteenth century, such as an anonymous combination of Dryden's *All for Love* and *Antony and Cleopatra* in 1813.[16] These later versions, however, were largely Shakespeare, greatly cut and combined with fragments of earlier adaptations, but still almost entirely taken from the original text. By the end of the eighteenth century, only Cibber's *Richard III*, Tate's *King Lear*, and Garrick's farcical *Catherine and Petruchio* were still consistently staged. Versions of the Davenant/Dryden *Tempest* appeared occasionally, but the original was regaining popularity and slowly ousted its adaptations. The original *King Lear* finally returned to the stage in 1838,[17] but permutations of Cibber's adaptation remained popular throughout the nineteenth century and even into the twentieth. After the eighteenth century, adaptation as I have defined it, involving rewriting and/or massive omissions, becomes a virtually dead form. Where the eighteenth century reworked Shakespeare's text, the nineteenth century chose to "adapt" his plays in a different manner, using them as the inspiration for different theatrical forms such as ballets and operas.[18]

Although the adaptations of the later half of the century are fewer in number and less blatant in their changes than the earlier adaptations (so that the resulting lack of critical comment is not surprising), the diminished changes represent an important but too frequently ignored development in the literary perception of Shakespeare. As literary "myth" (to use Graham Holderness's term) Shakespeare had been hallowed decades before, but during the later eighteenth century his text, rather than just his name, became sanctified. To extend the religious metaphor, Shakespeare had been beatified in the Restoration and early eighteenth century, and now, with the passage of time, his status was being elevated closer and closer to divinity. But the object as well as the nature of this glorification was changing, and the exaltation of Shakespeare now extended to the smallest fragments of his genius. What adapters did while espousing this praise for the Shakespearean word was often very different. By the last half of the century, Shakespeare was perceived as a semi-divine author and cultural hero whose works were fixed, rather than as a near-contemporary whose works were revered but not held sacred. The focus on Shakespeare's text made the distinction between what was accepted as Shakespeare and what was not more rigid, resulting in the eventual disinheriting of all words not penned by Shakespeare himself. By the end of the century, rewriting Shakespeare was no longer tolerated, for it violated the words of his text, the feature that was increasingly seen as the essence of his greatness.

Shakespeare Abbreviated

The increased regard for Shakespeare's language is most clearly seen in the abbreviated adaptations favored by the late eighteenth century. To form these adaptations, playwrights cut out large portions of each play, radically altering the plot, form, and themes, but they were careful to keep the actual rewriting to a minimum. The plays consist of scenes or acts taken almost verbatim from Shakespeare; any additions are relatively brief, no more than three to four hundred lines and often much less, consisting of new songs or explanatory passages which substitute for the sections deleted. Thus truncated, each play was very short, no more than three acts, and was usually performed along with another full-length play, frequently another adaptation. Stripped of troubling moral questions, the plays usually served as afterpieces, light comic accompaniments to the main attraction. Seven such adaptations were published and performed during the later eighteenth century, each taken from either *A Midsummer Night's Dream*, *The Taming of the Shrew*, or *The Winter's Tale*—the most popular group of adaptations to reach the stage during this period.

The structure of these particular works lends itself to such massive cutting. Each play contains plots that are distinct from the rest of the play and could be reduced to two or three acts without destroying the sense of the work and without adding large sections of new material to replace what was lost. While they present what could be seen as an eighteenth-century version of Shakespeare's greatest hits, they also avoid tainting the words of the Shakespearean scenes with non-Shakespearean dross. The result is Shakespeare made diverting and easily assimilable—and thus commercially successful. In general, the adaptations themselves are not moral pictures of good and evil like the adaptations of the Restoration and early eighteenth century but entertainments—short, comical pieces laden with songs and witty dialogue. They present vignettes of domestic morality, marriages properly ordered or families reunited, couched in Shakespeare's own words. These adaptations make no attempt to resolve moral ambiguities for the simple reason that all such ambiguity has been eradicated. What is left after the cuts are short lively dramatic sketches consisting largely of Shakespearean dialogue, with some explanatory additions and new songs. In their attempt to pick out favorite Shakespearean tidbits, these playwrights resemble earlier adapters such as Sir William D'Avenant who transplanted the popular figures of Beatrice and Benedict into his adaptation of *Measure for Measure*. Unlike D'Avenant, however, rather than rewriting and reshaping the Shakespeare, they leave the words almost unaltered and the plays brief but generally unadulterated.

The various adaptations of *A Midsummer Night's Dream*—John Frederic Lampe's *Pyramus and Thisbe* (1745),[19] Garrick's *The Fairies* (1755), and Colman's *A Fairy Tale* (1763)—most clearly embody the shift from mainpiece to entertainment. Each play uses one or two of the three plot lines and simply eliminates extraneous scenes, filling in with singing or dancing. Because the plot lines are so distinct, none of these playwrights needed to add new expository material to bridge gaps left by deletions. Consequently, all three adaptations are almost entirely verbatim, and even the new songs added to Garrick's and Colman's versions echo or quote Shakespeare.

The simplest of the adaptations is Lampe's *Pyramus and Thisbe*, a simple representation of the play-within-the play from Act V. No attempt is made to include other aspects of *A Midsummer Night's Dream* or to make the playlet more than a burlesque. Later adaptations by Garrick and Colman draw upon the current popularity of opera and pantomime and use the play as the basis for opera or musical comedy. Garrick's *The Fairies* uses the lovers and the fairy sections of *A Midsummer Night's Dream* beginning with Act I and concluding with IV.i as Theseus and Hippolyta wake the lovers in the wood. Mindful of the current predilection for opera, Garrick lavished twenty-eight songs upon his three acts and billed the resulting concoction not only as opera but as "A New English Opera." Even though Garrick's "English Opera" was performed by a variety of non-English singers, it was Shakespeare (more or less) and thus, Garrick reasoned, inherently better than the popular Italian operas. Critics disagreed, complaining that the piece was anything but English, and *The Fairies* was only moderately popular (it had eleven performances but was never revived).[20] Eight years later, Colman used a more successful combination of music and farce in his afterpiece, *A Fairy Tale*. Even more compressed than *The Fairies*, Colman's play consists of two acts rather than three, focusing primarily on the mechanicals.[21] Without actually rewriting *A Midsummer Night's Dream*, Colman's formula of songs and pantomime-inspired farce created a Shakespearean entertainment more to the public taste than benighted lovers wandering through an enchanted wood.

Different patterns emerge in the adaptations of *The Taming of the Shrew* and *The Winter's Tale*. *The Taming of the Shrew* has only one actual adaptation, Garrick's *Catherine and Petruchio*. Although James Worsdale's "ballad opera" *A Cure for a Scold* (1735) is often classed as an adaptation (as in George Branam's *Eighteenth-Century Adaptations of Shakespeare*), reading the play reveals that there is little of Shakespeare in it aside from the general outlines of plot in which a shrewish daughter is subdued by an unorthodox suitor.[22] Garrick's *Catherine and Petruchio*, however, is firmly rooted in Shakespeare's text. First performed in 1754 (published 1756), the play was the most popular of the shortened versions, appearing more than 230 times before the end of the century. It remained popular throughout most of the nineteenth century, appearing frequently until 1886, when *The Taming of the Shrew* was revived in its entirety.[23] The major changes are cuts, to be expected as Garrick's play has only three short acts. The Induction with Christopher Sly and the Lords disappears, as do the early scenes with Bianca's suitors, so that the play begins with Baptista and Petruchio discussing the marriage of Catherine. As indicated by Garrick's title, the play focuses exclusively on the story of Catherine and Petruchio; the story of Bianca and her various suitors vanishes, and we see her only as the wife of Hortensio (not Lucentio). What remains comes essentially verbatim from *The Taming of the Shrew*. Catherine storms on stage for her first confrontation with Petruchio; in the next act we hear the account of the wedding and the journey home; in the third act Catherine is thwarted in her attempts to eat and dress; and finally, when Baptista, Hortensio, and Bianca come to visit, she delivers her speech on a wife's duty to her husband. While some speeches are transferred to different speakers, in general the lines remain as Shakespeare wrote them. Changes in diction are infrequent, usually moderating lines that could be seen as indelicate (e.g., Petruchio's comment that he means to warm Catherine "in thy bed" [II.i.267] becomes "warm me in thy arms" [I, p. 12][24]).

The result of these changes is a lively farce rather than a comedy, a tribute to domestic happiness in a cozily patriarchal family. While the language remains Shakespearean, Garrick's alterations have a moralistic flavor characteristic of much later eighteenth-century drama. In addition to trimming out all subplots, Garrick also reshapes the play to focus almost exclusively on marital love and duty. Much of the talk of money is eliminated; Petruchio is not concerned with marrying a wealthy wife. In fact, in Garrick's version he tells Baptista that he was "Left solely heir to all [his father's] lands and goods, / Which I have bettered rather than decreased" (*CP*, I.i.9–10). This Petruchio is a model member of the bourgeoisie—a good business manager who, having made sure that his accounts were in order, goes in search of domestic happiness. (Garrick's inclusion of Shakespeare's I.ii.75–6: "I come to wive it wealthily in Padua; / If wealthily, then happily in Padua" undercuts this picture of prosperity by suggesting the mercenary adventurer.) Later, the wager between Petruchio, Hortensio, and Lucentio is similarly omitted; it was undoubtedly vulgar to bet upon your wife's behavior—especially if you were a loving husband.

Garrick adds fewer than one hundred lines of his own, most of them intended to soften the play's harsh edges. The most substantive addition appears at the end of the play, where Garrick provides new lines for both characters, placing them more firmly in their proper roles of paternal but loving husband and submissive and loving wife. After Catherine delivers part of Katherina's long speech on a woman's duty (*TS*, V.ii.136–179), punctuated by Petruchio's sounds of approval, Petruchio confesses that his autocratic behavior has been but a mask and that in reality he is a gentle and loving husband:

> My fortune is sufficient. Her's [sic] my wealth:
> Kiss me Kate; and since thou art become
> So prudent, kind, and dutiful a wife,
> Petruchio here shall doff the lordly husband;
> An honest mask, which I throw off with pleasure.
> Far hence all rudeness, wilfulness, and noise,
> And be our future lives one gentle stream
> Of mutual love, compliance, and regard. [III.266–73]

To which Catharine, transformed into both a proper wife and (rather implausibly) a meek and modest maiden, replies: "Nay, then I'm all unworthy of thy love, / And look with blushes on my former self" (III.274–75). On the surface, Petruchio's speech appears to be an example of what Lawrence Stone has called the "companionate marriage"; Petruchio seemingly stresses the mutuality of the marriage relationship. But he "doffs" the mask of brutish masculinity only after Catherine has proclaimed that a husband is a wife's rightful "keeper," "head," and "sovereign" (*CP*, III.i.250–51). Once the wife has internalized her subservient role ("I'm all unworthy") then the husband can afford to drop the "honest mask" of "lordly husband" and profess gentleness. Garrick's additions here expose the hierarchical foundation on which such an ideal of egalitarian marriage is built. This impression is strengthened when Garrick ends the play with another segment of Katharina's speech as Petruchio steps forward, hand in hand with his newly tamed wife, to give a lesson to the wives in the audience:

> How shameful 'tis when women are so simple
> To offer war where they should kneel for peace;
> Or seek for rule, supreme, and sway,
> Where bound to love, to honor and obey. [III.283–86]

Neatly exemplifying the power bases of domestic bliss, *Catharine and Petruchio* concludes with Petruchio as paternal sovereign, embodying the male role of "rule, supreme, and sway" by laying down the law to his loving and obedient wife.

A similar ideology of the family appears in the two adaptations of *The Winter's Tale* staged during this time, MacNamara Morgan's *Florizel and Perdita* and Garrick's play of the same name. The plays were staged at rival theaters for many years during the mid-eighteenth century, Morgan's play appearing at Covent Garden in March 1754 and Garrick's at Drury Lane in January 1756, and incorporate the elements that made the other abbreviated adaptations popular, namely music, farce, and domestic sentimentality.[25] Before this time *The Winter's Tale* had been performed only in 1741, at the peak of the Shakespeare revival, but these adaptations established it as a staple of later eighteenth-century theater.

As indicated by the titles, both versions of *The Winter's Tale* focus on the last two acts of Shakespeare's play, cutting the first three acts of the play completely. Morgan's *Florizel and Perdita* provides a broadly comic afterpiece, consisting of the pastoral scenes from Act IV, replete with a variety of songs. As with Colman's *A Fairy Tale*, emphasis is on the play's comic rather than romantic characters, as seen by the division of songs: Perdita has one, Autolycus, six. The entire Leontes-Hermione story vanishes apart from a brief comment near the end of the play. Although concern over the so-called unities was not in evidence, the sixteen-year break between acts III and IV was too jarring for any adapter of *The Winter's Tale* to stomach. Morgan evades the gap and change of scene by beginning with the pastoral scenes and recasting the old shepherd as Antigonus in disguise, who reveals all to Polixenes in the end. Garrick retains Leontes and Hermione but avoids the time and scene problems by having Leontes visit Bohemia, where Paulina had fled with Hermione many years before. After the removal of the first three acts, the only major deletion is that of Perdita and Polixenes's discussion of Nature and Art in IV,iv.; no eighteenth-century adaptation of *The Winter's Tale* retained these lines, presumably because Perdita's discussion of "nature's bastards" and "breeding" was seen as indecent.

Garrick's adaptation of *The Winter's Tale* was particularly popular and, unlike most of the abbreviated adaptations, appeared as a mainpiece. It has much in common with *Catharine and Petruchio* with which it was frequently staged.[26] Unlike Morgan's farcical afterpiece, Garrick's *Florizel and Perdita* is a mainpiece whose focus is distinctly domestic and sentimental. In contrast to Morgan's shepherdesses and clowns, Garrick's play focuses on Leontes, the role Garrick himself played. Even the play's pastoral scenes are seen through his eyes, as he watches the sheep-shearing and comments on its application to his bereaved state. What these pastoral scenes reveal is the redefinition of Leontes as family man, and many of the play's new lines reiterate his anguish over the loss of his wife and daughter (there is no mention of a son) and his ecstasy in having them restored to him. Leontes comes to the shores of Bohemia a broken man whose memories of his family haunt him. He does not need the prompting of Paulina to feel remorse, just the sight of Perdita causes him to weep:

> Haply such age, such innocence and beauty,
> Had our dear daughter owned, had not my hand—
> O had I not the course of nature stopped
> On weak surmise—I will not think that way—
> And yet I must, always, and ever must.
> *Cleomines.* No more, my liege—
> *Leontes.* Nay, I will gaze upon her; each salt dropt
> That trickles down my cheek relieves my heart,
> Which else would burst with anguish. [II.i.336–44]

Later in the scene, he refers again to his lost daughter in a slightly altered version of Shakespeare's original (V.i.132–34): "I lost a daughter that 'twixt heav'n and earth / Might thus have stood begetting wonder, as / Yon lovely maiden does"[27] (*FP*,II.i:56–58). Significantly, Garrick omits Leontes's reference to the loss of Polixenes's friendship that in *The Winter's Tale* follows the brief (and tearless) lament for his children. The effect of these repeated references to his daughter in a scene where Leontes speaks little is to establish Leontes not as King but as father. The loss of his domestic circle, not his betrayal of friends, is the source of his grief, a grief that Garrick's audience recognized and approved. Thomas Davies, the play's Camillo, stressed the emotional force of Garrick's Leontes; it was, he said, "extremely affecting."[28]

These elements of domestic sentiment culminate in the play's final scene, a combination of *The Winter's Tale*'s V.i and iii. Garrick expands the scene in order to emphasize the emotion of the family reunion. The characters themselves are awash in tears: Garrick's stage directions indicate that Leontes bursts into tears on at least two occasions (commenting the second time, "my penitence is all afloat again," III.iv.86); Perdita collapses with emotion; and even Hermione's voice is choked with tears. The scene's emotional climax comes with a family tableau as Leontes and Hermione embrace and Perdita kneels before them. Designed to incite as much emotion as possible, Garrick's adaptation exploits family ties to produce this emotion. The characters are properly respectful of the deities, but their true concern, like that of the English bourgeoisie who made the play a popular success, is domestic happiness. Garrick's loving patriarch and appropriately deferential wife and child constitute the ideal patriarchal family where lines of authority are hidden behind the rhetoric of sentiment. The characters, especially Leontes, prove their goodness of heart through displays of emotion while, in word and gesture, they embrace the patriarchal order outlined so clearly at the end of *Catharine and Petruchio*. (Garrick's Hermione exclaims in "transport": "my lord, my king,—there's distance in those names, / My husband!" [III.iv.215–16].)

This framework of bourgeois moral propriety necessitates reshaping the female characters as well as Leontes. To formulate this idealized family, Garrick touches up both Perdita and Hermione so that they constitute models of daughterly and wifely virtue. Perdita is a good daughter to both Leontes and the Old Shepherd; she is respectful, obedient, and devoted, hastening to obey her shepherd father's bidding and quickly transferring this filial piety to Leontes. Likewise, Hermione's role is retrofitted with all the appropriate trappings of domestic virtue. Visible only in the final scene, without the first three acts to show her as young, vivacious, and witty, she becomes an emblem of maternal and wifely love. Other characters describe her as a "matchless saint" or "paragon of virtue," while Garrick's additions carefully reiterate her maternal role. Florizel lauds her as the mother of Perdita, and Hermione's final speech to Perdita suggests that she lived only to see her daughter. Her only words not directed to her husband or daughter invoke the goodness of the gods for returning her to her family.

This redefinition of female characters is made possible by the virtual elimination of Paulina, the character who suffers the most by Garrick's abbreviation. She falls outside of the family circle and is further marginalized by Garrick's revised plot in which she flees Leontes's court after the catastrophic events sixteen years before. Garrick omits most of her caustic comments, reinventing her as a good-natured, if somewhat silly figure. We first see her weeping at the news of Leontes's arrival and later responding to the news of Leontes's reunion with Perdita. In the final scene, her comments, when Leontes responds emotionally to Paulina's reference to Hermione, are couched as the words of a foolishly garrulous woman:

> Touch'd to th' noble heart!
> What, my dear Sovereign, I said not well,
> I meant well; pardon, then, a foolish woman.
> The love I bore your queen—lo, fool again!—
> I'll speak of her no more. [III.iv.22–26]

Both sentimental and sentimentalized, Paulina's role is that of agent of good, the means by which the nuclear family is reunited. At the end of the play she is consigned to "live bless'd with blessing others," a domesticated and safer version of the acid-tongued, manipulative Paulina of Shakespeare's play.

With its serious treatment of moral issues and its status as a mainpiece, *Florizel and Perdita* provides a useful transition between the abbreviations of Shakespeare and the age's longer adaptations. Like *Catharine and Petruchio*, depictions of romance come second to portrayals of domestic virtue, and the play's sentimentality is dependent on family values akin to those lauded in conduct books such as Dr. John Gregory's *A Father's Legacy to his Daughters* (1774) as well as in sentimental novels and plays.[29] In direct contrast to the Shakespeare adaptations of an earlier generation, its plot depicts the restoration not of a monarch, but of a husband and father.

Domesticating Shakespeare

Sentimentality and Shakespeare intermingle as well in the full-length adaptations, all serious dramatic works that shunned the farce and song characteristic of the abbreviated adaptations. This second group of adaptations, Theophilus Cibber's *Romeo and Juliet* (1744), Garrick's and Colman's reworkings of *King Lear* (Garrick's first acted in 1756, Colman's in 1768), and Richard Cumberland's *Timon of Athens* (1771), are all versions of plays that had been previously adapted in the Restoration and early eighteenth century, and all make explicit use of those earlier adaptations. Less specifically Shakespearean than the shortened versions, they are nonetheless much closer in language and in form to their Shakespearean originals than their predecessors. In general, the playwrights do not seek new directions in their revisions. Rather, they attempt to reconcile the Shakespearean text with its earlier adaptation, often including lines or scenes from both, and in each case restoring large segments of Shakespeare that had been previously rewritten or eliminated.[30] Many follow Colley Cibber's example in *Richard III* and isolate the non-Shakespearean lines by the use of quotation marks or inverted commas. Even the earliest of these "restorations," Theophilus Cibber's *Romeo and Juliet* (1744), follows this pattern as Cibber integrates Shakespeare's tragedy and Thomas Otway's *The Fall of Caius Marius* (1680). The mid-eighteenth century marked the end of sweeping alteration, and from 1737 until the end of the century the only playwright who attempted to create a radically new adaptation was Colley Cibber, with the ill-fated *Papal Tyranny* (1745). Though these attempts to re-establish Shakespeare were usually successful, slowly pushing the early adaptations from the stage, the public was not always ready to accept a stronger dose of Shakespeare; Colman's rendition of *King Lear* failed to make any headway against Tate, and Garrick's attempt to replace portions of the Dryden/D'Avenant *Tempest* was a dismal failure.

What playwrights retained from the older adaptations—and what they rejected—reflects a change in priorities from those of an earlier generation. In general, Garrick's, Cibber's, and Cumberland's revisions retain the heightened emotions evident in the earlier adaptations as well as the increased attention given to female characters. Although these elements remain, they are transformed in the process of revision. Pathos shades into sentimentality as playwrights strive to move their audiences to amiable tears rather than to sexual titillation. Consequently, the role of the female characters is transformed from suffering victims into benevolent angels, good daughters rather than distraught wives. The adapters downplay or even reject the sensational and the erotic, a common feature of Restoration adaptations. They also pare down or eliminate the superadded love stories of earlier adaptations. Instead, they augment the domestic details of family life, trimming and reshaping the plays to highlight familial love, especially that of father and daughter. The audiences of the mid-eighteenth century, with their larger middle-class population, found such scenes particularly poignant.

The fate of *Romeo and Juliet*, the most popular Shakespeare play of the later eighteenth century, presents a vivid picture of adaptation's progress. Two adaptations vied for supremacy in the late 1740s, both adding to the play's already considerable emotional impact while claiming to have restored Shakespeare to the stage. Theophilus Cibber's *Romeo and Juliet* was one of the first that attempted to reinstate large amounts of previously unstaged Shakespeare. The play was first performed on September 11, 1744, at the Little Theater in the Haymarket and from the start was wildly successful.[31] Despite Cibber's cuts and the retention of passages from Otway's *Caius Marius*, the play was advertised as "written by Shakespeare," "a Play not acted once these 100 years." Only when the play was published in 1748 did Cibber advertize it as "Revis'd and Alter'd from Shakespear, by Mr. Theophilus Cibber."[32]

Stressing the revival of Shakespeare's *Romeo and Juliet*, Cibber implicitly sets his adaptation apart from *Caius Marius* (1680), even while covertly adding portions of Otway's play to his text. Unlike Otway, Cibber remains close to the original play; he shuns Otway's infusion of Roman politics with their English implications and focuses instead on young love and family tragedy. He accomplishes this through trimming the play to make room for his additions. As in most adaptations, the cast of characters shrinks; Lady Montague is cut completely, and the list of servants and minor characters is considerably reduced, with Gregory, Sampson, and Peter nonexistent. Many lines of the loquacious Nurse are trimmed and their indelicate portions omitted, subduing the comic interludes. Like Otway, Cibber removes any mention of Romeo's earlier love Rosaline, transferring the lines concerning Rosaline to Juliet and showing the two as professed lovers before the play begins. These omissions eliminate the element of love at first sight (the masked ball disappears in both Otway and Cibber) as well as dispelling Romeo's seeming fickleness in so suddenly falling out of love with Rosaline and into love with Juliet. Though Cibber retains Shakespeare's language, he reduces the scope of the play to a more intimate domestic circle, the conflicts between star-crossed lovers and their parents. Without the comic characters, and with fewer scenes of the Montague/Capulet conflict on a broader scale, *Romeo and Juliet* becomes a domestic tragedy.

While Cibber's additions, as is characteristic of the revised adaptations in general, are relatively simple, they establish the play's smaller scale. He adds few of his own lines, his most extensive original addition is the opening scene between Old Capulet and Paris, where Capulet gives the first hints of tragedy by mentioning his daughter's attachment to Romeo. Not only does this scene eliminate the unlikely element of love at first sight, but it also establishes a familial context for the tragedy that follows. Even the quarrel between the families is couched in intimate, domestic terms as Capulet explains:

> *Montague*, the ancient Enemy of our House,
> Thinking our Power greater, Sir, than his,
> Wish'd his Son, *Romeo* and our Daughter, married;
> Which so increas'd the Anger of our Wives,
> (Whose Quarrels we are ever apt to join in)
> The Rage of civil War, broke out more fiercely.[33]

In falling in love, Romeo and Juliet have only been following the wishes of their parents—it is the unnatural anger of their mothers that has caused all the problems. This addition redefines Romeo and Juliet as dutiful children, but, by describing the source of the current strife as a quarrel between two prospective mothers-in-law, it reduces almost to absurdity the scope of the strife that eventually kills not only the two lovers but also several of their kinsmen. Most of Cibber's additions, however, are taken from *Caius Marius*, and he occasionally follows Otway in changing

Shakespeare's diction. More often, however, he retains the original text, eschewing Otway's language for the wording in his own copy of Shakespeare.[34] Cibber's most substantive addition is in the final scene where he inserts over fifty lines from *Caius Marius* so that Juliet awakens before Romeo dies, thus increasing both the horror and the pathos of the scene. With the crazed distraction of a true Otway heroine, Juliet raves in a brief mad fit before stabbing herself. Cibber's concluding couplet stressing the heartrending sentiment of the conclusion, "Never true Lovers Story did impart / More real Anguish to a humane Heart" (p. 67), neatly summarizes the goals of this new scene and of Cibber's production in general.

Sparked in part by his dislike of rival Cibber, Garrick produced his own revival of *Romeo and Juliet* in 1748. Garrick's version of the play, published first in 1750 and then with a few additional changes in 1763, retains even more Shakespeare than Cibber's.[35] Garrick restores Shakespeare's opening scene and the masked ball, as well as the figures of Gregory, Sampson, and Peter. On stage, Garrick followed Cibber's portrayal of Romeo, purifying a potential "blemish in his character"[36] by removing all references to Rosaline. Aside from numerous omissions (most notably the quiet elimination of some of the play's elaborate figurative language), Garrick leaves the first four acts of *Romeo and Juliet* essentially unaltered. In the fifth act he adds a much touted "new scene" consisting of a funeral dirge for Juliet but containing no new dialogue. A similar scene was also staged in Covent Garden's productions of the play. It provided each theater with an opportunity for grand spectacle with bells tolling and an elaborate funeral procession. One German observer found this scene too realistic to be enjoyable,[37] another example of the emotional impact even non-speaking additions could add to a play.

In the final scene, Garrick, like all other eighteenth-century adapters of *Romeo and Juliet*, reunites the lovers in the Capulet tomb. Although Garrick's addition is longer and more impassioned than that in Cibber's adaptation, Juliet's lines frequently echo those of Otway's Lavinia and Cibber's Juliet. For example:

> *Juliet.* Oh my lord, my *Romeo*!
> Had'st thou not come, sure I had slept for ever;
> But there's a sovereign charm in thy embraces
> That can revive the dead— (V.iv.95–98)
> *Lavinia.* The Gods have heard my Vows; it is my *Marius*.
> Once more they have restor'd him to my Eyes.
> Had'st thou not come, sure I had slept for ever.
> But there's a sovereign Charm in thy embraces,
> That might doe Wonders, and revive the Dead. [V.iv. 364–81]

Garrick's most notable innovations come in his refiguring of Romeo's role in this scene. Where Cibber, drawing from Otway, used the scene to represent female pathos, Garrick's additions showcase the passion of Romeo. Otway's Marius (and Cibber's Romeo) die tranquilly soon after the lines quoted above, but Garrick prolongs Romeo's death throes so that he dies in both physical and spiritual agony. In contrast to Cibber's Romeo, who, like Otway's Marius junior, dies murmuring:

> This World's gross Air grows burthensome already.
> I'm all a God; such heav'nly Joys transport me,
> That mortal Sense grows sick, and faints with lasting. [*Dies*] [V.390–92]

Garrick's Romeo raves:

> *Romeo.*   My powers are blasted,
> Twixt death and love I'm torn, I am distracted!
> But death's strongest—and must I leave thee, Juliet?
> O, cruel, cursed fate! in sight of heaven—
> *Juliet.*   Thou ravest; lean upon my breast.
> *Romeo.*   Fathers have flinty hearts, no tears can melt 'em.
> Nature pleads in vain. Children must be wretched.
> *Juliet.*   O! my breaking heart!
> *Romeo.*   She is my wife; our hearts are twined together.
> Capulet forbear! Paris loose your hold!
> Pull not our heart-strings thus; they crack, they break.
> O! Juliet! Juliet! [*Dies*] [V.iv.124–35]

The emphasis on Romeo's suffering is not entirely surprising given that Garrick himself played Romeo, but it also indicates the movement away from dramatic focus on female pathos. Juliet's words are poignant and moving, but in this final scene she plays the supporting role, literally as well as figuratively. With their depiction of the agonized Romeo, Garrick's revisions were understandably popular; Francis Gentleman calls the addition of the tomb scene "a change of infinite merit": "Romeo's distraction and her tenderness are so excellently wrought up, that we cannot suppose any heart so obdurate as not to be penetrated."[38] Gentleman's praise pinpoints the elements of Garrick's adaptation which made it so popular: its ability to incite the sympathy of the audience and its depiction of female tenderness and male, not female, distraction.

These concerns, the shift from the pathetic to the tender female and the emotive rather than heroic hero, and the appeal these characters made to audience sympathy, underlie the ultimate success of Garrick's version.

In 1750, *Romeo and Juliet* was revived at both Covent Garden and Drury Lane in one of the great theater wars of the century. Covent Garden featured Mr. Barry and Mrs. Cibber in the title roles while Drury Lane countered with Garrick and Mrs. Pritchard. For twelve nights the productions ran head to head until Covent Garden finally gave up the battle, much to the relief of many theatergoers, and Drury Lane mounted a final triumphant performance.[39] Public opinion was divided over the merits of the two Romeos, Barry being commended for his "amorous harmony of features, melting eyes, and unequalled plaintiveness of voice" in contrast to "the superior grace of Mr. Garrick's attitudes, the vivacity of his countenance, and the fire of his expression."[40] In general, Barry was agreed to be stronger in the first three acts and Garrick in the last two, and some spectators made a practice of watching the first acts at Covent Garden, then rushing to Drury Lane for the final two. One unknown lady summed up the distinct allure of each production: "Had I been Juliet to Garrick's Romeo,—so ardent and impassioned was he, I should have expected he would have *come up* to me in the balcony; but had I been Juliet to Barry's Romeo,—so tender, so eloquent, and so seductive was he, I should certainly have *gone down* to him!"[41] Her emphasis on the emotional impact of each production indicates not only that this was the dominant feature of each production, but that it drove audience response to the play. Clearly emotion sold tickets; Garrick's version of *Romeo and Juliet* added enough audience-pleasing sensibility to remain popular well into the nineteenth century.[42] By the later eighteenth century, sentiment rather than politics seems to have been the key to commercial success.

A more acrimonious debate arose around *King Lear*. As with *Romeo and Juliet*, all productions of *Lear* staged during the eighteenth century included scenes from Tate's earlier adaptation. Tate, however, had deservedly never enjoyed the high reputation Otway had. Theater managers toyed with the idea of rejecting the happy ending or returning the fool but ultimately held back, largely because of fears of audience displeasure. (Samuel Johnson's approbation of the Tate ending suggests that their fears were probably justified: "I cannot easily be persuaded that . . . the audience will not always rise better pleased from the final triumph of persecuted virtue."[43]) Also, in this age of intense competition, theater politics had as much a hand in the version of *Lear* staged as popular taste. From 1756 when Garrick's *Lear* was first performed until his death in 1779, Drury Lane performed only Garrick's Tate-influenced version, with Garrick himself playing Lear for many years. His version was eventually published in Bell's *Shakespeare* (1773) as Shakespeare's *King Lear* "performed at the Theater-Royal, Drury Lane." Lacking a strong lead, Drury Lane dropped *Lear* from its repertoire for nearly ten years after Garrick's death, reviving it only after 1788.

During this time, Covent Garden continued to perform the Tate adaptation with a brief hiatus between 1768 and 1773, when, under the management of George Colman, the theater experimented with Colman's heavily Shakespearean version of *Lear*. After Colman left Covent Garden, the theater reverted to Tate's adaptation and staged it until the end of the century. Versions of Tate's adaptation persisted throughout the eighteenth century and, despite the opposition posed by Colman and Garrick, the presence of Tate's adaptation was felt well into the nineteenth century. Only in 1838 was Shakespeare's *King Lear* restored to the stage.

Incorporating parts of Tate's *Lear* into their own adaptations, both Garrick and Colman turned away from the bleakness of Shakespeare's tragedy by retaining Tate's happy ending (Colman the last act and Garrick the last two acts). As in the Restoration adaptations, moral ambiguities are resolved and motives clarified, although to a lesser extent. Of the two adaptations, Garrick's *Lear* stands closer to Tate.[44] The play begins with the first three acts of Shakespeare's play and concludes with the last two acts of Tate's. Aside from the Edgar-Cordelia love story[45] and some substantial omissions, including the Fool, Garrick follows Shakespeare word for word in the first three acts. His treatment of Tate's conclusion is more complicated. Garrick follows Tate's sequence of scenes but occasionally reverts to Shakespearean wording[46] as in the final scene in which he shifts back and forth between Tate and Shakespeare.

In addition to abandoning Tate's words, Garrick also revises Tate's characterizations, most notably that of Edmund, who in Tate is an inhumanly cruel, lecherous devil. In place of the Bastard's proud deathbed reference to Regan and Goneril ("Who wou'd not choose, like me, to yield his Breath / T'have Rival Queens contend for him in Death?" V.v.113–14), Garrick's Edmund dies after professing his desire that "some good I mean to do, / Despite of mine own nature" (V.iii.244–45). At Edmund's words, Edgar and Albany exit, and, in keeping with the Tate ending, rescue Lear and Cordelia. In reverting to a more Shakespearean representation of Edmund, Garrick eliminates some of the most lurid aspects of Tate's adaptation. Where Tate highlights the illicit relationship between Edmund, Regan, and Goneril, Garrick edits these intrusions out of his version. He omits the licentious scenes (such as IV.i: "A Grotto. Edmund and Regan amorously Seated") and most of the lines Tate had added for Regan and Goneril in the later acts.

While these revisions polarize good and evil less than in the Restoration adaptations, the play becomes not so much a moral or political lesson as an exercise in sympathy.[47] Not only does the play itself lack the political connotations it had in the Restoration, but such connotations seem unimportant. In the eyes of the mid-eighteenth century, *King Lear* is a family drama rather than a political drama. As with *Romeo and Juliet*, the erosion of the political function of the play leaves more room for sentiment, not superadded as with the tomb scene but achieved by replacing more of the Shakespearean text. The emphasis on emotion, accentuated by Garrick's acting, renders formerly dangerous subjects innocuous. With the audience sympathizing so strongly with Lear and Cordelia, Garrick can afford to make the bad redeemable and the good not wholly virtuous. Garrick does smooth over the most disturbing aspects of the play, most notably with the more comfortable happy ending, but despite the ending, he has not taken on Tate's sweeping moral simplification.

By including more of Shakespeare's language and characterization, Garrick also permits more ambiguity of the sort feared by earlier adapters. Doing so also shifted the play's focus back to Lear himself, an effect Garrick heightened by removing portions of Tate's love story, replacing them with segments from the original play. Garrick's Lear, a role for which he was famous, was the play's dominant figure. While this Lear was not a pathetic figure, his divisive family and descent into madness appealed strongly to the emotions of the audience. As with Garrick's *Romeo and Juliet*, his *King Lear* reverses the emphasis on female pathos and replaces it with an appeal to sympathy, particularly through the figure of the distraught father and his devoted daughter. With the Edgar/Cordelia romance abbreviated, the play's most important relationship is not that of lover and mistress, but of father and daughter; Garrick carefully retains Tate's references to Cordelia's filial piety, such as the scene in which Tate shows Cordelia begging Gloucester for succor "for a father and a King" (III.ii).

Colman's embrace of the Shakespearean text goes further than Garrick's as his version of *Lear* retains the first four acts of Shakespeare's play. His attempt, as he states in his "Advertisement," was "to reconcile the catastrophe of Tate to the story of Shakespeare."[48] In doing so he omits the attachment between Edgar and Cordelia which he describes as: "one of the capital objections to [Tate's] alteration ... the embraces of Cordelia and the ragged Edgar ... would have appeared too ridiculous for representation, had they not been mixed and incorporated with some of the finest scenes of Shakespeare."[49]

The only changes Colman makes in the Shakespearean segment of his play (Acts I-V.i) are omissions; as in Tate and Garrick, the Fool is cut, although Colman admits that only his fears that the character would "sink into burlesque" prevented him from restoring the Fool.[50] He diverges from Tate, Garrick, and Shakespeare in removing Gloucester's supposed fall from the cliffs at Dover, which he regarded as improbable. After Lear's reunion with Cordelia, Colman shifts to Tate's conclusion, and the last act is almost purely Tate. The thoroughness with which Colman followed Tate can be seen in the speech-prefixes for Edmund, who is cited as Edmund in the first four acts but suddenly becomes "The Bastard" (Tate's label) in the last act.[51] Occasional changes appear as Colman eliminates the love scenes and, like Garrick, restores Edmund's final repentant words. Overall, Colman's adaptation allows much of the pain of Shakespeare's play, discarding only what was necessary to attach a happy ending. Like Garrick, he abolishes the most sensational elements of the Tate ending, and the play itself presents a palatable solution to the popular demand for a happy ending. But while the contemporary critics praised Colman's version, public opinion, perhaps spurred by the lackluster performances of Quin and Barry, was not so favorable. The play survived only fifteen performances (in contrast to more than sixty for Garrick's), and in 1774 Covent Garden revived the Tate adaptation.

Both Garrick's and Colman's versions suggest that, within the theater at least, respect for the Shakespearean text was beginning to outweigh concern for *Lear*'s moral ambiguity and uncomfortable ending. Their adaptations show a similar distaste for the sensationalism that characterizes Tate's version, even to the point of Colman rejecting Gloucester's supposed fall at Dover because it also was too extreme. The willingness of both adaptations to accept verbal ambiguities so disturbing to an earlier generation of writers suggests that language in the later eighteenth century can be evocative without being dangerous. Its potential misleading qualities are defused by the role it plays in arousing sympathy, not political revolt. Although both Garrick and Colman modify Tate's rigid distribution of good and evil, reward and punishment, neither dares eliminate it completely. In the end, audiences seem to have found Garrick's version of Shakespeare more appealing, a tribute both to his acting and to his play's mixture of poignancy, filial piety, and triumphant happy ending. Not only does his Lear retire happily at the play's conclusion, but the inclusion of more elements from Tate makes his Cordelia a more likable daughter, explicitly devoted to her father and fetchingly in love with Edgar. She has laudable reasons for saying "nothing," more frequently displays her concern for her father, and does not invade England at the head of the French army. Overall, Garrick is more selective in his changes than Colman, searching for a calculated and carefully contrived effect. Where Colman tries to return to Shakespeare, Garrick seeks to satisfy his audience.

Timon of Athens, the last of the plays to be adapted, has never been a popular play, unlike *King Lear* or *Romeo and Juliet*. The bitter figure of Timon has attracted few admirers, and the rough verse and unfinished quality of the play have militated against it. Shadwell's adaptation (1678) was performed regularly in the early eighteenth century but was abandoned after 1745, and *Timon* in any version was not performed for several decades until Richard Cumberland produced a new adaptation in 1771. The play enjoyed a prosperous run, but was a critical failure and was never revived.[52]

In contrast to Garrick or Colman, Cumberland does not attempt to incorporate Shadwell's *Timon* into his adaptation, taking only the idea for a love interest from the earlier play. He combines Shakespearean passages with new material, retaining much more Shakespeare than does Shadwell (approximately half of the play is taken verbatim from Shakespeare's *Timon*.) As in the other later eighteenth-century adaptations, Cumberland's additions take the form of new scenes inserted into the Shakespearean text. He attempts to use the original language whenever possible and does not rewrite or alter the diction in his Shakespearean scenes. His additions arise solely from the changes he makes in the plot, in particular the sections dealing with the new figure of Evanthe, Timon's daughter. These additions seem to trouble Cumberland, and he comments uneasily in his advertisement: "I wish I could have brought this Play upon the stage with less Violence to its Author, and not so much Responsibility on my own Part. New Characters of Necessity require some Display. Many original Passages of the first Merit are still retained, and in the Contemplation of them, my errors, I hope, will be overlooked, or forgiven."[53] Making amends, at least textually, he carefully segregates these potential "errors" from the Shakespearean lines by the use of quotation marks, stressing the distinction between his words and those of Shakespeare.

Cumberland's *Timon* provides a textbook example of adaptation in an age of literary sensibility; while following the general pattern of textual restoration seen in both *Romeo and Juliet* and *King Lear*, the play incorporates the elements of the sentimental drama popular on the stage during the last half of the century. While staying within the basic outline of Shakespeare's tragedy, Cumberland simplifies and reorganizes the play, making the scope more intimate and the tone more conciliatory. The most obvious changes appear in the limited range of characters: Lucius and Lucullus take over the roles of all of Timon's false friends, while the bitterest railing of the play evaporates as Apemantus is virtually eliminated, appearing briefly in only two scenes. Other figures such as the Poet, Painter, Jeweller, and the Senators make fleeting appearances and then vanish. These omissions are necessary in order to make room for Cumberland's character, Evanthe, a modification of Shadwell's Evandra, now Timon's daughter rather than his mistress. Even more than Timon, she becomes the central figure of Cumberland's adaptation, and his desire to integrate her into the action necessitates changes not only in plot but in tone. By making Evanthe central to the play, Cumberland recreates *Timon* as sentimental drama.

Despite the similarity in names, Evanthe is markedly different from her predecessor Evandra. Whereas Evandra represents the exemplary pathetic heroine, virtuous and suffering, Evanthe is a sympathetic but not a pathetic figure. An extreme example of the fate of women in the later adaptations, she is a recognizable model of the sentimental heroine. A creature of almost impossible virtue and piety, she controls most of the play's action. Not only is she the lure that attracts the fortune hunters Lucius and Lucullus, but it is for love of her that Alcibiades is banished from Athens—he dares to plead Timon's case to the senate and is censured because of the "intemporate heat" with which he urges his suit (III.v). Ultimately, Evanthe saves Athens from sack and ruin in return for assistance for her father. In a scene reminiscent of Volumnia's plea outside of Rome in *Coriolanus*, she persuades Alcibiades not to attack the city. She then turns eagerly from the public realms to the private, remarking: "I've sav'd a city; grant me now, kind Gods, / To save a father" (p. 50). Unlike either Shakespeare or Shadwell, Cumberland downplays Timon's ravings in the woods in order to focus the final two acts on Evanthe's efforts to aid her father. As a dutiful and loving daughter, Evanthe embodies bourgeois values familiar to Cumberland's audience. Thrifty and obedient, with strong family ties and moral convictions, her role is not exploited for the titillation of pathos but featured because it upholds a new ideology dependent on domestic virtue and the patriarchal family. These values provide the foundation for sentimental drama, and, without her, Timon's story would be the same but Cumberland's play would have no coherence or impetus.

Timon's character itself changes as his function diminishes. He appears in fewer than half the scenes in the play. The major events are retained; Timon presides at his banquet of hot water and curses Athens, but the early scenes exhibiting Timon's extravagant generosity evaporate, leaving him a moderate figure rather than a man of extremes. This spirit of moderation is most apparent in the final scenes in which Evanthe finds Timon, led by his faithful servant Flavius. Father and daughter are briefly but blissfully reunited before Timon sinks peacefully into death. Timon's rage has dissipated: "We must be calm," he says, "Shatter'd with storms, at length I see my port, / And stretch for death's calm shore" (p. 58). His bitter anger was but a temporary phase, a passing madness, as Timon himself admits ("I much fear sorrow has shook my wits"). Although he says that he has "bandied curses to the moon" and "call'd malignant spirits to ensnare mankind," Cumberland shows nothing of this. Instead, he focuses the scene on Timon's tender exchanges with his daughter:

> *Timon.* All, all is well, for thou art in my sight,
> Mute as these scenes and calm as summer seas,
> Here will we sit and meditate a while,
> Then die and be at peace.
> *Evan.* Oh! talk not thus.
> *Timon.* Give me your pardon; I have suffer'd much,
> And much I fear sorrow has shook my wits;
> But in the bitterest moments of affliction,
> I have remember'd still to bless my child. [57-58]

The best thing that Timon can say about himself is that he has been a loving father: "I have remember'd still to bless my child." The father-daughter bond means more than any friendship, and the very presence of Evanthe rectifies all the damage done by the false friends. Because of her, Timon has no bitterness and can die at peace. Our last view of Timon is of a feeble old man who asks only to be buried by the sea, leaving no bitter epitaph to be delivered to the senate. The onetime misanthrope dies at the end of the scene, willingly embracing the good represented by his daughter and Alcibiades.

With this morally uplifting ending, Cumberland's *Timon* is as different from Shakespeare's as it is from Shadwell's play. Instead of Shakespeare's character of extremes, Cumberland creates a somewhat shadowy figure who is deserted by his friends and who, like Lear, goes briefly mad. This essentially passive figure cannot carry the play, and the central position is filled by the figure of Evanthe. Like Shadwell, Cumberland has added a love interest to his "tragedy" (Alcibiades and Evanthe), but this addition, rather than intensifying the emphasis on Timon, displaces it, shifting it again to Evanthe. Waning from a man of extremes to one of impotence, his caustic anger softened and controlled, Timon becomes a secondary figure in the play that bears his name. The addition of Evanthe creates a mood of tender emotion; the overwhelming sense is not of hatred and strident anger but of gentle pathos, a quality validated by emotion and exemplified most clearly in the scenes where Timon, like dozens of characters in sentimental drama before and after him, discovers the essential goodness of human nature and as a result evokes sympathy from the audience in a way Shakespeare's Timon never could. Where Shakespeare concludes with Timon's bitter epitaph, Cumberland provides a scene of reconciliation. Ironically, despite its melodrama and flagrant changes, Shadwell's *Timon, the Man-Hater* comes much nearer to Shakespeare in tone than does Cumberland's *Timon* with its blocks of Shakespearean dialogue, for, aside from the resurrection of larger portions of Shakespeare's play, the later *Timon*'s greatest similarity to Shakespeare lies mainly in its language.

DUTIFUL DAUGHTERS AND TRUE BRITONS

Cumberland's *Timon* represents the culmination of the later eighteenth century's reshaping of Shakespeare in the form of sentimentalized drama. Emphasizing domestic virtues and family ties, these sentimentalized plays eschew sensationalism, especially in the form of eroticism, and seek to incite sympathy in their audiences rather than titillating them with scenes of helpless female virtue. Written with these goals in mind, adaptation in the later eighteenth century takes a different form and deploys its female characters (the prime agents of sentiment) in a different manner. As these plays indicate, the dominant relationship is not that of lover and mistress, as in the Restoration adaptations which created new love stories and augmented existing ones, but that of father and daughter. Shakespeare provided a rich source of father-daughter bonds (22 of major importance, according to Diane Elizabeth Dreher); however, the representation of these bonds was often not appropriate to the ideals of sentimental drama. As Dreher observes, "[Shakespeare's] plays depict the father at middle life, reluctant to release his daughter into adulthood and face his own decline, while she stands at the threshold of adult commitment in marriage."[54] In Shakespeare's plays this conflict frequently results in defiant daughters. The conflict vanishes in the adaptations; these daughters are devoted, not defiant. They cherish their fathers and refuse to abandon them to old age, even rejecting love and marriage in order to minister to their needs.

The adaptations present ample evidence of properly compliant daughters who represent good models for the girls reading this new, sentimental Shakespeare, or seeing it on the stage. Any bad examples are revised or quietly edited out. Hermia's defiant escape into the forest appears only in Garrick's short-lived opera *The Fairies*, and Cordelia's harshness to her father, although partially excused because of her love for Edgar, causes her almost constant pangs of guilt. Cumberland's Evanthe is both the most prominent of these self-effacing daughters and the least Shakespearean. With the focus on the father-daughter relationship, *Timon of Athens* becomes a kind of attenuated *King Lear*; a father makes mistakes, runs mad, is found by his daughter who cares for him devotedly. But here the play's central figure is the daughter, not the father. Evanthe's father is the center of her life, and everything else, both material wealth and romantic love, must be put aside so that she can care for her parent. These qualities are perhaps epitomized most clearly in the form that her self-sacrifice takes. In a scene that prefigures a similarly sentimental moment in Sheridan's *School for Scandal*, Evanthe gives up her most prized possession in order to pay her father's debts:

> *Evan.* I have a picture,
> *Apelles* might have own'd it: 'tis my father.
> Lo, what a form he wears! A *Cretan* artist
> Trac'd out the living work. There was a time,
> Not all the treasure of the *Ephesian* fane,
> Had brib'd me to dispose on't. Here *Faminius*,
> Take it; get gold. Now I have nothing left. [25]

Evanthe's words convey the qualities appropriate in a sentimental daughter: self sacrifice, reverence, and affection. Even while remaining within the de-eroticized emotions of sentimentality, Evanthe's admiration of her father's "form" presents for a moment a Timon who is more than a impotent old man and recreates the image of the powerful father. The function of the daughter is not simply to serve but to elevate, recreate, and revere the image of the father.

As represented in the adaptations, the bond between father and daughter becomes a necessary pillar of patriarchy. These daughters represent no threat to the power of the patriarch; they never protest their subordinate role and indeed imbue it with a sacred aura, never swerving in their reverence for their fathers, no matter how feeble or frenzied these fathers might be. Unlike a son, with whom the father must negotiate a balance of power and to whom he must inevitably relinquish power, the dutiful daughter represents no threat. In these plays the power differential between father and child is both absolute and sacred. Not only do these daughters uphold the familial power structure, they also reject or subordinate romantic love in favor of their filial piety. Their subordinate position within society is built into their position within the family so that, unlike Catharine in *Catharine and Petruchio*, these women do not need taming; they have internalized the standards that Catharine must learn to observe.

Perhaps the most unusual variation on the theme of fathers and dutiful daughters occurred not within the text of an adaptation but in its performance. When Theophilus Cibber's *Romeo and Juliet* first played in 1744, Cibber himself played Romeo—and his fourteen year-old daughter Jennie played Juliet. The audience's attention was repeatedly drawn to this relationship. References to the father-daughter pairing appear first in the "Prologue," spoken by Jennie, later in an epilogue she allegedly wrote for subsequent performances, and, ultimately, in Cibber's *A Serio-Comic Apology for Part of the Life of Mr. Theophilus Cibber*, published with the adaptation in 1748. In these references, the audience is invited to envision actor and actress not as star-crossed lovers but as equally conventional characters, the needy father and the loving, supportive daughter. Cibber and his daughter recreate themselves as figures out of sentimental drama, a play for audience sympathy before the official play began. At the close of the prologue, Jennie described herself not as a lover, like Juliet, but as one "Who, full of modest Terror, dreads t'appear, / But, trembling, begs a Father's Fate to share."[55] Her "Epilogue," like the "Prologue" included in Cibber's *Apology*, takes the role of the sentimental daughter still further:

> For a kind Father fain I'd Pity move:
> Pardon the Fondness of my Filial Love.
> Reflect how oft' he pleas'd, oft' gain'd Renown,
> And varied Shapes to entertain the Town;
> While crouded Houses thunder'd his Applause:
> Ye bounteous Fair,—to you I plead his Cause.
> To your Protection, gen'rous *Britons*, take,
> Th'unhappy Father, for the Daughter's Sake.[56]

Jennie Cibber's words evoke those of a generation of rewritten Shakespearean daughters who would make equally emotional appeals for sympathy within the confines of the Shakespeare adaptations. Her plea is virtually identical with that of Garrick's Cordelia, pleading with Gloucester and Edmund to help her father, and later still, Cumberland's Evanthe pleading with the Athenian senators. That Cibber and his daughter felt that the representation of daughterly love was a more evocative subject than romantic love underscores the emotional potency of this relationship in the eyes of the average eighteenth-century playgoer.

Just as the later adaptations replace the love stories and pathetic heroines with the dutiful daughters, they also remove the earlier adaptations' explicit political lessons, replacing them with a more generalized appeal to British nationalism. Jennie Cibber's appeal to the sympathy of "gen'rous *Britons*" underlines the national context of this display of filial piety. In directing her appeal to the "Gen'rous *Britons*" of her audience, Jennie Cibber's "Epilogue" links national pride with support of family—because her audience is (ideally) composed of true Britons, they will come to the assistance of the equally British dutiful daughter. Their actions reinforce the hierarchical structure of the family,[57] and by extension the bases of patriarchal society. They are thus a quiet but integral part of the British vision of properly ordered society at a time when Britain was beginning to define itself in terms not only of its heroism and military prowess, but also in terms of its moral values.[58] As references in prologues and even the plays themselves indicate, it was difficult to separate the good daughter from the patriotic cause. She supports her father and her fatherland and does not create a schism between love and honor/duty, that favorite trope of Restoration drama. Through the vehicle of the adaptations, nationalism and the well-ordered family are sanctified by the words of Shakespeare.

The vision of Shakespeare as patriot and defender of family decency created a tension between reverence for his words and the desire to perpetuate this vision of Shakespeare, a tension that was eventually resolved in favor of Shakespeare's text. Though occasional new adaptations appeared, the mode of adapting Shakespeare shifted from verbal change to dramatic reinterpretation. In their concern not to lose a "drop" of Shakespeare, the playwrights of the later eighteenth century display a far greater tolerance for those aspects of Shakespearean language censored by earlier adapters, in particular Shakespeare's puns, archaic diction, and complex figurative passages. The legacy of Shakespeare's touch now endowed these formerly objectionable elements with an irreplaceable luster. Individual words took on a new importance as playwrights attempted to use as much of the original text as public taste would allow. In contrast to the adapters of Restoration and earlier eighteenth century, they viewed his language as fixed, instead of using the plays as plastic material that could be remolded when desired.

This shift toward viewing Shakespeare's words as immutable corresponds to the growing reverence for Shakespeare as Author. His audience in the later eighteenth century was aware that they were seeing—or more and more often reading—Great Poetry. This definition of Shakespeare as hero of English culture makes his works less dangerous; it defuses any explosive qualities by freezing them, like an exhibit in a museum. His plays can become dangerous only when the parallels between them and current events are overt, such as the parallel between the mad Lear and the mad George III or, later, between George IV's trial of his wife Queen Caroline for adultery and the accusations leveled at another English princess in *Cymbeline*.[59] Instead, managers enhanced the political undercurrent through interpretation rather than textual adaptation. No longer defined by their plot or moral stance, Shakespeare's works were conceived of as immutable collections of words, and as the century drew to a close, rewriting or tampering with these words became taboo. These changes not only shape the way the text of Shakespeare's plays was treated in the theater but also the way it was to be interpreted by critics, as we shall see in the following chapters.

4
Criticism at Mid-Century

In the period between 1740 and the publication of Samuel Johnson's edition in 1765, literary critics began to establish a new iconography of Shakespeare. To them, Shakespeare was a model of liberty, a sublime figure whose works were the result of powerful feeling. Ties with earlier criticism frayed and broke as critics formulated theories to accommodate a new national literature with Shakespeare as its figurehead. "With us islanders," wrote Arthur Murphy in 1753, "Shakespeare is a sort of established religion in poetry."[1] Murphy's statement, with its national identification and evocation of divinity, encapsulates a critical re-evaluation of Shakespeare as far-reaching as that which affected the adaptations during the later eighteenth century.

A series of economic and sociological changes, begun decades before but commonplace after 1740, shaped the ways in which critics of the mid-eighteenth century interpreted literature. In the first decades of the eighteenth century, with the publication of periodicals such as the *Tatler* and the *Spectator*, criticism had begun to move into the public sphere through open discussions, particularly in the popular coffee houses. The patronage system that had supported earlier critics such as Dryden and Howard decayed,[2] making critics dependent on an expanded literary marketplace rather than on a single aristocratic patron. As a result, critics directed their works toward a broader audience that included the growing middle class rather than the aristocratic circles that had previously controlled literary production. Appealing to this larger audience and to the financial support it offered, critics wrote fewer dedicatory prefaces and instead published widely in periodicals. At the same time, the sale of periodicals doubled, and this new marketplace attracted in turn an increasing crowd of would-be critics. The changed literary climate also supported numerous professional critics who had no personal connection with the theater. These critics, including such figures as Tobias Smollett and Samuel Johnson, made their living by writing, generating volumes of essays and new periodicals.

As the market for criticism changed, the nature of criticism changed as well. Neoclassical formalism with its ties to classical authorities had appealed to a relatively small educated elite; by contrast, the criticism practiced from the mid-eighteenth century on moved away from those learned precepts. With the greater movement toward interiority and critical standards based on subjective feeling, criticism became an inclusive rather than an exclusive practice. Depth of soul rather than breadth of learning became the basis of literary appreciation, a standard that allowed a larger, less educated audience to participate.[3] In this climate, the critical ideas of Dryden and Pope were no longer adequate. Gradually, the source of critical standards moved from classical authorities to individual authenticity, a shift in priorities which would be complete by the last decades of the eighteenth century. Mid-century critics, drawn to both methodologies, often found themselves directly in conflict with their critical forebears.

Shakespeare remained central to this critical debate; while the high opinion of his genius did not change, the methods of interpreting his works did. As Murphy's comment suggests, criticism and scholarship dedicated to the appreciation of Shakespeare's works had taken on a distinct note of reverence. For mid-century critics, he was no longer a near contemporary but an honored figure from the almost distant past. In the words of Johnson, "he has long outlived his century, the term commonly fixed as the test of literary merit" and thus "may begin to assume the dignity of an ancient."[4] Attaining the rank of "ancient" placed Shakespeare in the same class as the great Greek and Roman authors. The province of his works was now viewed as "literature," and expanded from the theater to the literary world in general. Novelists such as Horace Walpole derived new literary rules from Shakespeare's works while classicist Richard Hurd used a discussion of his language to gloss a line of Horace[5]—Shakespeare was at the same time a model for the gothic and an analogue for the classics. In addition, Shakespeare occupied a symbolic post as the father of English literature. He was not only an ancient but a *British* ancient, and as British literature was incorporated into the overall expression of nationalistic feeling, Shakespeare attained the prominence of a national hero.

With English literature a legitimate field of study, scholars began to expound upon native English poetry as well as the classics. Much scholarly discussion arose around Shakespeare, especially around the various editions of his plays. The debate over the proper editing of Shakespeare, along with his classification as the Homer of English literature, focused the attention of previously uninterested scholars upon his works. This phenomenon was noted (and ridiculed) by many, such as Thomas Seward, who described the effect of the Shakespeare editions in his "Preface" to the 1750 edition of the works of Beaumont and Fletcher: "No sooner therefore were *Criticisms* wrote on our *English* Poets but each deep-read Scholar whose severer Studies had made him frown with contempt on Poems and Plays was taken in to read, to study, to be enamour'd. He rejoiced to try his strength with the Editor, and to become a *Critic* himself."[6] Seward's comments chronicle the movement to include English literature within the scholarly canon—as well as the inclusion of popular forms of literature such as plays, the form in which Shakespeare's genius was expressed. As Seward suggests, Shakespeare's works were found in the study as well as on the stage, his printed text generating rapture rather than contempt. Scholars published erudite studies of Shakespeare's learning, and analyses of his works even appeared in learned footnotes.[7] Once again, these developments reflected the growing audience for works scrutinizing native English literature rather than the classics associated with the aristocratic values of a previous generation.

These gradual but inevitable developments grew out of the literary projects of an earlier age: the Shakespeare editions of Pope (1723) and Theobald (1733), and the literary essays of the *Tatler* and the *Spectator*. The criticism of Shakespeare's works slowly but inexorably moved away from the theater and into the public coffee house and private library. One consequence of the change in audience was the severing of the close connection between criticism and the stage. Criticism became a genre in its own right, with the result that essays no longer had to be justified by being attached to a play. The critical prefaces and prologues which had dominated criticism for over fifty years died out, and in their place a new generation of critics substituted periodical essays and learned book-length studies following the example of Lewis Theobald's *Shakespeare Restored* (1726). Prefatory essays did appear, but they were typically attached to editions of Shakespeare's works rather than adaptations of his plays.

Criticism of Shakespeare was thus the province of almost anyone, not simply dramatists. Anybody and everybody could write criticism—and did, as John Upton, for example, complains: "who more or less does not *criticize*?"[8] Such complaints demonstrate the new accessibility of literature to a wide audience which now included the bourgeoisie as well as the educated elite. At a time when familiarity with literature was a sign of social status, criticism represented a form of literature almost anyone could practice—not just aristocrats and the poets and playwrights they supported. Critics pointed with astonishment to the remarkable popularity of "criticizing," seeing the increased volume of Shakespeare commentary as an occasional blessing, but more often as a blight. The study of Shakespeare did prompt the search for a "genuine text" of his works, but to the indignation of many, the new movement produced its share of ignoramuses, who reduced his works to what William Dodd described as "a kind of stage for bungling critics to show their *clumsy activity* upon."[9] Often a useful foil for an argument, the figure of the idiotic critic became a favorite object of abuse. This familiar abuse, more than any serious gauge of public opinion, testifies to the ubiquitous nature of criticism and demonstrates the appropriation of Shakespeare by an ever-increasing audience.

A New Empire of Wit

Shaped by a new intellectual climate and answering to a different audience, mid-century critics responded uneasily to past critics. Though they rejected many aspects of earlier critical theory and recoiled with disgust to what they saw as immorality, they were not yet ready for a clean break with the critical precepts of the Restoration and early eighteenth century. They made use of a critical vocabulary similar to that of the critics they complain about, and one quality that defines this group of critics is their awareness of prior critics. Anxious to dissociate themselves from an earlier age, they attacked their predecessors in an age-old pattern of generational revolt, establishing their identity as writers and critics by distinguishing themselves from the immediate past. One form this revolt took was self-righteous critique of Restoration morality, a revolt compounded by middle-class distaste for aristocratic dissipation. Writing with an eye to the bourgeois sense of propriety, literary critics rejected an entire generation as corrupt. They thus defined themselves and their age in opposition to the rakes and profligates of the Restoration, an age whose literary taste they found as bankrupt as its morals. For these critics, Shakespeare is the standard not only of genius but of proper morality against which the frenchified and thus immoral writers of the Restoration could not compete.

Although responding to many of the same issues, mid-century critics generally chose to distance themselves from their predecessors. They viewed the age of Dryden with a kind of horror, emphatically rejecting the dramatic styles and critical standards of the Restoration. The works of Dryden, Rowe, and a host of lesser playwrights were seen as unnatural and sterile, "infected" by French criticism that "under the pretext of CORRECTNESS helped to extinguish SPIRIT."[10] To the new critics, the iniquities of these playwrights overshadowed any trivial errors of true genius. In *The Adventurer* no. 90 (15 September 1753), playwright George Colman demonstrated both the lingering influence of earlier writers and the equally strong reaction against them by relating a dream in which poets sacrifice their weaknesses to the muses so that "their names may descend spotless and unsullied to posterity."[11] Chaucer gives up his obscenity; Milton a few errors in *Paradise Lost*; while "SHAKE-SPEARE carried to the altar a long string of puns, marked 'Taste of the Age,' a small parcel of bombast, and a pretty large bundle of incorrectness"[12]—all familiar complaints. But Colman also envisions D'Urfey, Etherege, Wycherley, and their contemporaries making such a large contribution of bad drama that they set the entire altar ablaze.

Attacks on the previous generation seethed with moral outrage as writers represented Restoration playwrights as demonic and corrupt:

That an almost total extinction of genius and taste for poetry of every kind was the unhappy consequence of that event [the Restoration] is no less certain. Can any one then, who is sensible of the dignity of this divine art, and the excellent purposes it is capable of serving, with patience think on such a nest of pestilent vermin, as, warmed by the sun-shine of court favours, crawled forth at that time, and spread their poisonous influence around them? Who, I say, can, without indignation, behold such shameless profligates as *Carew, Killigrew, Howard, Sedley, Etherege, Sheffield, D'Urfey*, the hasty *Shadwell*, and even the slow *Wycherley*, corrupting the taste, and consequently the manners of an age, and arrogating to themselves the SACRED AND VENERABLE CHARACTER OF POETS?[13]

Here the offended critic explicitly attributes the degeneration of taste to a corrupt aristocracy's patronage. "Warmed by the sun-shine of court favours," poets become vermin who poison those around them, spreading their pernicious influence over an entire age. Worse yet, these "profligates" "arrogate to themselves" the name of poet, usurping literary control. The author of the essay offers Shakespeare's plays as an antidote to such depravity with the unspoken understanding that the current literary climate is itself morally and thus poetically superior to that of the Restoration.

Mid-century critics also condemned what they saw as the Restoration's improper assessment of Shakespeare. Not only did Restoration dramatists fail miserably to live up to his stellar example, but these same poets and critics also failed to appreciate his genius, abandoning "the sterling merit of Shakespear for the tinsel ornaments of the French academy."[14] Even the methodology of Restoration literary criticism came under fire as the once popular beauties-and-faults approach now provided evidence of degenerate taste, and to some, such as Arthur Murphy, even revealed a paucity of mind: "While the beauties of this admirable author are so brilliant and so numerous, I should be ashamed to own that

I had suffered my attention to be taken off from them long enough to discover any of his defects. For who indeed but the most dull and stupid of wretches would employ his time in a quarry of diamonds with raking after dirt and pebble stones, because such things might possibly be found there?"[15] The beauties-and-faults schema that Dennis had described as a necessary part of balanced criticism has become no more than "dirt and pebble stones" to those who follow him. For Murphy, there is no beauties and faults equation. In the case of Shakespeare the faults are trivial and the beauties stunning—to mention the two together would itself be grossly unbalanced. In sum, mid-century critics asserted that criticism had fallen into bad hands and that it was the duty of a new breed of critics to redeem it. Their outspoken disgust for the literature and standards of the Restoration may well be the original source of the critical truism that the Restoration and early eighteenth century could not appreciate Shakespeare, a view that has persisted into the twentieth century.[16]

The new critics focused their strongest objections upon the "mechanical rules," an easy target and a deliberate rejection of the taste of a previous generation. Although a few lone writers voiced tentative support for the unities,[17] even they expressed ambivalent feelings toward the idea of rules. Such acceptance of the rules, however lukewarm, was greatly overpowered by the strong antirule sentiment expressed by nearly every other critic. By this time, most critics saw rules as harmful restraints; where earlier writers decided the rules were valuable for modern drama, even though they should not be applied to Shakespeare, mid-century critics denied even this limited merit. Only a "genius of the lowest order" observes the rules, and only a fool would apply them to Shakespeare. The ancients wrote for their time, English poets and critics must write for their own. Trying to mingle the two involves a break with nature similar to that described by Alexander Gerard in *An Essay on Taste* (1759): "[Criticism] has fallen into the hands of incapable professors, who, without regard to the reality of nature, have attempted to prescribe rules, formed by their own imaginations. The accidental usage of an eminent author on a particular emergency, has been converted into a standing law, and applied to cases no way similar: arbitrary restraints have been imposed without necessity, and even shining faults have been recommended as beauties."[18] Gerard sees the rules not as reflections of nature (or "nature methodized," as Pope described them[19]), but as the creations of "incapable" but self-absorbed "professors" and thus the rules can only be arbitrary, not rational. They have no roots in reality—indeed they are but the result of accident. The overall result of adhering to these accidental laws is a corrupted taste in which "shining faults" are confused with genius.

Critics provided more proof for their rejection of the rules by denigrating tragedies that adhered to them. They claim that far from being natural and moving, these regular dramas are sterile and boring. As Guthrie complains, French and modern English playwrights "have peopled the poetic world with a race of mortals unknown to life."[20] Put simply, the rules make bad drama. The rigidity of the unities makes one plot much like another, and, worse yet, flattens variety and passion into mere declamation. Nature gets lost in artifice, which invalidates the rules as "Observations of Nature." Whereas critics and playwrights from Dryden to Addison had cautiously endorsed the rules for themselves if not for Shakespeare because they saw the rules as not only rational but aesthetically refined, their successors found this thought the ultimate example of artistic solecism. As Gerard explains, "a man would justly expose himself to a suspicion of bad taste, who approved a faultless, uninteresting tragedy."[21]

As in the earlier part of the century, adherence to the rules acquired a strongly negative political charge as critics developed the motif of the servile French versus the liberty-loving British. By mid-century, Shakespeare had been appropriated by both political parties as a political symbol of freedom and vitality, a representation of the British character. His works would not appeal to the French because, as Peter Whalley explains, a servile people cannot understand the nature of liberty: "It does not in the least abate my Veneration for our Poet that the *French Connoisseurs* have fixed on him the Imputation of Ignorance and Barbarism. It would agree, I believe, as little with their Tempers to be freed from a Sovereign Authority in the Empire of Wit and Letters as in their civil Government."[22] Whalley's words emphasize Shakespeare's role as political standard-bearer in a realm where the "Empire of Wit" is equated with "civil Government." The French need rules because they cannot handle freedom, whereas the opposite characteristic defines their British neighbors: "the dramatic poetry of this country is like our constitution, built upon the bold basis of liberty."[23] Shakespeare, the constitution, the Empire of Wit and civil government, all define the British national character. Not only do the British thrive upon liberty, but the very thought of restraint, whether in poetry or government, is antithetical to their nature and thus must be abolished. Ultimately, the rules and their practitioners are rejected for inherently political reasons. In the stirring words of playwright Samuel Foote:

But in general these bonds do not hit the Taste and Genius of the free-born luxuriant Inhabitants of this Isle: they will no more bear a Yoke in Poetry than Religion.

No political or critical Monarch shall give Laws to them. They have indeed sometimes given Proofs that they do not despise these Mandates of *Aristotle* because it is not in their Capacity to comply with them, but because they will not be indebted to any other Country for what they can obtain without its Assistance.[24]

Shakespeare, that "established religion in poetry," is of course Foote's example of "free-born" English genius as literary taste and literary criticism became as much of a patriotic statement as marching off to war.

This nationalistic fervor encompassed the sources of neoclassicism as mid-century critics not only decried the rules but rejected even the learning of foreign cultures. They did not need the classics because, as Foote argues, a true patriotic Englishman "will not be indebted to any other country." Their fear of a foreign "yoke" applied more generally to classical learning. Even limited acceptance of classical form became unpopular as critics began to consider learning itself a detriment to poetry. As Edward Young explains in *Conjectures on Original Composition* (1759), learning, like the rules, represents an infringement on poetic liberty: "[*Learning*] inveighs against natural unstudied Graces, and small harmless Indecorums, and sets rigid Bounds to that Liberty, to which Genius often owes its supremest Glory; but No-Genius its frequent Ruin. For unprescribed Beauties, and unexampled Excellence which are Characteristics of *Genius*, lie without the Pale of *Learning's* Authorities, and Laws; which Pale Genius must leap to come at them."[25] To Young and his contemporaries, too much learning was not only a disadvantage to the critic, who then "inveighs against natural unstudied Graces and small harmless Indecorums," but it also disables poets by fencing them into a narrow space. The audience to whom Foote and Young appealed would have appreciated this rejection of the elitist values of earlier critics, consisting as it did of people reading and practicing poetry who, like Shakespeare, might not have had a classical education but who did count themselves among the ranks of "free-born," liberty-loving Britons.

In this schema, genius becomes a corollary of liberty, that defining element of the British national character. Making even poetic genius dependent upon political and personal liberty, the British define themselves in opposition to all things foreign. As the title of Young's treatise indicates, the understanding of "genius," that quality that was best exemplified by Shakespeare's works, had become linked directly with originality, a concept that explicitly rejected the influence of learning, classical or otherwise.[26] In order to write with genius, poets must forget what they have learned. The hint that more of this unnatural learning might have dampened Shakespeare's genius appeared as early as Rowe's *Life of Shakespeare* in 1709. Within fifty years Rowe's idea was commonplace. Classical learning became a fatal error which could lead a poet, like Addison, to compose "lays . . . coldly correct," unlike Shakespeare with his "warblings wild."[27]

GENIUS, LIBERTY—AND FEELING

Genius and liberty were joined by a new criterion, feeling, which in the literary theory of the mid-eighteenth century became the core of both the author's and the audience's poetic experience. It was a mark of genius and a response to liberty as well as in itself a source of liberty. This triumvirate of excellences—liberty, genius, and feeling—come together in Shakespeare, firmly establishing him as England's literary and political standard-bearer. Using Shakespeare as their great exemplar, critics proclaimed the superiority of native British genius; British writers had no need of the classics because they possessed, when given the freedom to practice it, true depth of feeling, an individual response independent of class or education. Lack of this quality rendered the poetry of the ancients sterile. In Robert Lloyd's poem "Shakespeare: An Epistle to Mr. Garrick" (1760), Lloyd castigates the classics for exactly this want of feeling:

> Doubtless the Ancients want the art
> To strike at once upon the heart,
> . . . .
> Or need the Chorus to reveal
> Reflexions, which the audience feel;
> And jog them, lest attention sink,
> To tell them how and what to think?[28]

Like Young and Warton, Lloyd stresses the sterility of the classics and, implicitly, those who revered them so highly. Even more important, Lloyd's poem traces a shift from the autocratic standards of classical learning into the more subjective realm of feelings. To critics such as Lloyd, the classics lack the ability to move; they can only tell readers what to think—they cannot make them feel. In contrast to such an unnatural regimen, Lloyd lauds Shakespeare who "travers'd all the human heart, / Without recourse to Grecian art."[29] Shakespeare's greatness comes from his empathetic ability, and Lloyd sets this new standard in opposition to rigid rules and sterile imitation. Feeling thus occasions the liberty that has become a necessary part of genius.

With theory derived from classical authority fallen into disrepute, critics found themselves reassessing their conception of literature, especially dramatic literature. Where their predecessors had endorsed verbal clarity and moral order, mid-century critics were willing to overlook these qualities in favor of increased emphasis on characterization and on the newly popular concept of the sublime. Undeterred by Aristotle, they established new priorities, basing their critical standards on general sensitivity rather than formal principles. Emotional response, both the author's and the audience's, overruled formal considerations of plot, which became, like the rules that supposedly governed its shape, almost irrelevant. In this school of theory, well-drawn characters incite the strongest response, and only an author, like Shakespeare, with true depth of soul can create living, breathing characters.

Praise of Shakespeare's characters was hardly a new topic; critics since the Restoration (aside from Rymer) had applauded their naturalness. Even Dennis, whose theories of poetic decorum often involved strict definitions of character types, described his characters as "just" and "exact." Where the mid-century critics differed was in their emphasis on the primary importance of character. Experimenting with new ideas but expressing them in terms of outdated theory, they created a new dramatic unity—the unity of character. Whereas careful observation of the unities of time, place, and action leads to "starv'd, strait-lac'd Brats" of plays,[30] unity of character stands as the single greatest means of representing nature and can even induce moral instruction. By creating a consistent and thus realistic character, the playwright allows the audience to identify with the play's action in an immediate and emotional way, a quality seen in the mid-eighteenth century as foreign to "regular" drama. This concept of identification allowed critics to redefine the classical concept of pity and fear (catharsis), which in the *Poetics* arose from a realization of the plot, as a function of character, so that our pity is engaged for the persons represented, and our terror is upon our own account. This response, Arthur Murphy claims, cannot be achieved by plot, no matter how beautifully structured. As he explains, "the Art of constructing the dramatic Story should always be subservient to the Exhibition of Character. Our great *Shakespeare* has breathed another Soul into Tragedy, which has found the Way of striking an Audience with Sentiment and Passion at the same Time."[31] Murphy's "Sentiment and Passion" resemble the neoclassical pity and fear, somewhat reshaped to accommodate the language of sensibility familiar to his audience. Murphy's description of this experience "striking" the audience uses the same verb as Lloyd's poem and suggests an immediate, involuntary, and ultimately irrational response.

The creation of such rich and natural characters requires more than simple skill; it devolves from an empathetic quality inherent in the poet himself, a quality in which, critics asserted, Shakespeare surpassed all ancient and modern poets. Bonnell Thornton, minor poet and periodical editor, claimed that "Shakespeare with all his imperfections, is the only tragic poet that seems to have written from the heart," and that his insight into the heart yields true passion and nature rather than the "tinsel pomp of declamation."[32] Such pronouncements focus not simply on the work itself or on its affect in performance, but on the act of writing it. Reconstructing Shakespeare's personal qualities from his works, critics looked to the printed page in order to determine his sincerity.[33] The poet must feel the emotions he delineates, writing "from," not about, the heart; his feelings, not his mind, must inform his poetry. Without this authorial sincerity, the literary work will be "sterile," "soulless," unoriginal, and boring—the epitaphs that by mid-century were commonly directed toward the products of French neoclassicism and even toward the classics themselves.

Focusing on writing and sincerity, critical studies of Shakespeare moved away from considering his works in performance (where audience response was crucial). Predating Keats and the concept of "Negative Capability" by more than seventy years, William Guthrie and Henry Home, Lord Kames speculated on the role of authorial sympathy in poetic composition. Guthrie describes a model of the writing process based upon his impression of Shakespeare's particular genius: "The genius, forgetting that he is a poet, wraps himself up in the person he designs; he becomes him; he says neither more or less than such a person, if alive and in the same circumstances, would say; he breathes his soul; he catches his fire; he flames with his resentment. The rapid whirl of imagination absorbs every sensation; it informs his looks; it directs his motion . . . he is no longer himself; he flies from representation to reality."[34] Poetic composition here becomes intensely emotive, not a craft, but a quality of soul that can break down the barrier between "representation" and "reality." Becoming what he represents, the poet must experience that which he writes. Fifteen years later, Kames presents a similar vision in *The Elements of Criticism* (1762): "In order to reach such delicacy of execution, it is necessary that a writer assume the precise character and passion of the personage represented; which requires an uncommon genius. But it is the only difficulty; for the writer, who, annihilating himself, can thus become another person, need be in no pain about the sentiments that belong to the assumed character: these will flow without the least study, or even preconception; and will frequently be as delightfully new to himself as to his reader."[35] In both passages, the critic envisions the self-effacing poet swept away from himself into composition. Working backwards from the literary work, they construct the persona of the poet even while they imagine him ridding himself of this personality. This backformation testifies not only to the cult of the author[36] but also to the paramount importance theorists attached to emotion. It is not enough simply to be original; the ability to emote becomes the fountainhead of genius.

Because the force of emotion embedded in the literary work is the reality, it must have been created by some equally "real" part of the poet. Learning or "study" can have nothing to do with such "delicacy of execution" because the poet operates on a deeper level, feeling rather than writing to fulfill a plan. Shakespeare, the poet of nature, is the supreme example of this catalytic talent, and, predictably, he is the figure both Guthrie and Kames chose as the embodiment of genius.[37] Their speculations attempt to explain the artistic merit of Shakespeare's characters through specific personal traits of their author rather than through formal artistic criteria. Thus they argue that Shakespeare's characters live on the stage as consistent human beings because their creator, with his remarkable "whirl of imagination," experienced every aspect of their nature. As the result of this theoretical process of personification, Shakespeare becomes as much of a fictional creation as his own characters. At their most abstract, critics theorize a sort of literary transmigration of the soul from author to character and finally, through the medium of drama, to the audience.

Shakespeare's powerful effect on his audience prompted renewed discussion of his "sublimity," a term that became increasingly popular in the mid-eighteenth century. Translations of Longinus's *Treatise on the Sublime* had appeared in English as early as 1680, and early eighteenth-century translations (Leonard Welsted, 1712, and William Smith, 1739) occasionally used Shakespeare to exemplify the sublime, but not until mid-century does the term become current with critics.[38] Except when discussing Shakespeare's language (a topic to which I shall return), critics used the sublime as a generic term of praise, rarely attempting to explain why Shakespeare's works have this quality and using it instead as a catch-all compliment to the poet.[39] When considering the sublime, most mid-century critics focused their attention on its emotional effect, with the result that descriptions of the sublime object became less important. In terms of literary criticism, the sublime was thus recognized as an effect to be produced rather than as a concrete object,[40] a tendency that was particularly noticeable in references to Shakespeare. Richard Hurd, writing in 1765, illustrates this change in emphasis by claiming that Shakespeare is "greater when he uses *gothic* manners and machinery than when he employs classical; which brings us again to the same point, that the former have by their nature and genius the advantage of the latter in producing the *sublime*."[41] Providing yet another example of the shift away from formalist criticism, Hurd's comments appraise literary techniques by their ability to produce an effect and epitomize the overwhelming dominance of affective criticism in studies of Shakespeare.

This generalized notion of the sublime also plays a role in containing or domesticating aspects of Shakespeare that had previously been seen as barbaric, rough, or even dangerous. Even while critics emphasize the "greatness" and terror-inducing nature of the sublime, the easy use of such terminology makes Shakespeare knowable and thus controllable. The lack of theoretical rigor regarding Shakespeare and the sublime contributed to this tendency. What in earlier decades had been a blight or blemish, such as clearly fantastic situations or extravagant metaphoric language, now contributed to Shakespeare's greatness and, as Hurd suggests, aligns him with the native English tradition of "gothic" manners. Critics even see Shakespeare's sublimity as contributing to the moral impact of his works, a connection that underscores the taming nature of *this* vision of the sublime. The concern for morality that had so dominated Restoration and early eighteenth-century criticism had not vanished from critical discourse, although critics found themselves redefining the nature of morality in literature. John Upton, who had described "moral painting" as the greatest beauty in poetry, finds this quality inherent in the sublime: "everything in poetry should have manners and passions: and the moral should shine perspicuous in whatever aims at the sublime," for "descriptions without moral or manners, however designed by the poet to raise the passion of wonder and astonishment, are not instances of the *true* sublime."[42] With morality a part of the emotional impact of the sublime, it becomes an affective rather than a formalist concern. As critics label Shakespeare generally sublime, he becomes almost by definition moral, and one question that had troubled so many earlier critics is solved almost by sleight of hand.

TEXT AND MEANING

If the troubling question of the morality of Shakespeare's drama was subsumed into discussion of the sublime, criticism of his unrefined language also lost force. On the most basic level, the language of Shakespeare's age was no longer assumed to be rude and barbaric. Mid-century writers worried instead that their modern, refined English was somehow effete, trivial, or impotent. They looked back with nostalgia to previous centuries when great minds wrote with a strong, vibrant language lost to their successors. Murphy notes with relief Johnson's upcoming *Dictionary of the English Language*; it will, he feels, prevent further erosion of the language: "I should be glad that some means were devised to hinder the diction of *Bacon, Shakespeare, Milton,* and *Hooker* from being covered with the rush of time, and rendered useless by the quaint prettiness of modern innovation."[43] Dryden and his contemporaries' self-congratulatory claims of refining the language faded into the distance as Murphy's generation searched for the language its predecessors had eschewed. The nostalgia for the past evoked by Murphy's words is of a piece with the literary primitivism popular during the last half of the eighteenth century and exemplified most vividly by the craze for medievalism and the gothic. Each was a part of the literary nationalism that appropriated Shakespeare as symbol of liberty—the keystone in a national literature contradistinguished from the classics and French neoclassicism. The fundamental change in the perception of Shakespeare's language not only provided a clear break with earlier critics (as his language could no longer be reviled as crude or badly influenced by a barbaric age), but also invalidated a style of adaptation in which the "rude" dialect was rewritten and refined.

The numerous editions of Shakespeare's works published between 1730 and 1765[44] were a primary source of this new attitude toward Shakespeare's language. Commentary on specific editions formed a major segment of mid-century criticism, as writers attacked or supported each new edition. Everyone agreed on what an editor should do—provide a "genuine text" of Shakespeare's works—but each new edition spawned a swarm of would-be editors who irately pointed out the errors of the new text.[45] The complaints fall into two general categories, regardless of the edition reviewed. First, reviewers complain that rather than studying the text at hand, the editor has followed his own whims, egotistically foisting "chimeral conjectures and gross mistakes" upon an ignorant and unwary public.[46] Worse yet, his emendations may actually destroy the text he claims to save. Angry critics portray editors as eager to strike out every word they cannot comprehend, and in their lack of knowledge of Shakespeare's language and customs, "there is danger lest peculiarities should be mistaken for corruptions, and passages rejected as unintelligible which a narrow mind happens not to understand."[47] Illiterate editors were perceived as weeding the "vast Garden" of Shakespeare's works, pulling up flowers as they work.[48] The result was not the genuine text aspired to by critic and editor alike but a hybrid monstrosity "which is neither Shakespeare's nor English."[49]

These comments all evince a tremendous fear of disfiguring Shakespeare. To the critics, his plays were not general entities but bodies of minute particulars, and losing even one word meant losing a stroke of genius that could not be replaced. At the most fundamental level, these critics find Shakespeare's genius dependent on his words. Even a quibble or anachronism must be retained because it too partakes of the magic of Shakespeare's genius. The almost hysterical fear of "losing" Shakespeare even permeates reviews of plays in performance. As actor and manager of Drury Lane, David Garrick became the subject of numerous essays, poems, and reviews, many addressing not his adaptations of Shakespeare but the way in which he spoke Shakespeare's words. The tone of these essays varies widely. On one hand, an anonymous poet impersonates Shakespeare's ghost and addresses Garrick as "my great restorer" who repairs his "injur'd song" and places "each character in proper light."[50] Others were less pleased. Thady Fitzpatrick penned an extended complaint on Garrick's "improper" use of emphasis when reading, bemoaning "those mutilated lines of unhappy Shakespear."[51] With these personifications, Shakespeare becomes an entity in himself, larger than his works and yet defined by his words. Though earlier critics could and did differentiate between genius and words, for later writers mutilating Shakespeare's words, whether in print or on the stage, was a capital offense because it meant destroying "the Correctness of the Text, which is equally necessary to the right understanding him."[52]

New assumptions regarding the relation of text to meaning pervaded textual criticism, as seen in a review of Benjamin Heath's *A Revisal of Shakespeare's Text* written by George Steevens. Steevens states that Heath "has taken more pains to understand Shakespeare's meaning than his words, two studies which have so mutual a relation that they ought to be inseparable."[53] This comment distills one essential aspect of the mid-century perception of Shakespeare's language. On the most basic level, Steevens asserts that an author's meaning is dependent on the specific words that he or she wrote. The two cannot be separated as had been tried by the earlier critics who had praised Shakespeare's genius while deploring his language. This assumption lies behind the mid-century paranoia of losing Shakespeare, both the cultural construct and his works, and reveals a major shift away from the critics and adapters of the Restoration who used Shakespeare's language as an excuse to rewrite his plays. For critics and editors such as Steevens, such rewriting would be impossible, for by substituting new words, the early adapters were tampering with Shakespeare's "meaning" and thus diluting his genius. This emphasis on text also reflects the influence of the growing print industry. Reissued in inexpensive editions of single plays as well as scholarly editions, Shakespeare's works were by mid-century conceived of as books to be read, the source of yet more printed critical studies, rather than plays to be seen in the theater. No one yet would agree with Lamb that Shakespeare ought not to be acted,[54] but when reading Shakespeare in the privacy of the home, readers could not but view his works as a printed text.

Recognizing an inseparable connection between an author's own words and meaning also necessitated a different approach to Shakespeare by both critics and adapters. Where the adapters of the mid-eighteenth century kept their plays "Shakespearean" by retaining as many of the original words as possible, critics turned more and more to a specific examination of the same inviolable text. Detailed explications of scenes or speeches began to take the place of the general essays "on Shakespeare" popular with the playwright/critics of the Restoration. Instead critics insisted that by examining "little and almost imperceptible circumstances"[55] they could more truly understand Shakespeare's brilliance; in order to understand his works, a critic must "know more minutely his very words and genuine expressions."[56] At the same time, the new generation denigrated the older style of general appreciation: "General criticism is on all subjects useless and unentertaining; but it is more than commonly absurd with respect to SHAKESPEARE, who must be accompanied step by step and scene by scene in his gradual *developments* of characters and passions, and whose finer features must be singley pointed out if we would do compleat justice to his genuine beauties."[57] This emphasis on careful textual scrutiny was buttressed by the repeated insistence that the only real authority on Shakespeare is the poet himself, "for such authors are the best interpreters of their own meaning."[58] Ambiguous words or passages can best be explained internally, by reading more of the poet, rather than using an external critical apparatus. The focus thus falls heavily on the text itself, on the words as they stand, not as they ought to be. With critical theory linked so closely to the printed word, the "what might have been" school of criticism became invalid. Proper literary criticism, it was argued, should look carefully at the text, the closer and more specifically the better.[59]

With the specifics of the text (and not the general attributes of the text in performance) established as the tools of this new textual criticism, Shakespeare's imagery could be reclaimed. As in the past, figurative language was a popular topic of discussion, but, unlike their predecessors, critics now praised his use of metaphor and imagery. Though some still protested his overabundant metaphors, they pointed to specific passages rather than objecting to his figurative language as a whole.[60] A host of other critics elevated figurative language in general and Shakespeare's figures in particular to a point of poetic distinction. Hurd praises Shakespeare's ability to revitalize language, describing his use of language as "art."[61] Likewise, Daniel Webb claims that "allusions and images" distinguish poetic diction from "simple versification."[62] These comments display a new function for figurative language and a new understanding of what differentiates poetic diction from other forms of language. A growing number of critics equated figurative language with the sublime. The obscurity of figures and their association with emotion (as in the speeches of the mad Lear) made them an important source of sublimity. Gerard finds that "metaphor, comparison and imagery" often produce sublimity, even in a work "destitute of innate grandeur."[63] Implicitly, even while extolling the power of Shakespeare's language, critics suggested that such language was no longer dangerous. The obsession with verbal clarity that had obsessed earlier writers had been based on a fear of the destabilizing power of unclear language—words, such as those used in metaphors, that might have more than one meaning. By mid-century, such language, even if sublime, had been shorn of its larger significance so that despite its obscurity or duality, the threat of disorder, linguistic or political, no longer existed.

In emphasizing the verbal sublime, mid-century critics broke resolutely with their predecessors. By stressing the "sublime" power of Shakespeare's language, critics assessed not just the words themselves but the manner in which the reader responds to these words. Their theory of the power of figurative language not only invalidated the earlier rejection of figures, but also emphasized the ultimate importance of the written word. The earlier disparagement of Shakespeare's language was now seen as an example of frigid criticism and of minds so narrow that, as William Dodd argues, they would dare to tamper with an author's "sacred text": "[Shakespeare's] flights are sometimes so bold, frigid criticism almost dares to disapprove them; and those narrow minds which are incapable of elevating their ideas to the sublimity of their author's are willing to bring them down to a level with their own. Hence, many fine passages have been condemned in *Shakespear* as *Rant* and *Fustian, intolerable Bombast*, and *turgid* Nonsense which, if we read with the least glow as the same imagination that warm'd the writer's bosom, wou'd blaze in the robes of sublimity and obtain the commendations of a *Longinus*."[64] By implying that Shakespeare is by definition sublime and claiming every passage as the site of this sublimity, Dodd suggests that if problems are found with Shakespeare's language, it is the reader whose faculties are deficient, not the poet. When approaching Shakespeare's language the reader must strive to burn with the same flame of imagination which animated the poet, and only in this way can Shakespeare's followers elevate themselves to his level and experience his sublimity. The onus lies with the reader, not the poet. Details in Kames's *Elements of Criticism* reveal how much language theory has changed since the Restoration; when raising the issue of bombast, Kames reproves not Shakespeare, but the ever correct Jonson.

The perception of Shakespeare's text as "sacred" implicitly invalidates the concept of adaptation, which by definition changes the text. Most critics, however, did not hesitate to make the implicit explicit. Looking back to Addison's early attack on Tate's *King Lear*, critics found the very idea of altering Shakespeare repugnant, and said so with great force, reminding their readers that not only was it criminal to meddle with Shakespeare's plays (because by doing so great beauties were destroyed) but such meddling only reveals how infinitely superior Shakespeare is to his followers. The issue attracted a crowd of critics who bemoaned such desecration. In contrast to Dryden and his description of words as easily removable clothing, Upton argues that the genius of Shakespeare is of a piece with his "dress":

Our poets write to the humour of the age; and when their own little stock is spent, they let themselves to work on new-modelling Shakespeare's plays, and adapting them to the tast of their audience; by stripping off their antique and proper tragic dress, and by introducing in these mock-tragedies, not only gallantry to women, but an endeavour to raise a serious distress from the disappointment of lovers; not considering that the passion of love, which one would think they should understand something of, is a comic passion. In short, they make up a poet of shreds and patches; so that the ancient robe of our tragedian, by this miserable darning, and threadbare patchwork, resembles the long motley coat of the Fool, in our old plays, introduced to raise the laughter of the spectators. And I am afraid, if the matter were minutely examined into, we should find, that many passages, in some late editions of our poet, have been altered, or added, or lopped off, entirely thro' modern, and French refinement.[65]

Attacking the specific innovations of the Restoration adaptations, particularly the stress upon love and pathos, Upton presents the adapters as misguided tailors. His praise of Shakespeare personalizes the poet; Shakespeare wears a metaphorical robe (much like the robe of sublimity Dodd describes) and has talent and imagination far beyond the scope of "modern" poets. These modern poetasters stupidly destroy the integrity of Shakespeare's "proper tragic dress" by writing adaptations, replacing it with mere pastiche—"the motley coat of the fool." Upton's comments evince a distinct sense of nostalgia for "antique" times before the days of "modern and French refinement" and "new-modelled tragedy." Editors are complicit in this destruction of Shakespeare, like the adapters placing themselves and their taste ("modern and French refinement") before the text.

For Theophilus Cibber, the highly emotional association of text and poet provided a splendid opportunity for a brilliantly vituperative attack against rival David Garrick:

> Were *Shakespeare*'s Ghost to rise, wou'd he not frown Indignation on this pilfering Pedlar in Poetry who thus shamefully mangles, mutilates, and emasculates his plays? . . . Rouse *Britons*, rouse, for shame, and vindicate the Cause of Sense thus sacrific'd to Mummery! Think you see *Shakespeare*'s Injur'd Shade, with Patriot-Anguish, sighing over your implicit Belief and Passive Obedience, your Non-Resistance to this profanation of his Memory. He grieves to see your tame Submission to this merciless *Procrustes* of the stage who wantonly, as cruelly, massacres his dear Remains.[66]

"Emasculating" Shakespeare's plays by cutting the text, Cibber suggests, emasculates Shakespeare himself, leaving his venerable shade "injured" and the public taste corrupted. Cibber's indignant diatribe represents a logical extension of the appropriation of Shakespeare as a patriotic symbol where "mangling" or "mutilating" his words has become an anti-British act. His call to action ("Rouse *Britons*, rouse") sets patriotic action to prevent such desecration against un-English "passive Obedience." Injured by more than the "profanation" of his memory, Shakespeare's shade rises like the ghost of Hamlet's father in "Patriot-Anguish." Like Upton, Cibber argues that Shakespeare's works are beautiful as they were written, and to change these texts reveals the consummate idiocy if not outright criminal nature of the adapter. With every slash of the adapter's pen, Shakespeare's ghost shrieks aloud in agony.

The controversy reached its climax in the debate over *King Lear*.[67] Attacks on the Tate adaptation appeared as early as 1711 in Addison's *Spectator* essay, no. 40 (16 April 1711). One of the most frequently performed adaptations, *Lear* was a popular target, and as the regard for Shakespeare's text grew, the attacks on Tate intensified. Some readers (most notably Samuel Johnson) still preferred the reassuring happy ending, where "the catastrophe sends away all the spectators exalting with gladness."[68] For many others, the reign of Tate indicated the degeneracy of modern times, where the danger was no longer potential social disorder but the corruption of a specifically English sensibility. An assault on Tate's *Lear* even appears in the "Postscript" to *Clarissa Harlowe* (1748) as Richardson broods over the perverse taste of his contemporaries: "Yet so different seems to be the Modern Taste from that of the Antients, that the altered *King Lear* of Mr. Tate is constantly acted on the English Stage, in preference to the Original, tho' written by Shakespeare himself!— Whether this *strange* preference be owing to the false Delicacy or affected Tenderness of the Players, or to that of the Audience, has not for many years been tried."[69] Drawing upon the "patriot anguish" which had become an almost inevitable accompaniment to discussions of the adaptations, Richardson specifically addresses the "strange preference" of the "English" stage as if such atrocities were only to be expected in the more corrupt foreign theaters. He finds it unaccountable that Tate's *Lear* continues to be staged in favor of words penned by "Shakespeare himself." Using a form of circular logic dependent on the assumption of Shakespeare's transcendent genius, Richardson argues that Shakespeare's works should be preferred because Shakespeare wrote them. Charging Garrick and his fellow managers with preferring "the adulterated cup of *Tate* to the pure genuine draught offered by the master"[70] and thus corrupting the public taste, Richardson and others initiated a plea for returning the original *King Lear* to the stage. Although this particular campaign would not succeed, in its recognition of Shakespeare as "the master" and its desire for a "genuine" and "unadulterated" version of his works, it marked the growing popular resistence to the entire concept of adaptation.

JOHNSON AND SHAKESPEARE

It may seem odd that, in a discussion of Shakespeare criticism in the mid-eighteenth century, I make only glancing references to the century's best known discussion of Shakespeare, Johnson's "Preface" to his edition of Shakespeare. Published in 1765, at the end of the transitional period examined in this chapter, Johnson's edition with its famous "Preface" stands apart from the work of his fellow critics. Johnson's essay, eloquent and authoritative, reiterates the concerns of an earlier generation of critics: plot-based morality, poetic justice, errors of language. In this manner, the "Preface" is anachronistic and could be said to be representative of the period's ties to past critical theories. Yet Johnson was not a throwback to an earlier age; his comments on Shakespeare convey the same interest in the author that informed the work of his contemporaries. Johnson differs most from his contemporaries in his emphatic moral judgments, but where earlier critics had focused on the ethics of Shakespeare's plays, Johnson concludes by examining the morality of Shakespeare the man. In this, Johnson shares his contemporaries' growing fascination for the author, the figure behind the written word. Although his interest is moral rather than poetic, he too strives to reconstruct the mind of Shakespeare.

Although it appears at the end of the period during which the critical perception of Shakespeare underwent radical changes, Johnson's essay is in many ways closer to the form and sentiments of the age of Dryden than that of any other mid-century critic. Although it has become the eighteenth century's best known discussion of Shakespeare, the "Preface" itself is largely derivative; as Arthur Sherbo observes, "the belief, still persistent in some critics, that Johnson had something new to say on Shakespeare in the Preface must be discarded."[71] Even Johnson's defense of Shakespeare against the charges of irregularity leveled by earlier critics is a critical convention—despite Johnson's supposed trepidation ("I cannot but recollect how much wit and learning may be produced against me"). Similarities appear in the structure of the essay as well as in the topics Johnson chooses to discuss. Unlike any of his contemporaries, Johnson makes use of the beauties-and-faults method of carefully balanced, general criticism and explicitly denies the value of studying particular passages.[72] After establishing the need for an unbiased, rational evaluation of Shakespeare, he outlines the poet's beauties, most notably his ability to "hold a mirrour up to nature," and with equal rigor names his faults, a style of criticism that most mid century critics had denigrated as at best a waste of time, and at worst insensitive to Shakespeare's genius.

It is in his discussion of Shakespeare's faults that Johnson comes closest to the critical precepts of the early eighteenth century. He describes Shakespeare's plots as loosely formed and complains that Shakespeare made little attempt to produce a solid, satisfying conclusion, but to Johnson the most important manifestation of carelessness lies in his representation of morality. Lurking behind his references to Shakespeare's "sacrifice of virtue to convenience" (p. 71) is the assumption, common in the late seventeenth and early eighteenth centuries, that a poet must represent a just universe. Johnson states explicitly that "it is always a writer's duty to make the world better, and justice is a virtue independent on time or place" (p. 71). Although he avoids using the term, in his emphasis on "a just distribution of good and evil," Johnson laments Shakespeare's lack of poetic justice. Like Dryden and Dennis before him, he is acutely aware of the implications of leaving a play to "operate by chance."

Despite his strong views on the subject, Johnson avoids direct reference to poetic justice, and in this silence we can see two of Johnson's more strongly felt principles clashing head to head: his desire for justice, and his understanding of poetry as a "faithful mirror of manners and of life." Though the desire for order usually wins out, Johnson feels uncomfortable with the idea and cannot completely endorse it. Unlike Dryden and Dennis, however, he fears that a just distribution of good and evil may not be truly natural, as seen in his note on *King Lear.* "A play in which the wicked prosper, and the virtuous miscarry, may doubtless be good, because it is a just representation of the common events of human life: but since all reasonable beings naturally love justice, I cannot easily be persuaded, that the observation of justice makes a play worse; or, that if other excellencies are equal, the audience will not always rise better pleased from the final triumph of persecuted virtue" (704). Here, Johnson admits that just events are not always realistic but cannot reconcile himself to this realism in *King Lear,* admitting in a subsequent paragraph that he was "many years ago so shocked by Cordelia's death, that I know not whether I ever endured to read again the last scenes of the play until I undertook to revise them as an editor" (704). Despite his strong reaction, Johnson is curiously unable to deny the propriety of Shakespeare's ending.[73] His discussion of the conclusion is filled with evasions and equivocations as he avoids making a definite statement. He couches his desire for justice in roundabout, negative terms ("I cannot easily be persuaded") which argue only that the "observation of justice" will not hurt a play. He does not (or cannot) state with confidence that it will make the play better, only that it will not make the play worse. He rests his argument with hypothetical public opinion, imagining that "the audience will . . . always rise better pleased from the final triumph of persecuted virtue," once again relying on a negative construction as well as a hypothetical future tense. In the end, he avoids any conclusive statement, delegating authority to the eighteenth-century audiences whose verdict (although not necessarily Johnson's) has been that "Cordelia, from the time of Tate, has always retired with victory and felicity" (704).

Johnson's evaluation of Shakespeare's faults of language is less complicated. His outline of Shakespeare's weaknesses follows that of many Restoration and early eighteenth-century critics; the diction tends to be bombastic or turgid, the poet often gets caught up in "unwieldy sentiment," and he has a fatal weakness for "some idle conceit, or contemptible equivocation" (73–74). Johnson's condemnation of Shakespeare's language contrasts strikingly with the words of critics such as Hurd and Dodd who found these verbal qualities if not sublime at least inspired (for them, such objections would have revealed Johnson's personal failings not Shakespeare's). Johnson's argument comes to a head in the famous paragraph on Shakespeare's "quibbles" with which he concludes his examination of Shakespeare's faults:

A quibble is to Shakespeare what luminous vapours are to the traveler: he follows it at all adventures; it is sure to lead him out of his way, and sure to engulf him in the mire. It has some malignant power over his mind, and its fascinations are irresistible. Whatever be the dignity or profundity of his disquisitions, whether he be enlarging knowledge or exalting affection, whether he be amusing attention with incidents, or enchaining it in suspense, let but a quibble spring up before him, and he leaves his work unfinished. A quibble is the golden apple for which he will always turn aside from his career or stoop from his elevation. A quibble, poor and barren as it is, gave him such delight that he was content to purchase it, by the sacrifice of reason, propriety and truth. A quibble was to him the fatal Cleopatra for which he lost the world, and was content to lose it. [74]

In this passage, frequently cited by Johnson's contemporaries, we see the firm decisiveness absent in the discussions of poetic justice. Others have commented on Shakespeare's fondness for wordplay, but none with such rhetorical splendor. The passage's most distinctive quality, however, is its focus on the moral implications of the abhorred quibbles. Johnson's topic is not so much the quibbles themselves but rather what they reveal about Shakespeare. Johnson repeatedly portrays the quibble as a source of temptation; it is a "luminous vapour," a "golden apple," or a "Cleopatra." Its effects are expressed in explicitly moral terms as it has a "malignant power" which prompts the poet to "turn aside," "stoop," "leave his work unfinished," and finally "los[e] the world" by sacrificing "reason, propriety and truth." Shakespeare does not have the strength to resist temptation, and a weakness in the poetry reveals a weakness in the man, as Johnson conflates moral and literary criticism. Although the sentiments are different, Johnson's method resembles that of Guthrie and Kames as in Johnson's final judgment, the text becomes the man, the man the text, and Johnson the critic becomes Johnson the moralist.

In his discussion of Shakespeare, Johnson shows himself to be both a part of the cultural changes that shaped other critics and yet resistant to them. His moral concerns echo the critical standards of a previous generation, but he approaches these familiar topics from a new angle. He is antitextual in his vigorous opposition to the use of particular passages, but two of his largest literary endeavours involve the intensely textual work of the lexicographer or the editor. Even while censuring Shakespeare's use of language, Johnson works to preserve that language.

These paradoxes make Johnson's "Preface" an apt conclusion to the decades when neoclassical attitudes toward literature and the poet became intermixed with those frequently termed romantic, when emphasis on individual emotional response began to overwhelm that common consensus called taste, and when drama as text began to overshadow drama in performance.

5
The Search for a Genuine Text

This final chapter begins with the response to—and rejection of—Johnson's appreciation of Shakespeare. The content of the attacks on Johnson and his unromanticized approach to Shakespeare can be linked to that other great Shakespearean phenomenon of the 1760s, Garrick's 1769 Shakespeare Jubilee. The Jubilee, with its laudatory Ode and collection of appreciatory prose and verse[1] capped by a pilgrimage to Stratford-upon-Avon, is notable for its intense idolatry of Shakespeare and all things Shakespearean. Garrick's public adoration of Shakespeare as the "God of our idolatry" (Jubilee *Ode*, l.14) and the subsequent brisk market in Shakespeariana epitomize the extent to which Shakespeare, both his works and his name, had become a part of the public domain—a part of an increasingly bourgeois national ideology. Although Johnson's "Preface" has become the most famous discussion of Shakespeare to emerge from the eighteenth century, in its day it was an anachronism, and it was Garrick's Shakespeare that dominated critical discourse.

To the critics who followed Johnson, Shakespeare's plays as theater were now relatively unimportant; it was the individual's response to Shakespeare, in particular to reading the Shakespearean text, that was crucial. Rationalism and social consensus were rejected in favor of emotional response. The later eighteenth century saw Shakespeare as magician, as nature, and above all as divinity. Critics stressed the interplay among author, text, and reader, a dynamic vastly different from the manipulation of the audience's response to a visual and audible representation that typically concerned critics two generations before. The predominance of these qualities helped establish Shakespeare as an author and his text as a sacred object, a kind of secular bible. In this new literary marketplace, the reader is the consumer of printed texts, and literature is overwhelming perceived as text—not performed, but printed. All discussion of Shakespeare is predicated upon the assumption of the subjectivity of both author and critic, and the primary importance of the printed text.

The last decades of the eighteenth century mark the end of adaptation as I have defined it. The last substantially revised plays were written within six years of Johnson's "Preface," and most of those already written did not last out the century.[2] Critics rarely mentioned the actual adaptations, but the premises on which their discussions of Shakespeare were based eschew any alteration of what was by then considered the established text. My interest lies in examining the ways in which these very different modes of criticism assumed a fixed text of Shakespeare's works. Shakespeare's text, with its irregular beauties, became proof that literature must be approached intuitively and provided evidence of the superiority of "feeling" over the now outmoded and incomplete notion of "reason."

With the disparagement of reason, attempts to fit a literary work into a logical and ordered schema vanished, and the literary text disintegrated into smaller and smaller fragments. This new reliance on careful textual scrutiny took a variety of forms, from ignoring the general outlines of the plot and instead identifying a work's moral message and its portrayal of character as aspects of particular passages, to re-evaluation of figurative language. It culminated in the work of Walter Whiter, who treated the literary work as language isolated from plot. In each case, critics applied an increasingly fragmented view of the literary work. As formalist doctrines fell out of favor, critics chose to focus on words rather than plot, and insisted on the validity of Shakespeare's text over any critical model. In this sense, late eighteenth-century criticism was both a continuation and an extension of the ideas examined in the last chapter. Nowhere is this continuity more apparent than in the reaction to Johnson's "Preface" to Shakespeare.

THE RESPONSE TO JOHNSON

The publication of Johnson's edition in October 1765 provoked numerous reviews, many surprisingly negative. The edition, with its paucity of new textual scholarship, disappointed many readers, while the "Preface" itself incited more frowns than praise. Reviewers express almost universal admiration for Johnson's eloquence and sonorous style,[3] but after this polite compliment, they proceed to disagree with practically every other aspect of the essay.[4] Not surprisingly, critics attack Johnson's assessment of Shakespeare's faults, but, more crucially, they focus on the critical standards on which his essay is based, especially his search for balance and his insistence on the importance of a clear moral message. Each review hints that the issues Johnson raises are irrelevant; the subtext, implicit or explicit, is that literature should not be read in terms of plot and its moral corollary, poetic justice. In place of these now outdated ideas, the reviewers suggest new approaches, their rejection of Johnson demonstrating the upheaval in eighteenth-century critical thought. Through the response of Johnson's critics we glimpse the evolution of new critical lines that would burgeon near the end of the century and eventually prove incompatible with the adaptation of Shakespeare.

On a basic structural level, the form of Johnson's "Preface" confuses his readers. To their eyes, his essay discusses archaic issues in an archaic form, and they argue against his use of the once standard formula of beauties and faults, no longer seeing the importance of objectivity and consensus, and misunderstanding Johnson's attempt to provide evidence that such a consensus exists. Whereas forty years earlier this mode of argumentation would have been a necessary preliminary to a sound judgment, critics of the later eighteenth century misinterpret Johnson's inclusion of Shakespeare's faults. To many, he seems to be attacking Shakespeare, arguing against the playwright's genius. Even such critics as William Guthrie, who recognized Johnson's attempt to be impartial, accuse him of being "*immoderately* moderate." Guthrie argues that instead of enhancing Shakespeare, Johnson has "thrown the blemishes of his author in too odious a light, as some divines have given so much strength to the arguments of the atheist that their own reasoning appears weak when they attempt to confute them."[5]

Because he outlines the faults so decisively, his discussion of Shakespeare's beauties appears weak in comparison. His quest for balance confuses other readers, who interpret it as his inability to make up his mind, as in a review from the *Annual Register*: "If there is any fault in this piece, it is the almost paradoxical manner into which Mr. Johnson has contrived to throw his sentiments. Read first what he says of Shakespeare's beauties, and you will be apt to think he can have no blemishes, or only such as must vanish in the blaze of his beauties. Read first, what he says of his blemishes, and you will be equally apt to conclude, that he can have no beauties, or only such as his blemishes must eclipse."[6] To the reviewer, Johnson's "sentiments" are the issue, indicating that a subjective reading had become an expected part of literary criticism. As these examples show, an old convention has broken down, and broken down so completely that it makes no sense to those who read it. The critical standards that rested on a balance of beauties and faults have vanished, leaving in their place a new set of assumptions that do not necessarily base themselves on the ideal of rationality.

The reviewers took particular exception to Johnson's comments on Shakespeare's faults, for, in their eyes, the very act of finding fault was an affront to Shakespeare's genius. Although Colman recognizes Johnson's attempt to be impartial, he finds the discussion of Shakespeare's flaws "very disputable" and "infinitely too strong"; he proposes that the entire section be replaced with a discussion of some of Shakespeare's greatest plays, thus increasing everyone's appreciation of Shakespeare. Other reviewers share this sentiment, each reproving Johnson for his censure and correcting his lamentable mistakes in judgment, dismantling the list of Shakespeare's flaws piece by piece.[7] Two topics are singled out for special attention, Johnson's comments on Shakespeare's puns and his dismay over Shakespeare's "sacrifice of virtue to convenience." Reviewers portray faults of language as unimportant, certainly not deserving the attention that Johnson devotes to them. In their minds, he should accept Shakespeare's text as it stands. Ultimately, such minor flaws are not really Shakespeare's fault for "the humour and taste of the times had rendered a practice habitual to him, which his own better taste and judgment could not fail to condemn."[8]

Detractors complete the demolition by deconstructing Johnson's own argument on "quibbles": "Has not Mr. J. been as culpably fond of writing upon Quibble, as Shakespeare in pursuing it? and is not this laboured Paragraph upon Quibble as puerile as a Remnant of a Schoolboy's Declamation?"[9] or William Kenrick's sardonic footnote: "Doth not this whole paragraph serve egregiously to prove that altho' our Editor may not be fond of down-right punning, he takes full as much delight in starting and hunting down a poor conceit as he affirms Shakespeare did? We will venture to assert, indeed, that this is a species of quibbling which, barren and pitiful as it is, seems to give the critic himself so much delight that he is content to purchase it by the sacrifice of reason, propriety and truth."[10] As Colman and Kenrick observe, Johnson invalidates his own argument by falling into the same fault as Shakespeare, censuring Shakespeare's puns in a passage that is itself one long conceit.

The reviewers protest with equal vigor that Johnson's assessment of Shakespeare's moral vision is irrelevant. Implicitly or explicitly, they state that Johnson's arguments on the necessity of a formed moral vision are unimportant, or, at best, off the subject (Kenrick hints, rather nastily, that Johnson knows too little about drama to be able to write about it).[11] At the heart of this disagreement lies a clash between two different conceptions of the proper function of literature. Johnson adheres to the long-established dictum that literature should please in order to instruct, whereas for Kenrick such an illustration of morality is a subject for a moral philosopher, not a poet; strict adherence to the "narrow bounds" of poetic justice forces the poet to go against nature. Kenrick questions:

"Must a writer be charged with making a sacrifice of virtue because he does not professedly inculcate it? Is every writer *ex professo* a parson or a moral philosopher? It is doubtless always the *moralist's* duty to strive at least to make the world better, but we should think it no inconsiderable merit in a *comic-poet* to be able to divert and amuse the world without making it worse."[12] In arguing against Johnson's presentation of the moral laxity of Shakespeare's plays, Kenrick separates the poet from his traditional role as moral teacher. When the poet is no longer assumed to be a moralist, Johnson's discussion of Shakespeare's failure to provide moral instruction becomes irrelevant, a topic that has no place in literary criticism.

Even Johnson's praise of Shakespeare comes under attack. Critics appreciate his obvious admiration for the poet's talents, but his praise makes little sense to them. He seems to be praising trivial qualities or even insulting the poet through his injudicious approbation. In most cases, the critics fail to recognize that Johnson uses the terminology of an older generation. Guthrie finds Johnson "unjust and unhappy" in his praise of Shakespeare's plots, claiming that the excellency of Shakespeare's "fable" was "never before appropriated to that great writer."[13] As Guthrie's statement indicates, critical opinion has moved in new directions, misinterpreting older critics while making their favorite topics obsolete. Contrasting himself with Johnson, Guthrie implies not so much that Shakespeare's fables were faulty as that looking at plot is somehow a lesser, more superficial form of criticism.

Johnson's warm praise of Shakespeare as the poet of nature sparks more complaints as his contemporaries have problems comprehending his use of this expression. While Dryden, Rowe, and their contemporaries would understand the significance of Johnson's emphasis on the poet of nature, holding a mirror up to life, his reviewers see these comments as a trivialization of Shakespeare's genius. Colman complains that "there is a wide difference between drawing nature and painting life."[14] To Guthrie, the idea of "holding a mirror up to life" implies merely copying the events of day-to-day life. He questions (with a note of irritation): "Is the page of Shakespeare to be treated like that of a daily newspaper, as containing little more than a series of births and deaths, marriages, murders and misfortunes, bankruptcies and executions?"[15] For him, mirroring nature is nothing more than providing a nonselective reproduction of events. To praise Shakespeare for such a talent ranks him as a mere imitator, not as an imaginative genius, putting him on the same level as an ordinary hack writer. Such an equation was unsuitable for England's native genius, the divinity of English poetry. Imitating nature stands opposed to depth of feeling; to maintain proper literary hierarchies, Shakespeare's plays must be recognized as a higher form of print than a newspaper. Here Johnson's use of the critical terminology of the earlier eighteenth century no longer makes sense to a new generation of critics, and in this case even promotes misunderstanding. Guthrie and Colman in reality differ relatively little from Johnson in their praise of Shakespeare's ability to represent the essential stuff of human life, but the terms Johnson uses have fallen out of critical use.

In place of such outmoded theorizing, Johnson's reviewers propose a variety of new critical standards, focusing especially on the concepts of "character" and "feeling" discussed in the previous chapter. The establishment of these concepts does more than break with Johnson and the older school of criticism; they foreshadow the directions to be taken by almost all criticism for the rest of the century and for much of the nineteenth century as well. The opinions of the reviewers, unlike those of Johnson, harmonize with the majority view; aside from one rebuttal to Kenrick's attack (written by an Oxford undergraduate who resented the slight to Johnson, but addressed his essay to Kenrick's comments on the edition rather than to the "Preface"),[16] the reviews of Johnson's "Preface" went unchallenged. Guthrie notes with relief: "It is with no small pleasure we reflect that neither the criticism hazarded, nor the corrections and emendations proposed in the various reviews we have undertaken of Shakespeare's commentators have hitherto engaged us in any literary dispute worth mentioning; an uncommon piece of good-fortune, which we ascribe solely to the principles we have adopted in vindicating the text of that great poet."[17] This concern for "vindicating the text" of Shakespeare distinguishes Guthrie and his contemporaries from Johnson and from the critics of the early eighteenth century. It involves more than simply protecting Shakespeare from attacks against his figurative language, such as Johnson's comments about quibbles, opposing in general any attempt to subordinate portions of Shakespeare's text to reason and the demands of logical analysis. Time was to validate this concern; subsequent criticism based itself on the principles Guthrie and his fellow critics advocated and not on those of Johnson.

Acceptance of the Complete Text

New discussions of morality in literature exemplify the depth of the schism between Johnson and his contemporaries. Despite Kenrick's acerbic comments and the opinion of some scholars that much of Shakespeare's work had no moral purpose, the topic remained popular with many critics.[18] In contrast to Johnson, however, late eighteenth-century writers such as Martin Sherlock present Shakespeare as the model of moral writing: " 'Horace' says Bacon, 'is the most popular of all the poets of antiquity, because he contains most observations applicable to the business of human life.' Shakspeare contains more of them than Horace. . . . One of the chief merits of the Greek tragic poets (principally of Euripides) is that they abound with morality. Shakspeare has more morality than they."[19] As seen by Sherlock's praise of Shakespeare, "instruction" remains an important consideration, although couched in somewhat different terms. Sherlock finds Shakespeare "abounding" with morality, discovering this quality throughout Shakespeare's works, not simply in the outline of the action. For him, morality seems to be a quality similar to the "observations" which he finds in Horace, small pieces of the drama rather than sweeping patterns. This concern with the relocation of morality can also be seen in the comments of Francis Gentleman in *The Dramatic Censor* (1770), where, in contrast to many of his predecessors, he finds the much maligned grave-digger scene in *Hamlet* a source of "instruction." These admirers of Shakespeare's moral virtues approach the subject from a new direction. Where Johnson used the overall effect of the play and its observation of poetic justice[20] as the barometer of morality, his successors found moral messages in Shakespeare's "observations" and even in a single short scene still frequently excised from the play on the grounds that its levity seemed to destroy the play's moral tone.

It is Elizabeth Griffith, however, who most clearly demonstrates these changes in perspective where text overrules performance. In *The Morality of Shakespeare's Drama* (1775), she allows that "there is a Moral sometimes couched in [Shakespeare's] Fable,"[21] but dedicates the rest of her book to quoting passages from Shakespeare's works and then explicating the moral "maxims and sentiments" exemplified in each passage. To emphasize her point that Shakespeare's moral genius is located in his dialogue rather than his fable, she draws her examples from both dramatic interchanges and set speeches. In one example, she cites two speeches by the Ghost in *Hamlet* (I.v.84ff and III.iv.112ff) as finer than the "sublimest morality of Confucius" while concluding her book with a passage from *Othello* (IV.iii.18ff) in which she sees "comprehended the compleatest system of the oeconomical and moral duties of human nature that perhaps was ever framed."[22] Ostensibly, Griffith and her contemporaries merely reiterate an old theme, the portrayal of moral virtue in drama; in reality, they introduce a vastly different concept. Previous critics identified morality with the larger patterns of the plot: the "progress of the fable" and the representation of poetic justice. They interpreted "morality" visually, as if on the stage, viewing the play's actions within the larger context of the play and of the moral structure of the universe. By the later eighteenth century, this structural view of morality had broken down so completely that most critics no longer considered it a subject worthy of critical attention. Later critics use the term to represent a new concept which can be isolated in the basic elements of drama, in single scenes, speeches, or even gestures. As "morality" becomes an aspect of the text, the plot becomes irrelevant, and instruction, that composite effect long separated from the specifics of poetic language, in the end becomes an outgrowth of specific passages, its genius located in a grouping of words and dependent on textual interpretation.

With this change in theory, basing criticism on plot in any guise is perceived as narrow and confining. As seen by the reaction to Johnson's "Preface," critics revile any remnant of the so-called "rules of drama" regulating the conduct of the fable, and by association, criticism that emphasizes the beauties and consistencies of a play's fable and its ramifications (such as poetic justice) acquires a similar taint. Reacting against the critical establishment of their ancestors, critics plunge to the opposite extreme and find signs of genius in the very inconsistencies of Shakespeare's plots, as in George Steevens's comments on *Hamlet*: "In short, let it be said, more to the Honour of the Abilities of this astonishing Man, that notwithstanding all the Errors, Absurdities, and Extravagancies of the Play he alone could make it interesting without Progress in the Fable, and engage the Attention of an Audience by the Magic of his Imagery and Sentiments, by the wild irregular Sallies of an Inspired Imagination, unassisted by Probability, or even Connection of Events."[23] For Steevens, the very fact that Shakespeare's plays succeed even though the plots are incoherent proves the poet's powerful talents. He does not see this incoherence as a flaw, but as a measure of genius. Though he does not praise improbability as a virtue in and of itself, Steevens accepts it as part of literature and even finds it a useful way to indicate genius. In the work of a good poet, an improbable plot simply reinforces our recognition of his genius; in the work of an inferior poet, it remains a flaw. A stronger statement comes from the obscure figure of John Stedman, who holds that these "peculiarities" are an absolute sign of genius: "It is not Shakespeare's fables that please, but his peculiar manner of treating them; yea the improbabilities of these fables are a certain proof of the natural powers of the author."[24]

With eccentricity in plotting considered a near virtue, tidying up plotlines could no longer be justified as a means of clarifying Shakespeare's plays. Outcries against the adaptations of his plays still on the stage continued through the end of the century.[25] Only *King Lear* was occasionally "allowed" to want the assistance of an adapter. In general, however, the critical esteem for Tate's adaptation had fallen so low that when David Erskine Baker compiled his *Biographia Dramatica* from 1764 to 1782, he could write of Tate that "he is at present better known for his version of the Psalms . . . than for any other of his works," works that included the adaptation of *King Lear*.[26] But overall, critics spend little time discussing the adaptations. In their eyes, it is an accepted fact that altering Shakespeare is wrong and that the adaptations that remain on the stage are desecrations of his genius. By the late eighteenth century, the subject has become so much of a cliché that critics usually mention it only in passing.

Critics sought a new, more organic, standard by which to praise Shakespeare's works, a standard that could accommodate the text as well as avoid the formalism long associated with neoclassicism. Character analysis was an obvious choice, growing out of the more general interest in character demonstrated by mid-century critics, and between 1775 and 1800 practically every major critic tried his hand at examining Shakespeare's characters in isolation from the plot.[27] The trend began with the publication in 1774 of William Richardson's *A Philosophical Analysis and Illustration of some of Shakespeare's remarkable Characters*. Soon critics everywhere were examining characters or responding to someone else's analysis. A variety of essays emerged out of this plethora of paper. Some critics treated the characters as living people, creating plausible past and future employments that were supposed to have influenced the actions within the confines of the plays. Others argued for the existence of a single character trait, sometimes termed a ruling passion, such as Falstaff's cowardice, Hamlet's real or assumed madness, or Macbeth's possibly flawed courage. The critical standard of "consistency" lies behind many of these approaches, a term that has its roots in "unity of character," the unofficial fourth "unity" adopted by mid-century critics.

A Philosophical Analysis was Richardson's first work, a collection of essays including studies of Macbeth, Hamlet, Jacques, and Imogen. In subsequent years, Richardson added essays on Richard III, first published in the *Mirror*, no.66 (25 December 1779); King Lear; and Timon of Athens (1783);[28] Falstaff and Shakespeare's female characters (1788); and Fluellen (1812). Each essay uses the same approach: the character is isolated and examined as a representation of human psychology. In this manner, Hamlet's indecision is explained by examining the general conduct of the human mind when beset by indignation: "In its first emotion it may breathe excessive and immediate vengeance: but sentiments of justice and propriety interposing, will arrest and suspend its violence. An ingenuous mind, thus agitated by powerful and contending principles, exceedingly tortured and perplexed, will appear hesitating and undetermined. Thus, the vehemence of the vindictive passion will, by delay, suffer abatement; by its own ardour it will be exhausted; and our natural and habitual propensities will resume their influence."[29] Richardson's comments are not directly literary; rather, he treats Shakespeare's words as a guidebook to human behavior. Other characters are examined on equally abstract terms as Richardson balances his argument between general principles of psychology (such as the mind's behavior under contradictory impulses) and references to specific passages that exemplify these more general concepts. Imogen's behavior is glossed by a discussion of "the operations of memory and the illusions of fancy,"[30] while the subject of Macbeth's ambition spurs a lengthy discussion of the effect of "violent passions" (such as ambition) upon the mind.

Richardson's theory of character is dominated by the central concept of the ruling passion. Man's nature, he asserts, is controlled by one central trait: "Among the various desires and propensities implanted by nature in the constitution of every individual, some one passion, either by original and superior vigour, or by reiterated indulgence, gains an ascendant in the soul, and subdues every opposing principle; it unites with desires and appetites that are not of an opposite tendency, it bends them to its pleasure, and in their gratification pursues its own."[31] This model governs all human behavior, so that if a dramatic character is lifelike, he or she must exhibit a ruling passion. A large part of each essay consists of identifying this ruling passion and demonstrating the ways in which it shapes each character's words and actions. Macbeth is governed by the "vicious passion" of ambition, Hamlet by a sense of virtue, Jacques by "extreme sensibility," Imogen by "love," Lear by "mere sensibility undirected by reflection," and Timon by a "love of distinction." Focusing on these dominant traits, Richardson argues that Shakespeare's characters are consistent; what seems to be inconsistency (for example, Hamlet's inability to kill Claudius at prayer) can often be explained by the workings of the ruling passion upon the mind. Hamlet is governed in this scene by his sense of justice, which "in a moment when his violent emotions were not excited, overcame his resentment"—the hesitation is natural, it "arose from the inherent principles of his constitution."[32]

Despite the acuteness of most of Richardson's comments, his heavily psychological approach occasionally leads him to treat Shakespeare's characters as though they were real people and not fictive creations—a tendency observable in many of his fellow critics. Relying as he does on a psychological model, he occasionally moves beyond tracing character traits illustrated by the text and tries instead to provide the character with a history which would give a psychological explanation for his actions. In his eagerness to account for the seeming incongruity of Jacques's avoidance of society and his extreme sensibility (which by Richardson's reasoning is "the soil where nature has planted social and sweet affections" and thus should lead to a love of society), Richardson manufactures a past for Jacques that would explain and reconcile these contradictory passions. "Perhaps," he hypothesizes, "the excess and luxuriancy of benevolent dispositions, blighted by unkindness or ingratitude, is the cause that, instead of yielding us fruits of complacency and friendship, they shed bitter drops of misanthropy."[33] Over the course of several pages of psychological speculation, hypothesis becomes fact as Richardson later states emphatically that Jacques becomes reserved and censorious on account of disappointments in friendship.[34] This tendency to analyze Shakespeare's characters as if they were human beings with a past, present, and future, while marring the accuracy of the criticism, reveals the extent to which the later eighteenth-century critic tries to accommodate a complete text of Shakespeare's plays. Whereas in an earlier generation of playwrights, such inconsistencies could be resolved by judicious omissions or by rewriting a scene, for these later critics, a theory had to be invented which would accommodate the complete "unmutilated" text. Every scene or speech had to be explained, even if it led the critic into the realm of wild speculation.

Only by side-stepping theory in their attempt to accept the text could critics avoid this trap. In *Remarks on Some of the Characters of Shakespeare* (1784), Thomas Whately avoids extratextual commentary and focuses strictly on character as depicted within a play. He sees character as the soul of all drama; without it, the fable is meaningless and "the piece is at best a tale, not an action." He bases his analysis on the assumption that a fully-developed character distinguishes all men: "By that we know them, by that we are interested in their fortunes; by that their conduct, their sentiments, their very language is formed; and whenever, therefore, the proper marks of it are missing we immediately perceive that the person before our eyes is but suppositious."[35]

Although both more flexible and less specific than Richardson's theory of a ruling passion, Whately's argument derives everything from this central quality. When the "proper marks" are absent, we sense fiction in the real world and become conscious of it in literature. Such full representations are necessary for literary illusion because for Whately, realism is dependent on character. To him, the critic's most important task is examining character—all other aspects of literature evolve out of character; if they do not, then we recognize that the work is poorly crafted. Structuring his analysis on comparison, he examines the figures of Richard III and Macbeth, characters who possess many similar features (both are soldiers and usurpers and both are violent and ambitious), but who are inherently dissimilar. They share a similar plot, he argues, but they "agree in nothing but their fortunes" (6). Supporting his argument with appropriate quotations and references to the text, Whately claims that Shakespeare's plays evolve entirely out of a conception of character. Even when provided with two nearly identical plotlines, he can create two radically different literary works because of his "peculiar excellence of drawing characters" (91). It is character which distinguishes one man's life from another's, and by representing this law of nature in his drama, Shakespeare proves that he is the greatest of all poets. For Whately, character is the source of literary difference, and this ability to differentiate is crucial to Shakespeare's greatness. The poet's function is to create individuals and thus to appeal to his individual readers.

Illustrating the extent to which respect for a genuine text could take a critic as well as the privileging of individual response, Maurice Morgann's lengthy study of Falstaff (1777) underscores the connection between text and character. Like Richardson, Morgann bases his work on a theory of the mind, specifically on the distinction between mental impressions and the understanding. For Morgann, however, this model of the mind does not shape the poet's presentation of character, but rather the way in which the character is perceived by the reader. Morgann's argument develops from his conviction that criticism has been based for too long on the logical deductions of the understanding, ignoring an important aspect of the mind:

There are none of us unconscious of certain feelings or sensations of mind which do not seem to have passed thro' the Understanding . . . The Understanding and these feelings are frequently at variance. The latter often arise from the most minute circumstances, and frequently from such as the Understanding cannot estimate or even recognize; whereas the Understanding delights in abstraction, and in general propositions; which, however true considered as such, are very seldom, I had like to have said *never*, perfectly applicable to any particular case. And hence, among other causes, it is, that we often condemn or applaud characters and actions on the credit of some logical process, while our hearts revolt, and would fain lead us to a very different conclusion.[36]

The rejection of "Understanding" implies that it is not useful, a move that isolates literature in the realm of feeling. Morgann defines man by his ability to feel, not think, and uses this dichotomy between feeling and understanding to explain our reaction to Falstaff; logically, we know that he must be a coward and a disreputable old man, but we cannot help but love him. (Compare here Johnson's general assessment of Falstaff: "The moral to be drawn from this representation is, that no man is more dangerous than he with a will to corrupt, hath the power to please; and that neither wit nor honesty ought to think themselves safe with such a companion when they see *Henry* seduced by *Falstaff*.")

Morgann identifies these contradictory sensations as the result of minute "impressions" that make up Falstaff's character. We form our knowledge of character from these impressions, not from the understanding, just as we often love or hate at first sight with no abstract logic to support our feelings. Morgann's method emphasizes the purely subjective; he urges literary critics to throw out their logical deductions and go back to examine their impressions, no matter how minute. The process is particularly important in drama, for, Morgann argues, "in Dramatic composition the *Impression* is the *Fact*" (146). A play consists of a series of impressions felt by the audience; to consider it on a purely logical basis is to go against its natural form. Even worse, the understanding tends to ignore character: "it seems for the most part to take cognizance of *actions* only, and from these to infer *motives* and *character*, but the sense we have been speaking of proceeds in a contrary course; and determines of *actions* from the *first principles* of character, which seem wholly out of the reach of the Understanding" (147). Like Whately, Morgann rejects a plot-based critical method, but he goes beyond Whately in stating that examining action only distorts our comprehension of drama, a conviction that has important ramifications for his interpretation of character.

To Morgann's eyes, past criticism has misdesignated Falstaff a coward because, focusing only on what the understanding could perceive, it could not comprehend "the impression which the *whole character* of *Falstaff* is calculated to make upon the minds of an unprejudiced audience" (146). Morgann seeks to reverse this misapprehension and prove Falstaff a valiant man by ignoring logic and plot and focusing instead on the minute impressions made by the figure of Falstaff. He finds that, contrary to traditional accounts of Falstaff, Shakespeare has portrayed the knight as a figure of courage and that the conflict between outward cowardice and constitutional courage is but one more mark of Shakespeare's genius. He "has contrived to make secret Impressions upon us of courage, and to preserve those Impressions in favour of a character which was to be held up for sport and laughter on account of actions of apparent Cowardice and dishonour" (149). This conviction of Shakespeare's "secret Impressions" shapes Morgann's method; in order to discover these impressions at work, he examines in detail every passage which relates even peripherally to the issue of Falstaff's courage, for, he observes, only by looking at these details can we begin to discover "what *Impressions*, as to courage and Cowardice, he had made upon the persons of the Drama" (151). In yet another attack on conventional criticism, he refuses even to structure his argument logically, "as texts for comment," but proceeds impressionistically, "as chance or convenience shall lead the way" (155).

By rejecting rationalism and order, Morgann rejects any notion of critical consensus. The individual critic's impression is paramount, and there is no need to try to convince others (as indicated by his scorn for texts "for comment")—in essence each individual critic is divorced from a community. Locke's theory of the association of ideas, long seen as an argument for individual subjectivity, here becomes an argument for the individuality of the critic. By ignoring logic and basing his argument on his own impressions, Morgann is easily able to disprove Falstaff's cowardice. He reinterprets scenes such as Falstaff's feigned death (*I Henry IV*, V.iv) as the action of a sensible man who was clear-sighted enough to see honor for what it was and to "renounce its tyranny" (155), and points out that no character in the play accuses Falstaff of cowardice. He finds positive examples of Falstaff's courage in his military background and reputation, aspects of Falstaff that are often forgotten as Shakespeare presents him only during his "familiar hours." Although he stresses the importance of looking at details and not letting logic lead us away from the words of the play and the impressions they create, Morgann himself ranges far from Shakespeare's text. In order to move beyond the "familiar hours" presented in the history plays, he conjures up a picture of Falstaff's hypothetical youth and military prowess. The overall effect creates a Falstaff with a virtuous past, a figure who does not always correspond to the Falstaff of Shakespeare's plays. Thus he accommodates both the complete text and the individual response. The interplay between text and reader constitutes the reality of the literary experience, reader-response rather than audience response:

With a stage character, in the article of exhibition, we have nothing more to do; for in fact what is it but an Impression; an appearance, which we applaud or condemn as such without further inquiry or investigation? But if we would account for our Impressions, or for certain sentiments or actions in a character, not derived from its apparent principles, yet appearing, we know not why, natural, we are then compelled to look farther, and examine if there be not something more in the character than is *shewn*; something inferred, which is not brought under our special notice. In short, we must look to the art of the writer, and to the principles of human nature, to discover the hidden causes of such effects. [203]

Theater limits text by reducing it to a single impression, an interpretive dead end. The text itself is the source of "hidden causes" carefully planted by the author. Thus Morgann's extrapolations are simply an attempt to account for his impression that Falstaff is not a coward. They are derived from instinct, not the understanding, and we assess their validity not by weighing them as rational deductions but by determining whether they agree with our own impression of Falstaff's character. Not only does Morgann's critical method rely upon careful scrutiny of the text to discover the source of the "minute impressions," but in privileging feeling over reason it implies that logical proof is not necessary or even desirable for literary analysis.

Morgann's emphasis on inference rather than proof reflects a widespread shift away from the values of rational deduction and toward subjective analysis. His contemporaries, from Alexander Gerard to William Richardson, extolled the virtues of the emotions as a critical tool, and the capacity to feel, rather than to reason, was fast becoming the criterion for defining mankind. The emotions had long been cited as one seat of genius, and as the eighteenth century progressed, they usurped reason as the source of man's creative powers. For many eighteenth-century theorists, judgment and taste were no longer the domain of reason. Instead, philosophers such as Alexander Gerard argued that such properties were inborn, natural instincts rather than learned responses. By identifying judgment as a natural instinct, Gerard and his fellow critics implicitly (and sometimes explicitly) denigrate the use of any sort of a critical system. Because man can feel what is good, formal standards (such as the rules of drama) are irrelevant. It is not going too far to see this emphasis on innate talent as a statement of the rights of the individual set apart from social consensus, rights which were already being focused upon in political and economic areas, as well as in the world of publishing by the establishment of laws of copyright protecting the individual author.[37]

SHAKESPEARE AND SUBJECTIVITY

Along with judgment, the concept of taste undergoes a radical redefinition, again predicated on individual response rather than shared experience. As defined by Addison in 1712, taste is not only general, but can be acquired: "As this Word [Taste] arises very often in Conversation, I shall endeavour to give some Account of it, and to lay down Rules how we may know whether we are possessed of it, and how we may acquire that Fine Taste of Writing, which is much talked of among the Polite World."[38] Admitting later that this faculty "must in some degree be born with us," Addison discusses taste as an absolute standard and quantifies it by setting up a series of rules by which an "accomplished man" can obtain taste. In contrast, Gerard finds that taste (judgment of beauty) is an inborn trait that varies from person to person. There can be no general consensus of taste, because no two people have the same inborn qualities: "The tastes of different men differ extremely: we find in individuals, all the intermediate degrees between an almost total want of any of these qualities, and the almost perfection in it—A person may likewise possess one of these perfections while he is defective in the rest: or, without being remarkably defective in any of them, he may be eminent in one. Hence will spring dissimilar kinds of taste."[39] When critics describe taste as individually determined, it ceases to be a quality that can be acquired through education. Its connections with reason have been severed, and it becomes not only an emotional but a strictly personal quality. Echoing Gerard, Richardson proposes a theory of "consummate taste," an inborn trait, which allows man to feel what is excellent, both as a critic and as a moralist.

Likewise, a good poet feels what is good and writes with the prompting of this inborn trait. As Guthrie and Kames had asserted two decades before, the poet must become a Protean figure who, like the dervish of the Arabian tales, can throw his soul into the body of another person. It is this quality that makes Shakespeare's drama the work of genius; because he empathizes so closely with his creations, his works move us profoundly. The poet's experience translates itself into the experience of the audience through the medium of poetry. Emphasis on audience response is itself an old idea. Dryden and his fellow Restoration critics present the ability to move as a great and necessary talent in a poet, tracing it back to Aristotle and his description of the emotional effects of tragedy (pity and fear). In literary terms, the arousal of emotion was traditionally linked to a moral function. The poet moves his audience and thus spurs moral edification; he pleases in order to instruct. As the reading public for both Shakespeare and his critics grew and become more diverse, this broad focus shifted as the audience narrowed to the reader him- or herself. During the last decades of the century, critics reconsidered the idea of emotional response in terms of the sublime and its attendant sensations of fear and wonder, but in each case the effect is aroused within the reader. The moral imperative began to drop away as many critics promoted the emotional effect as an end in itself rather than the means to another (more virtuous) end.

As a result critics began to emphasize the irrationality of great poetry, recasting reason as a damper of poetic genius. When discussing *Othello*, Wolstenholme Parr writes that "the ardour and surprise of poetry have nothing in common with the rational and tranquil proceedings of prudence; where, without the aid of imagination, all that is to happen may be foretold by the simple force of sagacity founded on experience."[40] Setting imagination against reason (or at least sagacity), Parr indicates that man's reason has little to do with reading or writing poetry. Poetry is sublime in its effect on man; it surprises and it moves, while reason can incite nothing more than the static reserves of experience. Some critics take the concept even further, and move poetry completely out of the realm of the rational and into the supernatural, a development evident in the appearance of a new cliché describing Shakespeare's works as magical. George Steevens writes of *Hamlet* that only Shakespeare "could make it interesting without Progress in the Fable, and engage the Attention of an Audience by the Magic of his Imagery and Sentiments."[41] The audience should dislike the play because it does not go anywhere, but instead they are swept away from rational analysis by an irrational force—magic—in the form of imagery and feeling. Edward Burnaby Greene presents the same idea in more fulsome terms: "SHAKESPEARE's pen is the magician's wand commanding the soul of his reader."[42] Here the reader loses all power to control the supernatural force of Shakespeare's poetry, and Greene cites the totally irrational effect of Shakespeare's works as the highest possible praise. If the reader were able to reason his way to an appreciation of Shakespeare's genius, it would be a lesser literary experience than the sublime ecstasy of being overpowered by its magic. This parallels pictorial representations of Shakespeare as magician, in particular the popular equation of Shakespeare with Prospero.

Steevens's and Greene's comments are remarkable not only for evoking the supernatural qualities of Shakespeare's poetry, but also for their praise of the literary power of figurative language. Steevens's remark asserts that Shakespeare's imagery "engages the Attention of the Audience" rather than distracts it, as earlier writers such as Locke had avowed. Greene compares Shakespeare to the ancients, contending that both Shakespeare and the ancients used rhetorical devices, except that Shakespeare employed these figures far more effectively than did classical writers. Greene's theory exactly reverses the once popular belief that Shakespeare's figures were a result of living in a barbaric and vulgar age, an indication of the power Shakespeare's name now carried. A new crop of editors fostered this more liberal attitude toward figurative language by emphasizing the importance of the genuine text and by explicating Shakespeare's words without making value judgments on the language or style. The notes to Capell's edition (1780) include a lengthy section on Shakespeare's versification that never alludes to barbaric times or unrefined language. In his landmark 1790 edition, Edmond Malone openly attacks earlier critics and editors who "considered their own era and their own phraseology as the standard of perfection"; evaluation of Shakespeare's style, formerly an essential aspect of an editor's commentary, becomes obsolete.[43]

Although a few voices opposed the acceptance and canonization of the complete text of Shakespeare's works, usually stressing the illogical nature of his figurative language, these appeals to rationality are rare.[44] Most discussions of Shakespeare emphasize the important connection between literature and subjectivity, the individual and the text. In *An Essay on Genius* (1774), an exhaustive consideration of the workings of the creative mind, Alexander Gerard uses a psychological model similar to that of Morgann when examining Shakespeare's figurative language. The work is governed by the concept of the association of ideas, both in its description of genius and in its analysis of the representations of genius in literature. Gerard's essay could easily be retitled "An Essay on Shakespeare's Genius," for Shakespeare is one of the few figures Gerard finds who has both a wealth of ideas to associate and what he terms a "regulating" principle that focuses and orders these ideas according to some sense of a larger design. (Gerard even pairs Shakespeare with Euclid, attributing to the poet a sense of ordered composition ignored by other critics). The dual nature of Shakespeare's talent becomes an important feature of Gerard's discussion of poetic genius (Part II, Section iii "Of the Influence of the Passions on Association") when he examines the passions' effect on the way in which man thinks. This analysis becomes more literary criticism than psychological documentation, for Gerard takes most of his examples of human thought from Shakespeare's works: "To be able to select examples from real life and to set them in a striking light would require no small degree of one of the highest and rarest forms of poetic genius. It will therefore be the safest and best way to take our examples from such representations of the passions in poetry as are confessedly natural, and will approve themselves natural to the taste of the reader. Such examples have as great authority as instances which a person himself observes in ordinary life. Shakespeare alone will supply us with as many as are necessary" (150). Not an imitation of nature but nature itself, Shakespeare's text thus replaces life.

In a move that links figurative language to the issues of character analysis initiated by Richardson and Morgann, Gerard examines the speech of Shakespeare's characters. Determining whether the words they speak are natural or unnatural, he invariably concludes by commenting on the use of figurative language. Like his contemporaries, he differentiates between appropriate and inappropriate language, but he employs a very different standard of judgment. In place of the focus on the response of the audience seen in the works of earlier critics such as William Duff, Gerard uses the psychology of the character as the basis for judging the appropriateness of figurative language. Like Morgann he concludes that logic is a useless tool in such considerations, for passion robs man of his logic:

> It is a natural inference from the observations which have been already made that the passions, far from disposing us to follow order in the train of our ideas, render us incapable of preserving order . . . Abruptness, incoherence, fluctuation of thought are the consequences of passion; and these are the reverse of order. But it is worth while to observe that a passion even inverts the natural order of our ideas. As the imagination passes from one idea to another, so a passion once excited does not confine itself to its first object, but readily extends itself to other objects connected with that. [182–83]

Gerard argues that figurative language is a natural response for someone under the influence of passion, as "a passion once excited does not confine itself to its first object." This shift from the object of passion to other objects connected with it is the very essence of metaphor. Gerard finds figurative language improper only if it contradicts his model of the human mind's behavior under the influence of emotion. But he is cautious in his defense of metaphor, and warns that such "resemblances" are to be used with great care: "metaphors ought to be admitted with great reserve" (178). Overly elaborate figures of any sort are psychologically unrealistic; they show "an imagination disposed to seek amusement, not a mind intensely engaged by its subject."[45] Gerard uses these guidelines to evaluate Shakespeare's figures, and in most cases, he finds that characters speak naturally. Like Greene and Steevens, Gerard's comments demonstrate a new attitude toward Shakespeare's language. The fact that figurative language is no longer feared for its political impact suggests not only a calmer political climate but also, ironically, that the price of Shakespeare's canonization has been the taming of his works.

The Author in the Text

Published at the very end of the century (1794), Walter Whiter's *A Specimen of a Commentary on Shakespeare* goes further than any other eighteenth-century critical work, breaking completely with the emphasis on audience response prevalent in much Restoration and eighteenth-century criticism. In his essay, Whiter uses Locke's association principle as a tool to illuminate the workings of the poet's mind, emphasizing the subjective logic of the poet, as displayed in the individual words of the text, and thus of necessity privileging the text over any formalist questions of consistency or plot. With this emphasis on specific words, the literary work becomes fragmented into its smallest component parts and even the "plot" of grammar is ignored. This approach, he claims, had been previously unexplored:

We have seen the question totally exhausted as it refers to the general powers of the understanding, and the habitual exercize of the reasoning faculty; but we may justly be astonished that the effects of this principle should never have been investigated, as it operates on the *writer* in the ardor of invention, by imposing on his mind some remote and peculiar vein of language, or of imagery. If, in the ordinary exertions of the understanding, the force of such an association has been found so powerful and extensive, it may surely be concluded, that its influence would predominate with absolute authority over the vigorous workings of a wild and fertile imagination.[46]

Whereas Gerard's purpose was to explain the general workings of the human mind by showing how Shakespeare's characters, chosen as lifelike representations of human nature, exemplified the associating principles, Whiter focuses exclusively on Shakespeare and his own peculiar quirks of association, seeking to discover the author in the work. He differs from critics such as Gerard in refusing to apply general theories to Shakespeare's words. Such general applications are impossible in Whiter's eyes, for the poet's mind (like the minds of all other men) operates under the influence of its own peculiar associations, and thus cannot be expected to conform to any general pattern. Whiter stresses that his purpose is to give "a plain and concise definition of the *general principle* in its *peculiar application* to the object of my enquiry" (62). Explaining the meaning of the poet's words is not his goal; he hopes to explain the subliminal connections between seemingly unconnected words or images so that the text becomes purely an interplay of free signs.

The body of Whiter's work consists of a series of examples of these associating principles (what the twentieth century would call image clusters) at work. Whiter's targets are passages that combine seemingly incompatible ideas or metaphors. One such example is Shakespeare's use of imagery connecting "suits" and "weeds": "it is certain that those ideas are apparently very remote from each other, which relate to *dress*—to a *noisome plant*—and to that which is expressive of *asking* or *accommodating*; and yet the curious reader will be astonished to discover that the Poet is often led to connect some of these dissimilar objects" (72).[47] Whiter begins his discussion with a passage from *As You Like It* (II.vii.42–47),[48] which contains the words "coat," "suit," and "weed"; the words are connected by the common idea of clothing, even though in this case Shakespeare attaches a different meaning to "suit" and "weed." Whiter continues with a number of additional examples in which the same words follow each other in a variety of contexts, and he notes that the phenomenon is not affected by the sense in which any of the words is used. "The association arising from the same sound bearing an equivocal sense will be equally remarkable" (73). It does not matter that the word "dress" appears in the sense "address"; the train of associations evoked leads Shakespeare to another idea connected with clothing (e.g., *Henry V*, IV.i.8–12).[49] Whiter explores a variety of similar groupings (eye-facesbooks; reason/raisin and cooking, etc.), many of which he explains in topical terms, such as the construction of the Elizabethan theater, or practices in Elizabethan kitchens.

In their attempt to elucidate Shakespeare's text, Whiter's comments resemble the notes by Shakespeare's eighteenth-century editors, and, compounding the effect, the first portion of the *Specimen* consists of a series of "Notes" on *As You Like It*. But despite such apparent similarities, Whiter's work is not that of an editor. His comments make no attempt to clarify the meaning of a passage to the reader; instead, they trace the movements of the poet's mind. This distinction is crucial, for whereas an editor's notes are tied to the context of a passage, Whiter's commentary is not. In a radical shift away from the work of all previous critics, he ignores the constraints of plot and character in order to focus exclusively on Shakespeare's language. The text becomes for him the mirror of Shakespeare's consciousness, and his interest lies in the workings of the poet's mind as demonstrated through chains of signification, not in determining the effects of poetry upon an audience. He is emphatically nonjudgmental, for there can be no good or bad in the unconscious progress of imagination: "The rapid imagination of the unwary Poet, even when it is employed on sentiments the most tender and pathetic, is sometimes imperceptibly entangled in a chain of imagery, which is derived from the meanest subjects and the lowest occupations" (120).

The poet cannot be faulted for these seeming breaches of decorum, for he writes under the influences of uncontrollable trains of associations. Whiter's findings call into question the entire problem of decorum, for he argues that what in Shakespeare appears to be a flaw in the poet's taste (often blamed on the vulgarity of the Elizabethan age) is actually the result of the creative power of his mind. The poet may indeed even attempt to avoid all direct references to topical issues, but even a man of genius cannot avoid his subconscious and "the secret energy of local influence will continue to operate on his mind" (65). This irresistible power of association, Whiter suggests, explains the wealth of "quibbles" in Shakespeare's works. The use of a single word or image would suggest others seemingly unrelated except by a form of punning; following Whiter's explanations, these puns are not the result of a taste for low humor, but rather the inevitable result of a mind rich in ideas. They cannot be faulted, for they are, at least in part, unintentional. The novelty of Whiter's "metaphysical" examination lies not in setting up standards for a new definition of good poetry, but in its attempt to provide a new stratagem for reading literature. But when *A Specimen of a Commentary on Shakespeare* appeared in 1794, it was largely ignored by the literary community, and what response there was was overwhelmingly negative. Ironically, the charge leveled against the work by most reviewers was not that it was newfangled, but that Whiter's methods were old-fashioned because of their dependence on Locke, and the work went unnoticed until the mid-twentieth century.[50]

Although it was dismissed by his contemporaries, Whiter's *Specimen* shared the literary presuppositions of an age that defined literature as text and, in the case of Shakespeare, revered even minute portions of this text. The goal of the editor thus becomes to fix the unstable text and the task of the critic to perform an exegesis of the precious words. For if the clues to the working of a poetic genius lie within the words the poet writes, then changing any of these words, even those we do not like or understand, represents an act of wanton destruction. Without Shakespeare's words we cannot understand his mind, and we can only understand the larger body of his works if we first try to understand both the minute details of his poetry and the mind that lies behind it. This intellectual endeavour is useless if the words studied are diminished or altered in any way.

Whiter's homage to the text was overshadowed by a more flamboyant expression of England's obsession with the words of its national poet. In 1794, William Henry Ireland began producing a stream of forged "Shakespearean" documents: receipts, letters to and from the poet (including a love letter from William to Anne Hathaway), marginalia, and, eventually, the manuscript of a previously lost Shakespearean play, *Vortigern and Rowena*. The succession of documents, supposedly discovered in an old oak chest belonging to a mysterious gentleman, was avidly followed by the popular press, and, until publicly disproved by Edmond Malone, brought a horde of worshipers to the Ireland household. (One such worshiper was James Boswell, who fell on his knees in front of the blessed relics and declared that he could now die happy.)[51] Though Ireland produced some "manuscript" versions of previously existing works (*King Lear* and a few pages of *Hamblette*), most of the forgeries were new works, fresh examples of England's native genius. Ireland's creations were not imitations of Shakespeare but of his text, an example that goes beyond Foucault's "author-function" in its glorification of text before author. If Whiter's *Commentary* exalts the particulars of Shakespeare's text, Ireland's forgeries represent an attempt to satisfy the public desire for more of that text. As such, they call attention to Shakespeare's status as both sacred and profane, an object of worship and a moneymaker for forgers and critics alike. To Shakespeare's critics and readers, his works had become both secular Bible and England's literary constitution—an appropriation of Shakespeare that establishes the works as public institution and private inspiration, a source of universal knowledge as well as individual sentiment.

Conclusion

The disappearance of the adaptations returns me to the two central questions with which I began this investigation: why the adaptations were written, and why, less than one hundred years later, they vanished. As the body of this study indicates, there are no simple answers to these questions, for the adaptations themselves are but symptoms of much larger issues. Their existence does not imply a different perception of the quality of Shakespeare's genius, for the Restoration, like the twentieth century, perceived his works as the pinnacle of English poetry, but rather a different perception of where this genius is located. The issue thus becomes a question of whether the essence of Shakespeare's talent lies in *mimesis* or in *logos*, in representing nature or in language. Behind this distinction lies the explanation for adaptation, for where the word is perceived as the embodiment of genius, adaptation, or destruction of these drops of genius, is unthinkable. The greater the emphasis upon the word, the greater the outcry against change. As the eighteenth century progresses, this outspoken adherence to the text acquires a quasi-religious tone, for when the literary text of Shakespeare is perceived as sacred, it is subjected to the same sorts of exegeses formerly reserved for the Bible and certain classical works. Because the assumptions that govern the treatment of Shakespeare's works epitomize a generation's attitude to literature in general, the perception of Shakespeare as archetype establishes the important position of the adaptations in eighteenth-century studies.

The editions and criticism that culminated in Whiter's *Commentary* set the stage for the nineteenth-century deification of all things Shakespearean. As a literary figure, Shakespeare had been canonized in the Restoration, but not until the later eighteenth century was his text itself canonized. By the time of the Romantics, the concept of an inviolable text was taken for granted. Keats spent hours meditating on a single passage, whereas Lamb isolated the text, denying the possibility of performance by arguing that performance destroys the integrity of the text and that reading alone preserves Shakespeare's subtlety.[1] Hazlitt expatiated on the value of the specific word, claiming that in Shakespeare "a word, an epitaph paints a whole scene" and that Shakespeare "makes every word appear to proceed from the mouth of the person in whose name it is given"; nothing can be sacrificed.[2] A few decades later Arnold used Shakespeare as a favorite example of his theory of literary touchstones, in which genius is seen as distinguishable in particular phrases and which, because of its emphasis on the particular word, depends upon a set text.[3] These assumptions concerning the unchanging nature of the literary text become the basis for repudiating the previous age and its treatment of Shakespeare, an impulse still with us almost two hundred years later. The nineteenth century saw attempts to make Shakespeare's works gender specific in the form of Bowdler's *Family Shakespeare*,[4] and translated them into dance and song on the stage, but, whereas these Shakespearean ballets, skits, and operas were to flourish, rewriting his works would not.[5]

In contrast, Restoration adaptations reveal two general patterns of change: the removal or rewriting of much (if not all) of Shakespeare's language, and the removal of any moral ambiguity, a change that involved simplifying Shakespeare's characters into flat figures of good or evil and making the work conform more closely to the ideal of poetic justice. The playwright-critics of the Restoration and early eighteenth century, though they revere Shakespeare's genius, fault him for those very qualities that their adaptations attempt to remove, his barbaric language with its unrefined diction and vulgar fondness for puns, and the absence of poetic justice in the catastrophe of some plays. Decoding the attitude toward Shakespeare's language is the key to understanding the presence of adaptation in an age which revered its "English Homer." The perception of Shakespeare's words as the least part of his genius, a result of the barbaric age in which he wrote rather than an example of poetic genius, gave playwrights free license to meddle with his use of language. The actual text of Shakespeare's plays was not considered sacred because it did not represent an embodiment of his genius. This genius lay instead in his ability to represent general nature, to portray universal characters, and to move an audience; these virtues, it was felt, would not be altered if the poetry were rewritten in a more modern idiom, or if the offensive puns and quibbles were quietly edited out. The assumptions concerning Shakespeare's language also governed the structural revision of his plays. As with the rewriting of Shakespeare's dialogue, the reshaping of his plot to incorporate poetic justice was seen as a change which did not alter the genius of his works. Critics argued that by adding a "just" conclusion, in which good vanquishes evil and order is restored, an adaptation completed Shakespeare's representations of nature, for under the government of a benign deity all persons will inevitably receive their just deserts.

Determining why these adaptations eventually disappeared requires a more involved answer, for playwrights did not suddenly stop writing adaptations. By 1750, the Restoration adaptation, with its rewritten and restructured script, was replaced by a different form of adaptation. Shakespeare's text was no longer being substantively rewritten; instead, playwrights made their changes by simply cutting out portions of the original plays and retaining the Shakespearean language of the parts which remained, or by changing older adaptations, restoring large sections of original Shakespearean dialogue to the stage. As the adaptations indicate, interest in Shakespeare's language was growing, and even Garrick, the most prolific of the mid-century adaptors, could declare in his version of *The Winter's Tale* that he hoped "to lose no drop of this immortal Man." While alterations that involved little meddling with language were tolerated, changing Shakespeare's word was not. Even these deviations from the original play were handled apologetically, as playwrights felt a new sense of guilt over tampering with Shakespeare's text. Like their predecessors, these adapters revered Shakespeare, but the source of their reverence had shifted from his general greatness of thought to more specific greatness of language. In their concern not to lose a "drop" of Shakespeare, the playwrights of this period display a far greater tolerance for those aspects of Shakespearean language censored by earlier adapters, in particular Shakespeare's archaic diction, puns, and complex figurative passages. The legacy of Shakespeare's touch now endowed these formerly objectionable elements with an irreplaceable luster. Individual words took on a new importance as playwrights attempted to use as much of the original text as public taste would allow. In contrast to earlier periods, playwrights treated Shakespeare's language as a "given," a set of words that could be chopped or pieced out, but not subverted.

The critics approached this idea on more radical grounds. Prompted in part by scholarly editions of Shakespeare's works, mid-century critics began to turn against their predecessors and praise the elements of Shakespeare's language attacked so frequently only decades before. In doing so, they stress the importance of fixing a "genuine text" of Shakespeare's works. A schism develops between the critic and the playwright, as critics, unconcerned with the practical issue of box office sales, begin to call for an end to all adaptation. When critics praise rather than condemn Shakespeare's language, the justification for changing the hitherto scorned words vanishes. As Johnson observes, Shakespeare has "long outlived his century"; he has become an "ancient" whose works can be discussed by scholars, a text to be analyzed, not merely staged.

Finally, the gap between playwright and critic closes as, in the late eighteenth century, playwrights stop writing adaptations, and the taboo, which we feel today, against tampering with Shakespeare's works is irrevocably established. For these critics and for all others who follow them, Shakespeare's language has an intrinsic value that prohibits any alteration of the established text. The approaches to Shakespeare vary widely, but all depend upon careful textual analysis, where no passage is too minor to yield important facets of character, moral sentiments, or clues to the workings of the poet's mind. For the late eighteenth-century critic, Shakespeare's genius is clearly located within the words he wrote. The resulting reverence for all parts of the text precludes adaptation; even by cutting out minor scenes, we may lose essential "drops" of genius.[6] By this point, then, the establishment of Shakespeare's work as literary artifact is complete. His plays are perceived as masterpieces, unchanging and unchangeable, a national treasure to be studied and revered.

The pivotal figure in this development is Samuel Johnson, whose "Preface to Shakespeare" marks the end of an era when literature was defined generally. Johnson writes of Shakespeare: "His real power is not shewn in the splendour of particular passages, but by the progress of his fable and the tenour of his dialogue; and he that tries to recommend him by select quotation, will succeed like the pedant in Hierocles, who, when he offered his house to sale, carried a brick in his pocket as a specimen."[7] On the surface, Johnson firmly rejects his contemporaries' growing interest in holding minute parts of Shakespeare's works up for inspection and admiration. He argues that Shakespeare's works cannot be truly appreciated if read only in terms of the individual "bricks" or particular passages. Following the tradition of earlier critics, he states that Shakespeare's genius lies in *mimesis*, in the unfolding of the plot and the sense of the dialogue, not in the actual language. As some of Johnson's critics observe, however, Johnson's choice of metaphor tends to undercut this argument, for bricks, like particular passages, are crafted artifacts that can indeed represent genius. Extending Johnson's metaphor, William Guthrie pursues this inconsistency: "The bricks with which Shakespeare built did not owe their mould but their substance (as workmen call it) to him. The moulds of his tragedy are, if we mistake not, borrowed from historians and novelists; but he filled them with a clay which the Promethean fire alone could render fit for use, and a divine intelligence employ in building."[8] As Guthrie points out, bricks can be representative of quality, just as Shakespearean passages do indicate the brilliance of the poet's genius. Although Johnson argues that examining Shakespeare in this way is useless, he nonetheless creates a striking image of the literary work as crafted object (house) composed of equally crafted units (bricks) that can be taken down and examined individually in order to give some sense of the whole.

This ever-increasing perception of Shakespeare's genius in terms of language is graphically illustrated by a critical commonplace found from Restoration times until the later eighteenth century, the comparison of Shakespeare's works to gems and precious stones. In 1681, Nahum Tate described *King Lear* as a "heap of jewels, unstrung and unpolist; yet so dazling in their Disorder, that I soon perceiv'd I had seiz'd a Treasure"[9]—a description that exposes his lack of reverence for Shakespeare's text. The plot is not "strung" properly and the language needs polish; confident of his right to manipulate Shakespeare's text, Tate felt no qualms over remedying these blemishes. Nearly eighty years later, Johnson uses the same image in his "Preface": "Shakespeare opens a mine which contains gold and diamonds in inexhaustible plenty, though clouded by incrustations, debased by impurities, and mingled with a mass of meaner minerals."[10] The perception of Shakespeare's beauties has expanded from a finite heap of jewels to an inexhaustible mine, but these jewels are still seen as clouded, grand ideas cloaked in words that detract rather than gleam. But less than fifteen years later, Richard Cumberland redefines this critical commonplace in the "Advertisement" to his adaptation of *Timon of Athens* (1771). Speaking directly of the distinction between his own additions and the play's Shakespearean passages, he comments that "in examining the Brilliancy of a Diamond, few people throw away any Remarks on the Dullness of the foil."[11] To Cumberland, Shakespeare outshines anything his followers can write, and he put his reverence into practice by refusing to rewrite the Shakespearean scenes he uses. No longer perceived as unpolished or debased, Shakespeare's language appears as a polished and refined gem, dazzling and exquisite as originally crafted.

In these comments, as in the adaptations, we see a reversal of literary values. The age in which Dryden could say that "words are not like landmarks, so sacred as never to be removed,"[12] has vanished, giving way to a new conception of literature and its constituent parts. The evolving attitude toward adaptation emphasizes this shift. As Shakespeare's words are no longer considered easily replaceable, he becomes an established author with a specific, unchangeable canon. Critics and playwrights define his genius in terms of his words, focusing on characters in relation to his diction, language, and imagery. Such a change indicates a stress on text rather than performance, on defining the literary work in terms of its language rather than its plot. Although today such ideas are commonplace, the issue of adaptation remains alive in our own theatrical and literary productions. Like the Restoration and eighteenth century, we alter Shakespeare with every new performance.

Appendix

CHRONOLOGICAL LIST OF ADAPTATIONS

1662 *The Law Against Lovers*, Sir William D'Avenant (*Measure for Measure, Much Ado About Nothing*)
1664 *Macbeth*, Sir William D'Avenant
1667 *The Tempest, Or the Enchanted Island*, Sir William D'Avenant and John Dryden; with additions by Thomas Shadwell (1674)
1678 *Timon of Athens, the Man-Hater*, Thomas Shadwell
      Titus Andronicus, Or The Rape of Lavinia, Edgar Ravenscroft (1678)
      Troilus and Cressida, Or Truth Found Too Late, John Dryden (1678)
1679 *The History and Fall of Caius Marius*, Thomas Otway (*Romeo and Juliet*)
1680 *The History of King Richard the Second*, Nahum Tate (also known as *The Sicilian Usurper*)
      The Misery of Civil-War, John Crowne (*Henry VI, part II*)
1681 *Henry the Sixth, The First Part*, John Crowne
      The History of King Lear, Nahum Tate
      The Ingratitude of a Common-Wealth: Or The Fall of Caius Martius Coriolanus, Nahum Tate
1682 *The Injured Princess; Or, the Fatal Wager*, Thomas D'Urfey (*Cymbeline*)
1700 *Measure for Measure, Or, Beauty the Best Advocate*, Charles Gildon
      The Tragical History of King Richard III, Colley Cibber
1701 *The Jew of Venice*, George Granville
1702 *The Comical Gallant, Or the Amours of Sir John Falstaff*, John Dennis (*The Merry Wives of Windsor*)
1703 *Love Betray'd; Or, The Agreable Disapointment*, William Burnaby (*Twelfth Night*)
1716 *Pyramus and Thisbe*, Richard Leveridge (*A Midsummer Night's Dream*)
1719 *The Invader of his Country*, John Dennis (*Coriolanus*)
      The Tragedy of King Richard the II, Lewis Theobald
1723 *Humfrey, Duke of Gloucester*, Ambrose Philips (*Henry VI, part I*)
      King Henry the Fifth, Aaron Hill
      Love in a Forest, Charles Johnson (*As You Like It*)
1737 *The Universal Passion*, James Miller (*Much Ado About Nothing*)
1738 *Marina*, George Lillo (*Pericles*)
1744 *Romeo and Juliet*, Theophilus Cibber
1745 *Papal Tyranny in the Reign of King John*, Colley Cibber
      Pyramus and Thisbe, James Lampe (*A Midsummer Night's Dream*)
1748 *Romeo and Juliet*, David Garrick
1754 *Florizel and Perdita*, MacNamara Morgan (*The Winter's Tale*)

1755   *The Fairies*, David Garrick (*A Midsummer Night's Dream*)
1756   *Catherine and Petruchio*, David Garrick (*The Taming of the Shrew*)
        Florizel and Perdita, David Garrick (*The Winter's Tale*)
        King Lear, David Garrick
1759   *Cymbeline*, William Hawkins
1763   *A Fairy Tale*, George Colman (*A Midsummer Night's Dream*)
1768   *The History of King Lear*, George Colman
1771   *Timon of Athens*, Richard Cumberland
1777   *The Sheep-Shearing: A Dramatic Pastoral*, George Colman (*The Winter's Tale*)

Notes

NOTE: All references to Shakespeare's works are from *The Riverside Shakespeare*, ed. G. Blakemore Evans (Boston: Houghton Mifflin, 1974).

INTRODUCTION

1. Not all of Shakespeare was adapted, but adapted plays coexisted with the unadapted, many of them unaltered aside from minor omissions and an occasional new line. *Hamlet, Othello, Henry IV, parts I and II, Henry VIII*, and *Julius Caesar*, all popular plays during the Restoration and eighteenth century, appeared unadapted. All of these plays were cut, and some of them even advertised as "alter'd," but these alterations were mainly cuts, and little or no new material was added.

2. Adaptation, that is, as defined later in the Introduction. Of course, generally speaking, Shakespeare's plays have been adapted many times since the later eighteenth century in the form of operas, ballets, films, and so forth. The nineteenth century in particular specialized in Shakespearean ballets and operas; Verdi's *Macbeth, Otello*, and *Falstaff* are only three examples of this trend.

3. Performances of the original plays had been staged long before these dates. Charlotte Cushman revived *Romeo and Juliet* in 1845 while *The Taming of the Shrew* returned to the stage in 1844. *Catherine and Petruchio*, however, remained in performance in the United States until 1887.

4. Colley Cibber, *Richard III* (1701), IV.iv.198. The extent to which these lines (and others from Cibber's play) were seen as part of Shakespeare is vividly apparent in Dickens's description of "Private Theatricals" in *Sketches by Boz*: "Then the love scene with Lady Ann, and the bustle of the fourth act can't be dear at ten shillings more—that's only one pound ten, including the 'off with his head!'—which is sure to bring down the applause, and it is very easy to do—'Orf with his 'ed' (very quick and loud;—then slow and sneeringly)—'So much for Bu-u-u-uckingham!' Lay the emphasis on the 'uck;' get yourself gradually into a corner and work with your right hand, while you're saying it, as if you were feeling your way, and it's sure to do" (*Sketches by Boz* [London: J.M. Dent and Sons, Ltd., 1968]), 104).

5. Most notably Roland Barthes, "The Death of the Author" in *Image, Music, Text*, trans. Stephen Heath (New York: Hill and Wang, 1977). See also Michel Foucault, "What is an Author" in Josue V. Harari, ed., *Textual Strategies: Perspectives in Post-Structural Criticism* (Ithaca: Cornell Univ. Press, 1979), and *The Archeology of Knowledge*, trans. A.M. Sheridan Smith (New York: Pantheon, 1972).

6. John Dryden, "Preface to the Fables," in W.P. Ker, ed., *Essays of John Dryden* (New York: Russell and Russell, 1961), II, 267.

7. My personal favorite is a modern dress *Richard III* staged in 1978 at the Young Vic that featured Richard and his counselors in camouflage outfits, equipped with submachine guns, and which reached a low point when Hastings's head was brought on stage in a dripping porkpie bag.

8. Robert Witbeck Babcock, *The Genesis of Shakespeare Idolatry, 1766–1799*

(Chapel Hill: Univ. of North Carolina Press, 1931). Babcock argues that "the most prominent objection to Shakespeare in the seventeenth- and eighteenth-century criticism was that he violated the unities of time, place, and action" (46) and that critical praise of Shakespeare in opposition to the unities began only after Johnson.

9. See Gunnar Sorelius, *The Giant Race Before the Flood: Pre-Restoration Drama on the Stage and in the Criticism of the Restoration* (Uppsala: Uppsala Studies in English, 1966). By 1700 the number of Renaissance plays other than Shakespeare adapted or performed had decreased. During the eighteenth century, however, adaptations of Restoration drama appeared, such as *The Country Girl* (1766), Garrick's sanitized version of Wycherley's *The Country Wife*.

10. Hans Robert Jauss, *Towards an Aesthetics of Reception* (Minneapolis: Univ. of Minnesota Press, 1982), 21, 22. See also Terence Hawkes, *That Shakespeherian Rag: Essays in a Critical Process* (London: Methuen, 1986).

11. For a history of this tradition, see Arthur Sherbo's aptly titled *The Birth of Shakespeare Studies: Commentators from Rowe (1709) to Boswell-Malone (1821)* (East Lansing, Mich.: Colleagues Press, 1986).

12. In the "Advertisement" to his revision of Tate's *King Lear* (1768), iv, George Colman claims that by the later eighteenth century many of Shakespeare's plays "have long been refined from the dross that hindered them."

13. Frederick Kilbourne, *Alterations and Adaptations of Shakespeare* (Boston, 1906). Kilbourne's work was followed in 1925 by Hazelton Spencer's *Shakespeare Improved* (Cambridge: Harvard Univ. Press) and thirty years later by George C. Branam's *Eighteenth-Century Adaptations of Shakespearean Tragedy* (Berkeley: Univ. of California Press, 1956). *Shakespeare Improved* is still the best known study of Shakespeare adaptations. Spencer is primarily interested in cataloging the specific changes made in each adaptation; with a certain amount of distaste for his subject, he describes the ways in which the plays "improve" Shakespeare. Exceptions to this pattern have been the editorial work of Christopher Spencer, *Five Restoration Adaptations of Shakespeare* (Urbana: Univ. of Illinois Press, 1965); George Winchester Stone, Jr., "Garrick's Long Lost Adaptation of *Hamlet*," *PMLA* 44, no. 3 (1934): 890–921; and "David Garrick's Significance in the History of Shakespeare Criticism: A Study of the Impact of the Actor upon the Change of Critical Focus in the Eighteenth Century," *PMLA*, 65, no. 3 (1950): 183–97. More recently, the best study of the adaptations is Michael Dobson, *The Making of the National Poet: Shakespeare, Adaptation and Authorship, 1660–1769* (Oxford: Clarendon, 1992). See also David Wheeler, "Eighteenth-Century Adaptations of Shakespeare and the Example of John Dennis," *Shakespeare Quarterly* 36, no. 4 (1985): 438–49; Matthew H. Wikander, "The Spitted Infant: Scenic Emblem and Exclusionist Politics in Restoration Adaptations of Shakespeare," *Shakespeare Quarterly* 37, no. 3 (1986): 340–58; John M. Wallace, "Otway's *Caius Marius* and the Exclusion Crisis," *Modern Philology* 85, no. 4 (1988): 363–72; Catherine A. Craft, "Granville's *Jew of Venice* and the Eighteenth-Century Stage," *Restoration and Eighteenth-Century Theatre Research* 2, no. 2 (1987): 38–54; Michael Dobson, " 'Remember First to possess his books': the appropriation of *The Tempest*, 1700–1800," *Shakespeare Survey*, 43 (1991): 99–108.

14. Examples of this attitude appear in almost all general works discussing the history of Shakespeare production. In *Whatever Happened to Shakespeare* (New York: Barnes and Noble, Harper and Row, 1979), Kenneth McClellan cites the Restora-

tion as that "barbarous age." This idea is implicit in the title of Spencer's *Shakespeare Improved*.

15. Foucault, "What is an Author?" 141–60.

16. Raymond Williams, *The Long Revolution* (Westport, Conn.: Greenwood, rpt. 1975), 76.

17. See Jurgen Habermas, *The Structural Transformation of the Public Sphere: An Inquiry into a Category of Bourgeois Society*, trans. Thomas Burger with the assistance of Frederick Lawrence (Cambridge: MIT Press, 1989). As this idea relates to criticism, see Terry Eagleton, *The Function of Criticism from The Spectator to Post-Structuralism* (London: Verso, 1984).

18. Raymond Williams, *Keywords: A Vocabulary of Culture and Society* (New York: Oxford Univ. Press, 1976), 135. See also Williams, *Culture and Society, 1780–1950* (New York: Columbia Univ. Press, 1958), and *Long Revolution*.

19. See Mark Rose, *Authors and Owners: The Inventions of Copyright* (Cambridge: Harvard Univ. Press, 1993), and "The Author as Proprietor: *Donaldson v. Becket* and the Geneology of Modern Copyright," *Representations* 23 (Summer 1988): 51–85; Martha Woodmansee, "The Genius and the Copyright: Economic and Legal Conditions of the Emergence of the 'Author,'" *Eighteenth-Century Studies* 17, no. 4 (Summer 1984): 425–48.

20. The growth of the print industry can be charted through the number of London publishing houses: 60 at the time of the Restoration; 75 by 1724; 150–200 by 1757 (Williams, *Long Revolution*, 161). Much has been published on the growth of the book trade in the eighteenth century. See for example Isabel, Rivers, ed., *Books and Their Readers in Eighteenth-Century England* (New York: St. Martins, 1982); John Feather, "The Commerce of Letters: The Study of the Eighteenth-Century Book Trade," *Eighteenth-Century Studies* 17, no. 4 (Summer 1984): 405–24; Deborah D. Rogers, "The Commercialization of Eighteenth-Century English Literature," *CLIO* 18, no. 2 (1989): 171–78. For the implications of developments in writing and publishing see Walter J. Ong, *Orality and Literacy: the Technologizing of the Word* (London: Methuen, 1982).

21. Brian Vickers's collection of seventeenth- and eighteenth-century commentary on Shakespeare reflects this development. In his six-volume collection, the first volume covers forty-nine years (1623–1692), the second forty years (1693–1733) and the last four volumes in the series cover slightly more than a decade apiece (*Shakespeare: The Critical Heritage*, 6 vols. [London: Routledge and Kegan Paul, 1974]).

22. See, for example, Nahum Tate, who in the "Epilogue" to his *King Lear* describes himself as "this play's reviver."

23. Despite the wealth of material, few general examinations of eighteenth-century Shakespeare criticism exist: Augustus Ralli, *A History of Shakespeare Criticism*, 2 vols. (London, Oxford Univ. Press, 1932), and F.E. Halliday, *Shakespeare and his Critics* (London: Gerald Duckworth, 1949). Both see criticism as "advancing" when the praise of Shakespeare becomes more effusive in the later eighteenth century. Brian Vickers's *Shakespeare: The Critical Heritage* is a welcome addition to this much neglected field. More recently in *The Birth of Shakespeare Studies*, Arthur Sherbo deals with those who wrote notes on Shakespeare's text for the various eighteenth-century editions of Shakespeare.

24. Unless they are actual adaptations, as when Bell prints Garrick's adaptations.

25. In *Shakespeare Verbatim: The Reproduction of Authenticity and the 1790 Apparatus* (Oxford: Clarendon, 1991), Margreta de Grazia deals explicitly with the effects of Malone's edition on the study of Shakespeare. For discussions of related topics, see Nicola Watson, "Kemble, Scott and the Mantle of the Bard" in Jean I. Marsden, ed., *The Appropriation of Shakespeare: Post-Renaissance Reconstructions of the Works and the Myth*, (Hemel Hempstead: Harvester Wheatsheaf, 1991), and Gary Taylor, *Reinventing Shakespeare: A Cultural History from the Restoration to the Present* (New York: Weidenfeld and Nicolson, 1989).

1. Radical Adaptation

1. During the first decades after the Restoration, plays by Beaumont and Fletcher were probably performed more often than those by Shakespeare. John Freehafer claims that D'Avenant was bound by the Lord Chamberlain's stipulations to adapt any Renaissance plays the Duke's company performed (*Theatre Notebook* 20, no. 1 [1965]: 27). This is an interesting point and would certainly absolve D'Avenant of the stigma of tampering with Shakespeare. The Lord Chamberlain's permission, however, only says that D'Avenant asked to produce certain "ancient plays" and "make them, fitt"; as the published versions of these plays prove, "making fitt" did not necessarily involve major revision, sometimes requiring only a little judicious cutting and the addition of new scenery, elaborate costumes, and special effects.

2. See for example Dryden's praise of English drama in *The Essay of Dramatic Poesy* (1668), written well before most of the adaptations.

3. D'Avenant began the trend of incorporating new stagecraft into Shakespeare's plays. Taking advantage of new machinery to create special effects, D'Avenant added a series of new witch scenes to *Macbeth* and an elaborate storm scene to *The Tempest*. D'Avenant's witches exit and enter flying, accompanied by much thunder and lightning, which was highly effective; Downes describes the play as being "in the nature of an opera." The changes included the addition of a new ghost scene and several new witch scenes, including an extravaganza in III.viii where Heccate and the witches sing and dance and that reaches its climax when the machine descends and Heccate exits, called by a "little spirit" who "sits in a foggy Cloud" (III.vii.21). Sir William D'Avenant, *Macbeth* in Spenser, *Five Restoration Adaptations of Shakespeare*. All further references to *Macbeth* will be from this edition. D'Avenant's 1663 production of *Henry VIII* advertised "new Cloath'd and new Scenes." This is most likely a reference to the new scenery that adorned the production rather than to adaptation. D'Avenant's "version" of *Henry VIII* was never published. Betterton's *Henry VIII* was published in Dublin in 1734 and, aside from cutting, is virtually unaltered.

4. One such character is Valerie in Tate's *Ingratitude of a Common-Wealth*, who in *Coriolanus* has one line. Added for comic relief, she appears as an aging coquette, "Gawdily and Fantastically Drest, follow'd by Six or Seven Pages" (9). Her dialogue is drawn directly from the stock comic figure of the elderly flirt; she babbles unrelentingly about her dress, her supposed gallants, and the life of a society lady: "Val. *Come, I must have you forth with me: I have some Nineteen Visits to make, and all of 'em old Debts upon my Honour: Well, I'll swear there's an intollerable deal of Patience requir'd to common Civility: Because an impertinent Lady comes and teazes me three Hours at my House to Day, therefor I must go to be teazed three more at her House to Morrow; I swear*

'tis most Unreasonable. How I wish my self at Athens *again! We had no such Doings at* Athens; *no idle chat of Tires and Fans, but of Secrets in Nature, and stiff Points of* Philosophy" (9). Valerie's speeches are all printed in italics—and she speaks the epilogue—Tate's indication that she is his own creation. Her prominence suggests that neoclassical theories such as the rigid separation of comedy and tragedy had relatively little impact on theatrical practice; when theory conflicted with popular demand, popular demand won easily. As the play moves to its tragic conclusion with the death of Coriolanus and, in Tate's version, Virgilia, Valerie appears incongruously out of place, chattering of her lovers as Virgilia and Volumnia learn of Coriolanus's mortal danger.

5. One reason that Renaissance literature has played such an important part in much twentieth-century criticism, particularly in the work of the New Critics where ambiguity was a key term and even a sign of genius.

6. Raymond Williams observes that "from the [late seventeenth century] the use of *class* as a general word for a group or division became more and more common" (*Keywords*, 51).

7. Aaron Hill's *King Henry the Fifth. Or, the Conquest of France by the English* (1723) had sixteen performances between 1723 and 1746.

8. In contrast to the effect of new dramatic technologies such as the so-called "machines" that has been thoroughly documented, these topics have been largely overlooked. Recent work concerning the political function of adaptation include: Wikander, "Spitted Infant"; Michael Dobson, "Accents Yet Unknown: the Canonization and Claiming of *Julius Caesar*," and Nancy Klein Maguire, "Nahum Tate's *King Lear*: 'the king's blest restoration' " in Marsden, *Appropriation of Shakespeare*; Dobson, *Making of the National Poet*. The subject of women, as well as the more general topic of rewritten morality, has been almost entirely neglected.

9. Nicholas Rowe's edition was published in 1709, many years after most of the adaptations were written.

10. On the political implications language in D'Avenant's *Macbeth*, see Richard Kroll, "Emblem and Empiricism in Davenant's *Macbeth*," *ELH* 57, no. 4 (1990): 835–64.

11. Nahum Tate, *King Lear* in Spencer, *Five Restoration Adaptations of Shakespeare*, II.ii.69–71. All further references to *King Lear* will be from this edition.

12. Francis Bacon, *New Organon*, ed. with an Introduction by Fulton H. Anderson (New York: MacMillan, 1985), 56.

13. Thomas Sprat, *The History of the Royal Society of London*, edited with critical apparatus by Jackson I. Cope and Harold Whitmore Jones (St. Louis: Washington Univ. Press, 1958), 41. See also the chapter, "Language and Ideology," in Robert Markley, *Two Edg'd Weapons: Style and Ideology in the Comedies of Etherege, Wycherley and Congreve* (Oxford: Clarendon Press, 1988).

14. This note first appears in the 1676 edition of *Hamlet*: "As it is now acted at his Highness the Duke of *York*'s Theatre," and appears in a similar form in acting versions of *Hamlet* printed throughout the early eighteenth century. Although given a slightly different title (*King Henry IV, with the Humours of Sir John Falstaff*), Betterton's *Henry IV, part 1* is an acting version, not an adaptation.

15. Colley Cibber, "Preface" to *Richard III* in Spencer, *Five Restoration Adaptations of Shakespeare*. All further references to *Richard III* will be taken from this edition.

16. In his edition of *Richard III*, Spencer provides a chart giving the number of lines from Shakespeare in each scene, as well as a detailed account of the plays other than *Richard III* from which Cibber incorporates lines (*Five Restoration Adaptations of Shakespeare*, 452).

17. George Granville, *The Jew of Venice* in Spencer, *Five Restoration Adaptations of Shakespeare*. All further references to *The Jew of Venice* will be taken from this edition.

18. Though most adaptations followed this trend, Aaron Hill's *Henry V* (1723), the one truly popular new adaptation after *The Jew of Venice*, makes extensive changes to Shakespeare's play and does not attempt to distinguish non-Shakespearean passages.

19. For a discussion of Shakespeare and quotation see Margreta de Grazia, "Shakespeare in Quotation Marks" in Marsden, *Appropriation of Shakespeare*.

20. Even Coleridge comments that there is "some little faulty admixture of pride and sullenness in Cordelia's 'nothing' " (*Lectures and Notes on Shakespeare*, 1818).

21. Lear's abrupt behavior is also given a partial justification through the concept of humors—like Cymbeline in D'Urfey's *Injured Princess*, he is a "chol'rick" king and thus subject to powerful fits of rage.

22. Tate completely omits the King of France.

23. G. Wilson Knight observes, "no tragic movement is so swift, so clearcut, so daring and so terrible," (*The Wheel of Fire* [London: Methuen, 1954], 221).

24. In the beginning of the play, we see Evandra as the virtuous mistress rejected unfairly in favor of the shallow Melissa, and this undeserved rejection blackens Timon's otherwise generous character. Not only does he display faulty judgment in selecting Melissa over Evandra, but the pain he inflicts on her justifies some of his own suffering.

25. The term first appears in Thomas Rymer's *A Short View of Tragedy; It's Original, Excellency, and Corruption. With Some Reflections on Shakespear, and other Practitioners for the Stage* (1692).

26. But not, one might add, to the still earlier play of *King Leir*.

27. For more on the political implications of Tate's *Lear*, see Maguire, "Nahum Tate's *King Lear*."

28. John Downes describes one adaptation (unfortunately never published) that gave *Romeo and Juliet* a happy ending similar to that in Tate's *Lear*: "Th[e] Tragedy of *Romeo* and *Juliet*, was made some time after into a Tragi-comedy, by Mr. *James Howard*, he preserving *Romeo* and *Juliet* alive; so that when the Tragedy was Reviv'd again, 'twas Played Alternately, Tragical one Day and Tragicomical another" (*Roscius Anglicanus*, ed. Montague Summers [London: Fortune Press, 1928], 22).

29. Actresses had long since been performing in other parts of Europe. Spain, for example, had never used boy actors to play women's parts whereas in France actresses had been on the stage throughout the seventeenth century, even appearing occasionally on the English stage, as in 1635 when Queen Henrietta Maria imported a troupe of French actors and actresses.

30. This development has been documented by many feminist historians, beginning with Alice Clark's landmark study *The Working Life of Women in the Seventeenth Century* (1919; rpt., New York: Augustus M. Kelley, 1968). See also Robert

D. Hume's discussion of the position of women and its effect on comedy in the later seventeenth century, "Marital Discord in English Comedy from Dryden to Fielding," *Modern Philology* 74 (1977): 248–72. The essay has been reprinted more recently in a collection of Hume's essays, *The Rakish Stage: Studies in English Drama, 1660–1800* (Carbondale: Southern Illinois Univ. Press, 1983), 176–213.

31. *As You Like It* appeared as Charles Johnson's *Love in a Forest* (1723) and *Twelfth Night* as William Burnaby's *Love Betray'd; Or, the Agreable Disapointment* (1703).

32. Critics and historians have approached the topic from a variety of angles. For two different views see Clark, *Working Life of Women*, and Lawrence Stone, *The Family, Sex and Marriage in England, 1500–1800* (New York: Harper and Row, 1977).

33. See Laura Brown, *English Dramatic Form, 1660–1760* (New Haven: Yale Univ. Press, 1981); "The Defenseless Woman and the Development of English Tragedy," *Studies in English Literature, 1500–1900* 22, no. 3 (Summer 1982): 429–43; and *Ends of Empire: Women and Ideology in Early Eighteenth-Century English Literature* (Ithaca: Cornell Univ. Press, 1993).

34. Richard Allestree, *The Ladies Calling* (Oxford, 1673), 29.

35. Allestree, "The Preface" to *Ladies Calling*.

36. George Savile, Marquis of Halifax, *The Lady's New-Years Gift: Or, Advice to a Daughter* (1688), 26.

37. Anon., *The Vertuous Wife is the Glory of her Husband* (1667), 9.

38. Allestree, *Ladies Calling*, 49.

39. Ibid, 81.

40. Conduct books stress that a woman's strongest weapons are her passive virtues. When wrongfully accused of adultery, for example, a woman should not defend herself with angry words but with an additional show of meekness and modesty (see Allestree, "Of Wives" in *Ladies Calling*).

41. John Dryden, *All for Love* in *The Works of John Dryden* (Berkeley: Univ. of California Press, 1984), IV.1.91–96.

42. Thomas Otway's *Caius Marius* is the one exception as Otway sacrifices some of the focus on the love plot to a new emphasis on politics. In arguing that domesticity and politics can coexist I differ from Matthew H. Wikander who downplays this juncture.

43. The list of new love interests is long. By my calculations, new or augmented love interests appear in at least nine of the approximately sixteen adaptations of Shakespeare that appeared before 1700.

44. John Dryden, *A Defence of the Epilogue, Or, An Essay on the Dramatique Poetry of the Last Age* (1672) in *Of Dramatic Poesy and Other Critical Essays*, ed. George Watson (London: J.M. Dent and Sons, Ltd., 1962), 182.

45. *The Ladies Dictionary; Being a General Entertainment for the Fair Sex* (1694), 136.

46. Nahum Tate, "Dedication" to *The History of King Lear* in Spencer, *Five Restoration Adaptations of Shakespeare*.

47. "You have more strength in your *Looks*, than we have in our *Laws*; and more power by your *Tears*, than we have by our *Arguments*" (Halifax, *Lady's New-Years Gift*, 28).

48. The Trojans thus become the heroes of the play, in keeping with Dryden's patriotic promise to tell "how *Trojan* valour did the *Greek* excell" and "Your great forefathers shall their fame regain" ("Prologue" to *Troilus and Cressida* in *Works of John Dryden*, vol. 13, l.38, 39).

49. Dryden, *Troilus and Cressida*, IV.ii.254–61.

50. Anon., "A Letter to *Colley Cibber*, Esq; On His Transformance of King *John*" (1745), 12. In contrast to his praise for Tate's *Lear* and Hill's *Henry V*, the author of the pamphlet is unrelentingly critical of Cibber's adaptation.

51. In *Henry V* Catherine's character appears only in two broadly comic scenes that turn upon bilingual play of language; in Aaron Hill's version she becomes a central figure whose love for Henry V, as the author states, "improves" her character and thus "raises" the entire play.

52. Brown, "Defenseless Woman," 443.

53. *The London Stage* cites only the following: *The Comedy of Errors* (evidence that it was acted, probably in the 1670s); *Merry Wives of Windsor* (1660, 1661, 1667, 1675, 1691); *A Midsummer Night's Dream* (1662, later the play was used as the basis for Purcell's opera *The Fairy Queen*, 1692–93); *Twelfth Night* (1661). As these figures indicate, the comedies appeared most frequently shortly after the theaters opened when the repertoire was limited and managers needed ready-made plays. Many of the other comedies were assigned to companies, but there is no evidence that they were ever acted. The tragedies and histories were performed at least two or three times as often. Although the records for the later seventeenth century in *The London Stage* are not complete, these listings suggest that Shakespearean comedy was not popular at this time.

54. Three essays in Robert D. Hume's *The Rakish Stage* deal directly with this topic: " 'Restoration Comedy' and its Audiences, 1660–1776" (with Arthur Scouten), "Marital Discord in English Comedy from Dryden to Fielding," and "The Multifarious Forms of Eighteenth-Century Comedy."

55. Jane Spencer, *The Rise of the Woman Novelist* (Oxford: Basil Blackwell Ltd., 1986), 58.

56. Laura Brown discusses the role of the exemplary female character in *English Dramatic Form*. See especially chapter 3 ("Affective Tragedy") and chapter 5 ("Dramatic Moral Action").

57. Actual rape (as opposed to symbolic rape) is rare in Shakespeare. The only rape that occurs is that of Lavinia in *Titus Andronicus*. Two other contemplated rapes are mocked: In *Pericles*, the attempt to ravish Marina by selling her to a brothel backfires ridiculously when rather than losing her virtue, she manages to convert all potential ravishers, thus destroying the brothel's formerly profitable business. In *Cymbeline*, Cloten declares his intention to kill Posthumus and rape Imogen in a burst of bravado—a boast he does not put into effect.

58. Nahum Tate, *The Ingratitude of a Commonwealth* (1681), 60.

59. Ibid., 61.

60. My discussion of the function of rape in the adaptations is indebted to Susan Staves and her discussion of attempted rape in the works of Fielding in a paper given at the Houghton Library in February 1987.

61. The two exceptions, D'Urfey's *The Injured Princess* and Dryden's *Troilus and Cressida*, could be said to refer negatively to the politics of the time by their stead-

fast avoidance of any topic that might be seen as inflammatory. Although Shakespeare's *Troilus* and *Cymbeline* are set against a backdrop of war, these conflicts almost disappear from the two adaptations. In both plays, the love plots of Imogen and Posthumous and Troilus and Cressida are made the single focus of the play, and the confrontations and battle scenes (which get equal billing in Shakespeare) recede into the distance. D'Urfey also claims in the play's Epilogue that he actually wrote it nine years earlier, well before the Exclusion Crisis.

62. Edward Ravenscroft, *Titus Andronicus, Or the Rape of Lavinia* (1687). As is evident by Ravenscroft's words here, *Titus* was produced several years before its publication.

63. See Jessica Munns, " 'The Dark Disorders of a Divided State': Otway and Shakespeare's *Romeo and Juliet*," in *Comparative Drama* 19, no. 4 (Winter) 347–62.

64. For a more detailed account of the changes made to specific plays, see Wikander.

65. As both Wikander and Christopher Spencer observe, Tate was lucky to avoid having his version of *Lear* suppressed as the play points to the ramifications of a ruler's ill-advised arrangement of the succession (Spencer, *Five Restoration Adaptations of Shakespeare*, 2). I suggest also that the spectacle of the rightful king being restored to the throne at the end of the play overshadowed the "stupidly arranged" succession at the beginning.

66. Thomas Shadwell, *Timon of Athens, or the Man-Hater* in *The Complete Works of Thomas Shadwell*, ed. Montaque Summers (Fortune Press, 1927), vol.III, p. 250.

67. Dryden's adaptation of *Troilus and Cressida*, which was to appear the following year, uses a similar situation to make a very different point. In a moral tacked on to the final scene, Ulysses declares:

> Hayl *Agamemnon*! truly Victor now!
> While secret envy, and while open pride,
> Among the factious Nobles discord threw;
> While publique good was urg'd for private ends,
> And those thought Patriots, who disturb'd it most;
> Then like the headstrong horses of the Sun,
> That light which shou'd have cheered the World, consum'd it:
> Now peacefull order has resum'd the reynes,
> Old time looks young, and Nature seems renew'd:
> Then, since from homebred Factions ruine springs,
> Let subjects learn obedience to their Kings. [V.ii.316–26]

68. Nancy Klein Maguire speculates that Tate sought to appeal to both Whig and Tory interests. Maguire, "Nahum Tate's *King Lear*."

69. In the preface to the first printed edition (1700), Cibber complains about this censorship: "This play came upon the Stage with a very Unusual disadvantage the whole first Act being Intirely left out in the Presentation; and tho' it had been read by several persons of the first Rank and Integrity, some of which were pleas'd to honour me with an offer of giving it under their hands that the whole was an Inoffensive piece, and free from any bad Paralel, or ill manner'd reflection, yet this was no satisfaction to him, who had the Relentless power of licensing it for the Stage. I did not spare for intreaties; but all the reason I could get for its being refus'd, was,

that *Henry* the Sixth being a Character Unfortunate and Pitied, wou'd put the Audience in mind of the late *King James*: Now, I confess, I never though of him in the Writing it, which possibly might proceed from there not being any likeness between 'em."

70. A final example of political adaptation appears with Colley Cibber's adaptation of *King John*. Originally written in 1736, but not staged until 1745, under the title *Papal Tyranny in the Reign of King John* it played off the anti-Catholic sentiments aroused by the Rebellion of 1745.

71. For examples of other modes of political production of Shakespeare, see Dobson, "Accents Yet Unknown: Canonization and the Claiming of *Julius Caesar*," in Marsden, *Appropriation of Shakespeare*.

72. As seen in the response to Jonson publishing his plays as "works" earlier in the seventeenth century: Henry Fitzgeoffry scoffs at "books made of ballads; works, of plays"; John Boys mentions that "the very plays of a modern poet are called in print his *Works*"; and an unknown writer asked: "To Mr Ben Jonson demanding the reason why he called his plays works": "Pray tell me, Ben, where doth the mystery lurk, / What others call a play, you call a work?" (cited by Rosalind Miles in *Ben Jonson: His Life and Work* [London: Routledge and Kegan Paul, 1986], 177).

2. The Beginnings of Shakespeare Criticism

1. In the six volumes of *Shakespeare: The Critical Heritage*, covering the years 1623–1801, Brian Vickers includes only three selections written before 1660: Jonson's eulogy from the First Folio and a few paragraphs from *Timber*, part of another poem by Leonard Digges; and two short paragraphs from the commonplace book of Abraham Wright.

2. The most egregious example of this attitude is Branam's *Eighteenth-Century Adaptations*, which traces a cause-and-effect relationship between the criticism and the adaptations. Though certain elements of this argument are plausible, Branam tends to ignore much Restoration criticism. However, there are some excellent works on specific critics, among them Robert D. Hume, *Dryden's Criticism* (Ithaca: Cornell Univ. Press, 1970); Curt A. Zimansky, "Introduction" to *The Critical Works of Thomas Rymer*, ed. Zimansky (New Haven: Yale Univ. Press, 1956); and Edward N. Hooker, "Introduction" to *The Critical Works of John Dennis*, ed. Hooker (Baltimore: Johns Hopkins Press, 1939).

3. Dryden, Dennis, and Gildon, among the most prolific critics, have often been noted for their inconsistencies. All three were advocates of the rules at one time or another, but each one also upheld independence from these same rules for English drama (and Shakespeare in particular). Because of fluctuations in opinion such as these, I have avoided outlining a set model of each critic's theory.

4. John Dennis, "An Essay on the Genius and Writings of Shakespeare" (1712), in *Critical Works of John Dennis*, ed. Hooker, II, 17. All further references to Dennis's critical works will be taken from this edition.

5. I regretfully diverge from Brian Vickers on this point. Vickers finds the Restoration and early eighteenth-century critics far too harsh on Shakespeare and argues that this shows the limitations of their critical methods ("Introduction" to *Shakespeare: The Critical Heritage*, ed. Vickers, vols. 1 and 2).

6. Robert Gould, "The Play-House. A Satyr," in *Poems Chiefly of Satyre and Satyric Epistle* (1689), 177.

7. John Dryden, "Preface" to *All for Love* in *Of Dramatic Poetry and Other Critical Essays*, ed. George Watson (New York: Dutton, 1962), I, 224. All further references to Dryden's works will be taken either from this edition or from the as yet incomplete University of California edition *The Works of John Dryden*, vol. 17, ed. Samuel Holt Monk (Berkeley: Univ. of California Press, 1971).

8. Joseph Addison, *The Spectator*, no. 161 (3 September 1711).

9. Nicholas Rowe, "Some Account of the Life, &c. of Mr. William Shakespeare," prefixed to *The Works of Mr. William Shakespeare* (1709), I, vi. All further references will be to this edition.

10. Lewis Theobald, *The Censor*, No. 10 (2 May 1715).

11. Ibid.

12. "There are few of our English Plays (excepting only some few of Jonson's) without some faults or other; and if the French have fewer than our English, 'tis because they confine themselves to narrower limits, and consequently have less liberty to erre" (Richard Flecknoe, *A Short Discourse of the English Stage*, prefixed to *Love's Kingdom* [London, 1664]).

13. Anon., "A Defence of Dramatic Poetry: Being a Review of Mr. Collier's View of the Immorality and Profaness of the Stage" (1698) in *Shakespeare: The Critical Heritage*, ed. Vickers, II, 91.

14. Thomas Purney, "Preface" to *Pastorals* (1717). Purney stresses that despite their regularity the French are not superior to English writers. He identifies a genius special to the English, what he terms the "gloomy," which the French are incapable of producing.

15. Dennis, "The Usefulness of the Stage, to the Happiness of Mankind, to Government, and to Religion. Occasioned by a Late Book, Written by Jeremy Collier, M.A." (1698), and "The Stage Defended from Scripture, Reason, Experience, and the Common Sense of Mankind for Two Thousand Years. Occasioned by Mr. Law's Late Pamphlet Against Stage Entertainments" (1726).

16. Taylor, *Reinventing Shakespeare*, 134.

17. Zimansky, "Introduction" to *Critical Works of Thomas Rymer*, xxiii. All further references will be to this edition.

18. "Heads of an Answer to Rymer" (this title originally given by Edmond Malone in his 1800 edition of Dryden's prose works) was first printed without title in the preface to Jacob Tonson's 1711 edition of *The Works of Mr. Francis Beaumont, and Mr. John Fletcher* (I, xii–xxv). Though in the past, some scholars have cited "Grounds of Criticism in Tragedy" (1679) as Dryden's diluted revision of "Heads," Robert D. Hume effectively puts this theory to rest in chapter 4, "Rymer and Others," *Dryden's Criticism*.

19. See for example Addison's jibe that Rymer's play was so bad that it was being shredded for use as artificial snow: "Mr. *Rimer's Edgar* is to fall in Snow at the next acting of King *Lear*, in order to heighten, or rather to alleviate, the Distress of that unfortunate Prince; and to serve by way of Decoration to a Piece which that great Critick has written against" (*Spectator* No. 592, 10 September 1714).

20. Charles Gildon, "Some Reflections on Mr. Rymer's *Short View of Tragedy* and an attempt at a Vindication of Shakespear, in an Essay directed to John Dryden, Esq." in *Miscellaneous Letters and Essays, on Several Subjects* (1694), 110.

21. Ibid, 84.

22. Ibid., 106–7.

23. Shaftsbury discusses Shakespeare's language in some detail in volume I, part III of *Characteristics*, "Soliloquy, or Advice to an Author," (part II, section i), where he laments the "natural Rudeness" of Shakespeare's style, his "antiquated Phrase and Wit," and his "deficiency in almost all the Graces and Ornaments of this kind of Writing" (217). Shaftsbury's work is only one of the more illustrious works to express this idea—by the time he wrote, it was a convention which appeared almost any time Shakespeare's works were mentioned.

24. See "Defense of the Epilogue: Or an Essay on the Dramatic Poetry of the Last Age" (1673, second edition). "To begin with Language. That an alteration is lately made in ours, or since the writers of the last age (in which I comprehend Shakespeare, Fletcher and Jonson), is manifest," Watson, I, 170.

25. Dryden, "Preface" to *All for Love; or The World Well Lost*, Watson, I, 231. Many others shared this amazement (at least at times). Dennis comments that Shakespeare's expression "is in many Places good and pure after a hundred Years" ("Essay on the Genius and Writings of Shakespeare," Hooker, II, 4). Others took exception to Dryden's remarks on Shakespeare's rudeness, such as Gerald Langbaine, who in *An Account of the English Dramatick Poets* (1691) wrote that "I might easily prove that his [Dryden's] Improprieties in Grammer are equal to theirs [Shakespeare, Fletcher, Jonson]: and that He himself has been guilty of Solicicms in Speech, and Flaws in Sence, as well as *Shakespear, Fletcher* and *Johnson*," 150. For further discussion of Restoration theories of language, see Markley, *Two Edg'd Weapons*.

26. Gildon, "An Essay on the Art, Rise, and Progress of the Stage in Greece, Rome, and England," Prefixed to vol. 9 of *The Works Of Mr. William Shakespeare* (1714), xlviii.

27. Quoted by Allardyce Nicoll in *A History of English Drama, 1660–1900* (Cambridge: Cambridge Univ. Press, 1952), I, 173.

28. Dryden, "An Account of the Ensuing Poem, in a Letter to the Honorable Sir Robert Howard," Prefixed to *Annus Mirabilis* (1667), Watson, I, 97–98. Dryden uses the same image in another essay, the "Epistle Dedicatory" to *The Rival Ladies: A Tragi-Comedy* (1664): "For imagination in the poet is a faculty so wild and lawless that, like a high-ranging spaniel, it must have clogs tied to it, lest it out run the judgment" (Watson, I, 8).

29. Addison, *Spectator* no. 61 (10 May 1711).

30. Thomas Hobbes, *Leviathan*, ed. C.B. Macpherson (Harmondsworth: Penguin, rpt. 1985). Metaphor as deceit or obfuscation (the second abuse of words) counters Hobbes's second use of words: "to show to others that knowledge which we have attained."

31. John Locke, *An Essay Concerning Human Understanding*, ed. Peter H. Nidditch (Oxford: Oxford Univ. Press, 1979), 506. Locke's discussion of metaphor appears in Book 3, chapter 10, "Of the Abuse of Words."

32. "What a pudder is here kept in raising the expression of trifling thoughts! Would not a man have thought that the poet had been bound prentice to a wheelwright, for his first rant? and had followed a ragman for the clout and blanket, in the

second? ... Wise men would be glad to find a little sense couched under all these pompous words; for bombast is commonly the delight of that audience which loves poetry, but understands it not: and as commonly has been the practice of those writers who, not being able to infuse a natural passion into the mind, have made it their business to ply the ears and stun their judges by the noise" ("Grounds of Criticism in Tragedy," Watson, I, 258).

33. Addison, *Spectator* no. 39 (14 April 1711).

34. See *Poetics*, VI.14–19.

35. Edward Ravenscroft, "Preface" to *Titus Andronicus* (1679).

36. Dennis, "The Advancement and Reformation of Modern Poetry," Hooker, I, 200. Dennis makes even grander claims for poetic justice in his letter to the *Spectator*, "To the Spectator, upon his Paper on the 16th of April" (1712): "For what Tragedy can there be without Fable? or what Fable without a Moral? or what Moral without poetical Justice? What Moral, where the Good and the Bad are confounded by Destiny, and perish alike promiscuously. Thus we see this Doctrine of poetical Justice is more founded in Reason and Nature than all the rest of the poetical Rules together. For what can be more natural, and more highly reasonable, than to employ that Rule in Tragedy without which that Poem cannot exist?" (Hooker, II, 19–20).

37. Addison, *Spectator* no. 40 (16 April 1711).

38. Lewis Theobald, *The Censor*, No. 10 (2 May 1715).

39. In contrast, Dryden's adaptation of *Troilus and Cressida* not only recreates Cressida as unswervingly true to Troilus, but provides a noble death for each of the lovers.

40. Dennis's comments suggest his conservative political bias, seeing Brutus as a regicide rather than a protector of freedom. For a political reading of eighteenth-century productions of *Julius Caesar*, see Dobson, "Accents Yet Unknown."

41. For a fuller discussion of eighteenth-century editorial practices and their implications, see de Grazia, *Shakespeare Verbatim*; and Peter Seary, *Lewis Theobald and the Editing of Shakespeare* (Oxford: Clarendon, 1990). Also, Ronald B. McKerrow, "The Treatment of Shakespeare's Text by His Earlier Editors, 1709–1768," in *Studies in Shakespeare: British Academy Lectures*, directed and introduced by Peter Alexander (London: Oxford Univ. Press, 1964), 105; Stanley Wells and Gary Taylor, *William Shakespeare: A Textual Companion* (Oxford: Oxford Univ. Press, 1987).

42. Alexander Pope, "Mr Pope's Preface" in *The Plays of William Shakespeare*, ed. Samuel Johnson and George Steevens (Fourth Edition, 1793), I, 117.

43. Ibid., 124–25.

44. Ibid., 125.

45. Theobald, *Shakespeare Restored* (1726), viii.

46. For Theobald's theories on editing, see Seary, especially chapter 8, "Theobald's Edition: Establishment of the Text and Principles of Emendation," 131–70.

47. Theobald, "Mr. Theobald's Preface" in *Plays of Shakespeare*, ed. Johnson and Steevens (1793), I, 147–48.

48. Ibid., 153.

3. ADAPTATION IN DECLINE

1. Between the years 1740 and 1775, six major editions of Shakespeare's plays appeared: *The Works of Shakespeare*, ed. Thomas Hanmer (Oxford, 1744); *The Works of Shakespeare*, eds. Alexander Pope and William Warburton (1747); *The Plays of William Shakespeare*, ed. Samuel Johnson (1765); *Twenty of the Plays of Shakespeare*, ed. George Steevens (1766); *Mr William Shakespeare his Comedies, Histories, and Tragedies*, ed. Edward Capell; and *The Plays of William Shakespeare*, eds. Samuel Johnson and George Steevens. In addition, the first acting edition of Shakespeare was published by John Bell in 1774: *Bell's Edition of Shakespeare's Plays, as they are now performed at the Theatres Royal in London. Regulated from the Prompt Books of each House by Permission; with Notes Critical and Illustrative; by the Authors of the Dramatic Censor* [ed. Francis Gentleman].

2. Before 1719, only two new adaptations were staged, John Dennis's ill-fated Comical Gallant in 1702 (*The Merry Wives of Windsor*) and William Burnaby's *Love Betray'd; Or, the Agreable Disapointment* in 1703 (*Twelfth Night*). The years between 1717 and 1723 saw four new adaptations, part of a larger resurgence of Shakespearean drama. In 1719, Lewis Theobald wrote a moderately successful version of *Richard II* and Dennis produced another unsuccessful adaptation, this time a tragedy, *The Invader of His Country: Or, the Fatal Resentment* (*Coriolanus*). Four years later, Drury Lane staged four new adaptations of which only Aaron Hill's *Henry V* was ever revived: *Love in a Forest* (*As You Like It*), by Charles Johnson; *Humfrey, Duke of Gloster* (*Henry VI, pt. II*), Ambrose Philips; *An Historical Tragedy of the Civil Wars in the Reign of King Henry VI* (*Henry VI, pt. III*), Theophilus Cibber; and *Henry V*, Aaron Hill. See Michael Dobson, *The Making of the National Poet: Shakespeare, Adaptation and Authorship, 1660–1769* (Oxford: Clarendon Press, 1992), 94–98, 131–33. On Dennis's adaptation, see Wheeler, "Eighteenth-Century Adaptations," 438–49.

3. This is particularly true of Revd. James Miller's *The Universal Passion* (*As you Like It*, 1737) and George Lillo's *Marina* (*Pericles*, 1738), two adaptations that appeared in the late 1730s during an even more widespread revival of Shakespeare's plays. Both playwrights assure their audiences of the upliftingly moral nature of their plays. Miller stresses that "sacred Decency's his constant Aim" and that in his version of Shakespeare there appears "No sentence that can wound the chastest ear." Likewise, Lillo's "Prologue" claims that his adaptation of *Pericles* should incite "pleasures" which "as they charm the sense, improve the mind."

4. One obvious reason behind the high percentage of Shakespeare plays staged after 1737 is the restrictions placed on the theaters by the Licensing Act. Though the years leading up to the Licensing Act had produced large numbers of new plays, this surge of literary productivity was curtailed by the Act's provisions for censorship. In their search for material, theater managers turned to the ready stock of Shakespearean drama. See also L.W. Connoly's *The Censorship of English Drama, 1737–1824* (1976).

5. The epilogue to George Lillo's adaptation of *Pericles* (1738) lauds the Shakespeare Ladies Club:

> A sacred band, determin'd, wise, and good,
> They jointly rose to stop th'exotic flood,
> And strove to wake, by Shakespear's nervous lays,
> The manly genius of Eliza's days.

6. This trend began at Goodman's Fields, where Henry Gifford evaded the strictures of the Licensing Act by charging patrons for "concerts" and providing theatrical entertainment gratis. But performances of Shakespeare soon spread to both Drury Lane and Covent Garden.

7. Theophilus Cibber, *Two Dissertations on the Theatres* (1756), 34. See also Cibber's resentment when this "rule" was broken during the staging of Colley Cibber's *Papal Tyranny in the Reign of King John* (Theophilus Cibber, *A Serio-Comic Apology for Part of the Life of Mr. Theophilus Cibber, Comedian, Written by Himself* [1748], 89–92).

8. The best recent discussion of Garrick's relationship with Shakespeare is Dobson, *Making of the National Poet*, chapter 4 ("Embodying the Author") and chapter 5 ("Nationalizing the Corpus").

9. Only one such play, George Colman the Elder's version of *The Winter's Tale, The Sheep-Shearing* (1777), premiered after 1763.

10. Along with the thirteen plays that fall into these two groups (seven abbreviated versions and six revised adaptations), a few slightly altered plays appeared that remain essentially as Shakespeare wrote them but contain an occasional short new scene or scattered new lines. Two such plays are: Benjamin Victor's *Two Gentlemen of Verona* (1763), which adds approximately 150 new lines scattered throughout the play, and Thomas Hull's *The Twins*, a version of *The Comedy of Errors*. As first published, *The Twins* added only thirty new lines and was performed only once. It was revived and republished in 1793; the "New Edition" adding thirty more lines and making occasional verbal changes. Perhaps the most notorious of the later eighteenth-century adaptations is David Garrick's unpublished version of *Hamlet*, staged in 1772, late in his career. Retaining most of the first four acts, Garrick cuts almost all of the last act. The last act of Garrick's *Hamlet* was published for the first time by George Winchester Stone from a promptbook in the Folger Shakespeare Library in "Garrick's Long Lost Adaptation of *Hamlet*," *PMLA*, 49, no. 3 (1934): 890–921. Stone argues that Garrick's *Hamlet* is as much a restoration of Shakespeare as an adaptation. In such, the additions are brief as the playwright aims to accommodate Shakespeare to the stage rather than to bring about major changes, aside, of course, from the compressed ending. See also Jeffery Lawson Laurence Johnson, "Sweeping up Shakespeare's 'Rubbish': Garrick's Condensation of Acts IV and V of *Hamlet*," *Eighteenth-Century Life* 8, no. 3 (1983): 14–25.

11. Nahum Tate, "Dedication" to *King Lear*.

12. James Miller, "Prologue" to *The Universal Passion* (1737).

13. George Colman, "Advertisement" to *King Lear*, iv.

14. David Garrick, "Advertisement" to *Romeo and Juliet* (1750).

15. David Garrick, "Prologue" to *Florizel and Perdita, a Dramatic Pastoral* (London, 1758), ll. 54–55.

16. George Odell speculated that Kemble wrote this adaptation but does not discuss Kemble's connection with the play, *Shakespeare from Betterton to Irving* (New York: Charles Scribner's Sons, 1920), II, 66.

17. William Macready revived Shakespeare's *King Lear*, complete with Fool, on January 25, 1838. Edmund Kean restored the tragic ending in 1823, but omitted the Fool as well as retaining Tate's love scenes.

18. Operatic versions of Shakespeare have been staged since Purcell's *The Fairy Queen* (1692), but the nineteenth century produced an especially large number of such operas. The best known are Italian and French versions, such as Verdi's *Macbeth*, *Falstaff*, and *Otello* or Gounod's *Romeo et Juliette* (or even Ambroise Thomas's *Hamlet*, 1869). England produced its share, especially during the first decades of the nineteenth century: H. Bishop's *A Midsummer Night's Dream* (1816), *Comedy of Errors* (1819), *The Tempest* (1821), and *The Merry Wives of Windsor* (1824); M.W. Balfe's *Falstaff* (1838); C.V. Stanford's *Much Ado About Nothing* (1901). See Eric Walter White, *A Register of First Performances of English Operas and Semi-Operas from the 16th Century to 1980* (London: Society for Theatre Research, 1983); Gary Schmidgall, *Shakespeare and Opera* (Oxford: Oxford Univ. Press, 1990).

19. Although the authorship of *Pyramus and Thisbe* is uncertain, the play was advertised as a "Mock Opera, set to Musick by Mr. Lampe" and is usually attributed to Lampe. Lampe's playlet closely resembles the earliest of the abbreviated adaptations, Richard Leveridge's *Pyramus and Thisbe* which appeared briefly at Lincoln's Inn Fields in 1716 and 1717. Both plays focus exclusively on the mechanicals and the Pyramus and Thisbe play; in Lampe's version, the one act farce exists solely as a burlesque, without explanation or background.

20. On Garrick and Colman's treatment of *A Midsummer Night's Dream* see George Winchester Stone, Jr., "*A Midsummer Night's Dream* in the Hands of Garrick and Colman," *PMLA* 54 (June 1939): 467–82.

21. It begins with I.iii (the mechanical's first assembly) and continues through IV.i. The cuts, however, are substantial; the Pyramus and Thisbe play is never acted, and, in the end, Bottom (described as "the body") is dragged off the stage, still sleeping.

22. Set in eighteenth-century England and written in prose with an occasional Shakespearean line, the play portrays the adventures of Worthy, Heartwell, Manly, and Peg. The names as well as most of the lines are lifted directly from John Lacy's *Sauny the Scot* (1698). Although Worsdale states in his "Preface" that he has "abbreviated" Shakespeare, the title page announcement ("founded upon Shakespeare's *Taming of a Shrew*") is much more accurate.

23. On March 16, 1844, a revival of *The Taming of the Shrew* appeared, acted in the Elizabethan style, at the Haymarket. The production was popular, but it did not force *Catherine and Petruchio* off the stage.

24. The text for all of Garrick's adaptations was taken from *The Plays of David Garrick*, ed. Harry William Pedicord and Fredrick Louis Bergmann (Carbondale, Illinois: Southern Illinois Univ. Press, 1981), vols. 3 and 4 ("Garrick's Adaptations of Shakespeare").

25. Twenty years later, in 1777, George Colman produced another version of the last acts of *The Winter's Tale*. *The Sheep-Shearing*, a play in three acts, pared Shakespeare's romance even more than Garrick's *Florizel and Perdita*, completely removing the story of Hermione and focusing on Florizel, Perdita, and the antics of Autolycus, the Old Shepherd, and the Clown. Colman's additions follow Garrick closely, and he includes several new songs taken from *Florizel and Perdita* (advertised as having "Musick by the most eminent composers"). Colman's play was short-lived, however, and, according to *The London Stage*, appeared only three times, twice as a mainpiece, once as an afterpiece. See Harry William Pedicord, "George Colman's

Adaptation of Garrick's Promptbook for *Florizel and Perdita*," *Theatre Survey*, 22, no. 2 (1981): 185–90.

26. This combination, with its cast list featuring Garrick as Leontes, Mrs. Cibber as Perdita, Woodward as Petruchio, and Kitty Clive as Catherine, moved even a staunch anti-adaptationist like George Odell to envy: "Though, from a point of view of fidelity to the original text, it may seem heretical to say so, I confess I should like to have attended that double bill; I envy the Londoners of 1756, who enjoyed that unique privilege" (*Shakespeare from Betterton to Irving*, I, 360).

27. The corresponding lines in Shakespeare's *The Winter's Tale* read:
I lost a couple, that 'twixt heaven and earth
Might thus have stood, begetting wonder, as
You, gracious couple, do.

28. Thomas Davies, *Dramatic Miscellanies* (1784), II, 260.

29. See particularly Dr. John Gregory, *A Father's Legacy to His Daughters* (1774), and Rev. James Fordyce, *Sermons for Young Women* (1765). The "Preface" to Dr. Gregory's book assumes that Gregory's status as a father makes the book particularly appealing: "That the subsequent Letters were written by a tender father, in a declining state of health, for the instruction of his daughters, and not intended for the Public, is a circumstance which will recommend them to every one." Similar ideals of family can be found in most of the conduct books published during the eighteenth century. For an opposing point of view, see Mary Wollstonecraft, *Vindication of the Rights of Women* (1792), especially chapter 10, "Parental Affection," and chapter 11, "Duty to Parents." On the characteristics of sentimental drama see Frank H. Ellis, *Sentimental Comedy: Theory and Practice* (Cambridge: Cambridge Univ. Press, 1991).

30. The one exception to this rule is William Hawkins's short-lived adaptation of *Cymbeline* (1759). There are some similarities between Hawkins' version and D'Urfey's *The Injured Princess* (such as the characterization of Pisanio as a misogynist), but in general connections between the two plays are few. (See Dobson, *Making of the National Poet*, 205–7.) Performances of *Coriolanus* were, on the other hand, strongly influenced by James Thomson's play of the same name (1749), a play based on Shakespeare's story, although not an actual adaptation. In 1754, Thomas Sheridan combined the two plays, and as a result, most eighteenth-century productions of *Coriolanus* contained several scenes from Thomson's version.

31. In fact, the popularity of Cibber's *Romeo and Juliet*, and the revival of *Cymbeline* that followed it, resulted in the closing of the theater for violations of the Licensing Act. See Arthur H. Scouten, "The Increase of Popularity of Shakespeare's Plays in the Eighteenth Century: A *Caveat* for Interpreters of Stage History," *Shakespeare Quarterly* 7 (1956): 200.

32. Cibber also advertized his published play as "now Acted at the Theater-Royal, in *Drury Lane*" although it is unlikely that his version of *Romeo and Juliet* was revived after its 1744 appearance. The production to which Cibber refers was almost certainly of Garrick's version. The cast list includes characters such as Gregory, Sampson, and Peter whom Cibber cut from his adaptation, and it is highly unlikely that Garrick would agree to stage the work of a man whom he so strongly disliked. Cibber probably added the connection to Drury Lane in an attempt to increase sales of his play.

33. Theophilus Cibber, *Romeo and Juliet* (1748), 2. All further references to this text will be made parenthetically.

34. Cibber apparently used one of the Pope editions of Shakespeare. See, for example, Romeo's second speech in II.ii.27 where Cibber uses "night" rather than Theobald's emendation of "sight" and 1.31 "lazy-pacing" used by Pope and Theobald [taken from Quarto 1] rather than the Quarto 2–4 and Folio reading of "lazy-puffing." Otway keeps "lazy-puffing" but rewrites the rest of the passage:
> She speaks.
> Oh! speak agen, bright Angel: for thou art
> As glorious to the Night, as Sun at Noon
> To the admiring eyes of gazing Mortals,
> When he bestrides the lazy puffing Clouds,
> And sails upon the bosom of the Air.

Thomas Otway, *The Fall of Caius Marius*, in *The Works of Thomas Otway*, ed. J.C. Ghosh (Oxford: Clarendon, 1932), II.ii.261–66.

35. On Garrick's *Romeo and Juliet* see George C. Branam, "The Genesis of David Garrick's *Romeo and Juliet*," *Shakespeare Quarterly* 35, no. 2 (1984): 170–79; Nancy Copeland, "The Source of Garrick's *Romeo and Juliet* Text," *English Language Notes* 24, no. 4 (1987): 27–33.

36. David Garrick, "Advertisement," published with the second edition of *Romeo and Juliet* (1750). Garrick originally retained the references to Rosaline but removed them in the 1750 edition of the play and in all subsequent editions.

37. A German observer described the scene at Drury Lane as spectacular but too realistic: "The funeral dirges and the choirs made the whole ceremony too solemn for theatrical representation, especially on the English stage, which has no superior in the world, and on which everything is produced with the highest degree of truth." Count Frederick Kielmansegge, *Diary of a Journey to England, 1761–1762*, trans. Countess Kielmansegge (1902), 221–22.

38. Francis Gentleman, *The Dramatic Censor* (1770), I, 187.

39. After several nights of *Romeo and Juliet*, the *Daily Advertiser* printed this short expression of boredom:
> "Well, what's today," says angry Ned
> As up from bed he rouses.
> "Romeo again!" and shakes his head,
> "Ah, pox on both your houses."

Cited by William Cooke, *Memoirs of Charles Macklin* (London, 1804), 160.

40. Francis Gentleman, *The Dramatic Censor* (1770). Gentleman remembers these performances as the finest he had ever seen and admits that he saw both productions three times. He goes on to catalogue the strengths of each actor: "Mr. BARRY in the garden scene of the second act—Mr. GARRICK in the friar scene in the third—Mr. BARRY in the garden scene in the fourth—Mr. GARRICK in the first scene, description of the Apothecary, etc. fifth act—Mr. BARRY first part of the tomb scene, and Mr. GARRICK from where the poison operates to the end" (I, 189). Overall, Gentleman concludes, "Mr. GARRICK commanded most applause—Mr. BARRY most tears" (I, 190).

41. Quoted by John Doran in *Their Majesties' Servants: Annals of the English Stage, from Thomas Betterton to Edmund Kean* (London: William H. Allen and Co., 1864), I, 511.

42. Garrick's version, however, was rarely acted after Charlotte Cushman restored Shakespeare's text to the stage in 1845.

43. Samuel Johnson, "Notes" to *King Lear* in *The Works of William Shakespeare* (1765), in *Johnson on Shakespeare*, ed. Arthur Sherbo, vol. 7 and 8 of *The Yale Edition of the Works of Samuel Johnson* (New Haven: Yale Univ. Press, 1968), 704.

44. On Garrick's *King Lear* see Leigh Woods, "Garrick's King Lear and the English Malady," *Theatre Survey* 27, no. 1–2 (1986): 17–35; Leigh Woods, "Crowns of Straw on Little Men: Garrick's New Heroes," *Shakespeare Quarterly* 32, no. 1 (1981): 69–79; Harry William Pedicord, "Shakespeare, Tate, and Garrick: New Light on Alterations of *King Lear*," *Theatre Notebook* 36, no. 1 (1982): 14–21.

45. Two brief additions of less than ten lines in acts I and II and two scenes of Cordelia on the stormy heath in Act III.

46. Charles Beecher Hogan overlooks several of these restorations in his summary of Garrick's *Lear* (*Shakespeare in the Theater, 1701–1800* [Oxford, Clarendon, 1957], II, 334) as does Odell (*Shakespeare from Betterton to Irving*, I, 377–78). Garrick's role as restorer of Shakespeare has been debated. See Stone, "David Garrick's Significance," 183–97. Arthur John Harris opposes the view of Garrick as restorer in "Garrick, Colman, and King Lear: A Reconsideration," *Shakespeare Quarterly* 22, no. 1 (Winter 1971): 57–66.

47. Sympathy as a response to perceived emotion is the foundation for Adam Smith's *Theory of Moral Sentiments*: "As we have no immediate experience of what other men feel, we can form no idea of the manner in which they are affected, but by conceiving what we ourselves should feel in the like situation" (I.i.1). *The Theory of Moral Sentiments*, ed. D.D. Raphael and A.L. Macfie (Oxford: Oxford Univ. Press, 1976), 9.

48. George Colman the Elder, "Advertisement" to *The History of King Lear* (1768), iv.

49. Ibid., ii–iii.

50. Garrick also considered restoring the fool, but, like Colman, feared that the character would be too broadly comic. Thomas Davies relates: "It was once in contemplation with Mr. Garrick to restore the part of the fool . . . but the manager would not hazard so bold an attempt; he feared, with Mr. Colman, that the feelings of Lear would derive no advantage from the buffooneries of the parti-coloured jester." *Dramatic Miscellanies* (1784) II, 172.

51. These changes in nomenclature can be found in the 1768 edition of Colman's play. Later editions, i.e., his collected works, use "Edmund" throughout the play.

52. Fifteen years later Covent Garden staged a single performance of an adaptation by Thomas Hull. Although Hull's version was never published, the cast list implies that Hull based his adaptation largely on Shadwell. Hull's cast includes Shadwellian figures such as Melissa and Evandra.

53. Richard Cumberland, "Advertisement" to *Timon of Athens* (1771). All further references to the play will be taken from this edition.

54. Diane Elizabeth Dreher, *Domination and Defiance: Fathers and Daughters in Shakespeare* (Lexington: Univ. Press of Kentucky, 1986), 1.

55. In *A Serio-Comic Apology for Part of the Life of Mr. Theophilus Cibber* (1748, published with his version of *Romeo and Juliet*), 74.

56. In Cibber, *A Serio-Comic Apology*, 87.

57. See for example James Fordyce: "The world, I know not how, overlooks, in our sex, a thousand irregularities, which it never forgives in yours; so that the honour and peace of a family are, in this view, much more dependent on the conduct of daughters than of sons." *Sermons for Young Ladies* (1774), 15.

58. See Gerald Newman, *The Rise of English Nationalism: A Cultural History, 1740–1830* (New York: St. Martin's, 1987), especially chapter 6, "The Moral Elevation of the English National Identity." For a larger picture of the growth of English nationhood, see Linda Colley, *Britons: Forging the Nation, 1707–1837* (New Haven: Yale Univ. Press, 1992). As Newman notes, generosity and sincerity were traits that began to be associated with the British national character in the mid-eighteenth century. A generalized appeal to the values commonly associated with the British character appears as well in Cumberland's *Timon of Athens* where Cumberland projects onto ungrateful Athenians the degeneracy associated with the French, as opposed to the British, character:

> Alcibiades.   No, ye are Lords:
> A lazy, proud, unprofitable crew,
> The vermin, gender'd from the rank corruption
> Of a luxurious state.—No soldiers, say you?
> And wherefore are ye none? Have you not life,
> Friends, honour, freedom, country to defend? [15]

Without ever mentioning England, in Alcibiades's speech Cumberland draws upon traits associated with Britain—honour, freedom, defence of country—and opposes them to those traits commonly associated with foreigners, particularly the French, lazy, degenerate, luxurious. His final exclamation ("How is our fathers antient spirit fled") expresses the same yearning for a purer national past as that in the many prologues to plays performed during the Shakespeare revival when Shakespeare himself represented the "manly genius of Eliza's days" against "rank corruption of a luxurious state." In the case of a play such as Cumberland's *Timon*, we see the work (more or less) or England's great national poet espousing an implicit but recognizable statement of national identity.

59. Productions of *Lear* halted between 1811 and 1820 during the last period of George III's madness—the parallel between the mad kings was too strong. In 1820, during the adultery trial of Queen Caroline, performances of *Cymbeline* were interrupted by supporters of both the Queen and King who cheered and hissed lines they thought reflected on the ongoing trial. See Jonathan Bate, *Shakespearean Constitutions* (Oxford: Oxford Univ. Press, 1989), 87–88.

4. Criticism at Mid-Century

1. Murphy, *Grays-Inn Journal*, no. 41 (Saturday, July 28, 1753).

2. Paul Korshin observes that patronage in the eighteenth century became "relatively insignificant" because of the vast number of writers and the relatively small number of patrons. Its place was taken, in part, by subscription, which was to affect editors of Shakespeare more than critics ("Types of Eighteenth-Century Literary Patronage," *Eighteenth-Century Studies* 7 [1974]: 453–73). See also Deborah D. Rogers, "The Commercialization of Eighteenth-Century English Literature," *CLIO* 18, no. 2 (1989): 171–78; Eagleton, *Function of Criticism*, especially chapters 1 and 2.

3. See Habermas, *The Structural Transformation of the Public Sphere*. Habermas comments: "However exclusive the public might be in any given instance, it could never close itself off entirely and become consolidated as a clique; for it always understood and found itself immersed within a more inclusive public of all private people, persons who—insofar as they were propertied and educated—as readers, listeners, and spectators could avail themselves via the market of the objects that were subject to discussion. The issues discussed became 'general' not merely in the significance, but also in the accessibility: everyone had to *be able* to participate" (37).

4. Samuel Johnson, "Preface" to *The Works of William Shakespeare* (1765), in Sherbo, *Johnson on Shakespeare*, 61. All further references to Johnson's writings will be taken from this text.

5. In the "Preface" to *The Castle of Otranto*, Horace Walpole claims that "my rule was Nature" and boasts a historical precedent: "I had higher authority than my opinion for this conduct. That great master of nature, *Shakespeare*, was the model I copied." Horace Walpole, "Preface" to *The Castle of Otranto*, second edition (1765), viii-ix. Walpole makes these claims in reference to his depiction of the "domestics" in his novel, which, he says, he patterned on Shakespearean characters.

6. Thomas Seward, "Preface" to *The Works of Mr. Francis Beaumont, and Mr. John Fletcher* (1750), I, lviii.

7. See for example Richard Hurd's notes to Horace in *Q. Horatii Flacci Ars Poetica. Epistola ad Pisones. With an English Commentary and Notes* (1749). Also, Christopher Smart and Peter Whalley both re-examined the issue of Shakespeare's learning, Whalley in *An Enquiry into the Learning of Shakespeare with Remarks and Several Passages of his Plays. In a Conversation between Eugenius and Neander* (1748), and Smart in "A Brief Enquiry into the Learning of Shakespeare" in *The Universal Visitor and Monthly Memorialist* (Jan. 1756). Both critics assert that Shakespeare was much more learned than originally believed. Smart cites passages that he says echo classical works while Whalley asserts that Shakespeare must have known Danish (along with both Latin and Greek) in order to write *Hamlet*. He attributes the rumors of Shakespeare's "unlearned wit" to the degenerate taste of the age of Dryden (10–11).

8. John Upton, *Critical Observations on Shakespeare, The Second Edition, with Alterations and Additions* (1748), v.

9. William Dodd, "Preface" to *The Beauties of Shakespeare. Regularly Selected from each Play* (1752), xv.

10. William Guthrie, *An Essay upon English Tragedy. With Remarks upon the Abbe le Blanc's Observations on the English Stage* (1747), 17.

11. George Colman, *Adventurer*, no. 90 (15 September 1753).

12. Ibid.

13. N.S., "Remarks on the Tragedy of *The Orphan*," in *The Gentleman's Magazine* 18 (Dec. 1748): 552.

14. Guthrie, *Essay upon English Tragedy*, 10.

15. Arthur Murphy, *London Chronicle* (Oct. 12/14, 1758), 367.

16. See for example Richard Hurd's comments on the age of Dryden, which could almost be a gloss to such works as Spencer's *Shakespeare Improved* (1925): "There was a time, when the art of JONSON was set above the divinest raptures of SHAKESPEARE. The present age is well convinced of the mistake. And now the genius of SHAKESPEARE is idolized in its turn. Happily for public taste, it can

scarcely be too much" ("Notes on the Art of Poetry" in *Q. Horatii Flacci Ars Poetica. Epistola ad Pisones. With an English Commentary and Notes* [1749], 149).

17. Joseph Warton, *Adventurer*, no. 93 (25 September 1753), Anonymous, *An Examen of the Historical play of Edward the Black Prince* (1750). Warton states: "The time which the action takes up is only equal to that of the representation, an excellence which ought always to be aimed at in every well-conducted fable, and for the want of which a variety of the most entertaining incidents can scarcely atone." Nonetheless, Warton, who had praised *The Tempest*'s three hour time span, refuses to mention the unities in his comments on *The Tempest*, whereas the author of *An Examen*, who decried Shakespeare's irregularity, asserts that he prefers "the End to the Means" and would rather toss out the rules "than lose one start of Nature or exalted Sentiment" (7).

18. Alexander Gerard, *An Essay on Taste* (1759), 185–86.

19. "Those rules of old discovered, not devised, / Are Nature still, but Nature methodized" (Alexander Pope, *Essay on Criticism*, ll. 88–89).

20. Guthrie, *An Essay on English Tragedy*, 20.

21. Gerard, *Essay on Taste*, 155.

22. Peter Whalley, *An Enquiry into the Learning of Shakespeare*, 16–17.

23. Murphy, *Grays-Inn Journal*, no. 73 (Saturday, March 9, 1754). For more on this topic, see Bate, *Shakespearean Constitutions*.

24. Samuel Foote, *The Roman and English Comedy Consider'd and Compar'd* (1747), 20.

25. Edward Young, *Conjectures on Original Composition* (1759), 27–28.

26. For an account of the changing application of the term "genius" to Shakespeare see Jonathan Bate, "Shakespeare and Original Genius," in *Genius: The History of an Idea*, edited by Penelope Murry (Oxford: Basil Blackwell, 1989), 76–97. In an anonymous essay published originally in the *Literary Magazine, or Universal Review* 3 (January 1758), the author assesses the genius, judgment, learning, and versification of twenty-nine poets; on a scale of one to twenty (with a score of twenty "never yet attain'd to"), only Shakespeare achieved a score of nineteen in terms of genius, "those excellencies that no study or art can communicate."

27. Joseph Warton, *The Enthusiast: Or, the Lover of Nature* (1744), ll.130–31.

28. Lloyd, "Shakespeare: An Epistle to Mr. Garrick" (1760), ll.115–16, 127–30.

29. Ibid., ll. 33–34.

30. Foote, *Roman and English Comedy*, 21.

31. Murphy, *Grays-Inn Journal*, no. 41, "A Letter to Voltaire" (28 July, 1753); and no. 52 (24 August 1754). In a later edition (1786) of the *Grays-Inn Journal*, Murphy revised this paragraph to read: "To conclude: *Aristotle* tells us that fable is the soul of tragedy, and there can be no doubt but that the great critic is right. Tragedy represents the misfortunes of the great, and misfortune is the consequence of human action. *Shakespear*, with all his rudeness, was fully aware of the doctrine, and accordingly we find that no man better knew the art of bringing forward great and striking situations. He was not versed in *Aristotle*'s art of poetry, but he had what was better than art; a genius superior to all mankind." Murphy's revision is a vague reversal of his claim that plot is not the central feature in tragedy, but it defines plot

very generally as dependent on character. The praise of Shakespeare remains, although in slightly different form.

32. Bonnell Thornton, *Have at You All, or the Drury Lane Journal*, no. 6 (20 February 1752).

33. de Grazia, "Shakespeare in Quotation Marks," 57–71.

34. Guthrie, *Essay upon English Tragedy*, 19.

35. Henry Home, Lord Kames, *Elements of Criticism* (1762), II, 151.

36. On the implications of the cult of the author, see Foucault, "What is an Author?" 141–60.

37. In his discussion of genius, Guthrie finds Shakespeare "a greater authority than the antients," using as an example the legend that in order to "feel" the ghost in *Hamlet*, Shakespeare locked himself in Westminster Abbey overnight. In chapter 16, "Sentiments," Kames opposes Shakespeare's characters ("the legitimate offspring of passion") to those of Corneille who writes as a spectator rather than feeling the passions of his characters.

38. See for example Addison's occasional general references to the "Sublime in Writing," as in *Spectator* no. 592 (10 September 1714).

39. Rigorously theoretical analyses of the sublime were more likely to appear in discussions of Milton's poetry with its fantastic landscapes and epic figures than in those of Shakespeare's plays. Edmund Burke's *A Philosophical Enquiry Into the Origin of Our Ideas of the Sublime and the Beautiful* (1756) seems to have been the dominant influence in references to Shakespeare and the sublime.

40. Samuel Holt Monk remarks this change in reference to the sublime and traces it to David Hume's *Treatise on Human Nature* (1739). *The Sublime: A Study of Critical Theories in XVIII-Century England* (New York: Modern Language Association of America, 1935), chapter 4, "The Sublime in Transition." See also Thomas Weiskel, *The Romantic Sublime: Studies in the Structure and Psychology of Transcendence* (Baltimore: Johns Hopkins Univ. Press, 1976), 4–22; Neil Hertz, "The Notion of Blockage in the Literature of the Sublime," *The End of the Line: Essays on Psychoanalysis and the Sublime* (New York: Columbia Univ. Press, 1985), 40–60; Paul H. Fry, "The Possession of the Sublime," *Studies in Romanticism* 26 (Summer 1987): 187–207. On the nationalistic overtones of the sublime in eighteenth-century literary theory, see Michael Cohen, "The Imagery of Addison's *Cato* and the Whig Sublime," *CEA Critic* 38 (1976): 23–25; "The Whig Sublime and James Thompson," *English Language Notes* (September 1986): 27–35.

41. Richard Hurd, *Moral and Political Dialogues; with Letters on Chivalry and Romance* (1765), 265–66.

42. Upton, *Critical Observations*, 85.

43. Murphy, *Grays-Inn Journal*, no. 63 (29 December 1753).

44. Four scholars edited Shakespeare during this period: Theobald (1733), Hanmer (1744), Warburton (1747), and Johnson (1765).

45. For more on the relationship between editors and their critics, see de Grazia, *Shakespeare Verbatim*.

46. Thomas Edwards, *Canons of Criticism, and Glossary, being a Supplement to Mr. Warburton's Edition of Shakespear. Collected from The Notes in that Celebrated Work, and proper to be bound up with it*, 7th ed. (1765), 259.

47. Samuel Johnson, *Proposals For Printing, by Subscription, the Dramatick Works of William Shakespeare, Corrected and Illustrated by Samuel Johnson* (1756), in Sherbo, *Johnson on Shakespeare*, 56.

48. Thomas Seward, "Preface" to *The Works of Beaumont and Fletcher* (1750), lxxii.

49. Edwards, *Canons of Criticism*, 259.

50. Anonymous, "Shakespeare's Ghost," *The London Magazine*, no. 19 (June 1750).

51. Thady Fitzpatrick, *An Enquiry in the Real Merit of a Certain Popular Performer, in a Series of Letter, First published in the Craftsman or Grays-Inn Journal, with an Introduction to D——d G——K, Esq.* (1760), 20.

52. Peter Whalley, *An Enquiry in the Learning of Shakespeare*, 16.

53. George Steevens, *Critical Review*, no. 19 (March 1765), 255. Murphy makes a similar statement in the *Gray's-Inn Journal*, no. 9 (16 December 1752): "Thinking is so intimately connected with what is called stile."

54. "I cannot help being of the opinion that the plays of Shakespeare are less calculated for performance on a stage than those of almost any other dramatist whatever." Lamb admits that seeing Shakespeare performed is pleasurable, "but dearly do we pay all our life afterwards for this juvenile pleasure. When the novelty is past, we find to our cost that, instead of realizing an idea, we have only materialized and brought down a fine vision to the standard of flesh and blood. We have let go a dream, in quest of an unattainable substance" ("On the Tragedies of Shakspeare").

55. Joseph Warton, *Adventurer*, no. 97 (9 October 1753). Warton makes this remark after quoting four lines of *The Tempest* and finding in them a solid proof of Shakespeare's genius.

56. Upton, *Critical Observations*, lx.

57. Warton, *Adventurer*, no. 113 (4 December 1753).

58. Upton, *Critical Observations*, 137. John Holt makes a similar statement in his pamphlet on *The Tempest*: "In pursuing this Attempt *Shakespeare* alone shall be considered; and where any Ambiguity arises it shall be explained by the Poet himself" (Holt, *Remarks on the Tempest: Or an Attempt to Rescue Shakespeare from the Errors falsely charged on him by his several Editors*, second edition [1750]).

59. See, for example, John Upton's complaint: "The misfortune seems to be, that scarcely any one pays a regard to what Shakespeare *does* write, but they are always guessing at what he *should* write; nor in any other light is he look'd on, than as a poor mechanic; a fellow, 'tis true, of genius, who says, now and then, very good things, but very wild and uncultivated" (*Critical Observations*, 8).

60. Tobias Smollett complains of the "excess of figures" in Hamlet's "to be or not to be" soliloquy and of "extravagant hyperbole" in the Queen Mab speech, but elsewhere praises Shakespeare's figures (*The British Magazine*, III [April, May, June, and November 1762]).

61. Richard Hurd, "Notes" to *Q. Horatii*, etc. Hurd's comments on Shakespeare's language come as an explication of a line from the *Ars Poetica*: "Dixeris egregie, notum si callida verbum/ Reddiderit junctura novum." ("You will express yourself most happily if a skillful setting makes a familiar word new.")

62. Daniel Webb, *Remarks on the Beauties of Poetry* (1762), 77. Webb devotes much time to a discussion of imagery and figure which he claims impart a "high de-

gree of beauty" to poetry. He supports his views almost exclusively with quotations from Shakespeare: "It is by the frequency and degree of these beauties, principally, that an original Genius is distinguished. Metaphors are to him, what the Eagle was to Jupiter, or the Doves to Venus, symbols of his Divinity; the sure indications of Majesty and Beauty" (74).

63. Gerard, *Essay on Taste*, 26–27.

64. William Dodd, "Preface" to *The Beauties of Shakespeare* (1752), vi. Dodd adds: "the text of an author is a sacred thing; 'tis dangerous to meddle with it, nor should it ever be done, but in the most desperate cases" (vii).

65. Upton, *Critical Observations*, 7–8. Other critics use similar images: Seward, "Preface" to *The Works of Beaumont and Fletcher*, xv; and Smollett, *The Critical Review*, I (March 1756): 144.

66. Theophilus Cibber, *Two Dissertations on Theatrical Subjects* (1756), 36–37. The occasion for this flow of rhetoric was Garrick's adaptation of *The Winter's Tale*. Cibber seems to have conveniently forgotten his own adaptation of *Romeo and Juliet* staged eleven years earlier.

67. The argument over adaptation was not entirely one-sided, and a small but determined group of critics were eager to defend it. These writers focused on the need to weed out Shakespeare's overabundant "garden" left "choaked up with Weeds through the too great Richness of the Soil" (Eliza Haywood, *The Female Spectator*, Book 8, ii, 91 [1745]). Without exception, however, the "weeds" they want to uproot are verbal "errors," Shakespeare's "*Clinches, False Wit* and "low *Vein of Humour*" (Anonymous, *A Letter to Colley Cibber, Esq; on his Transformation of 'King John'*, 1745). By applying the "shears" without mercy and removing these blemishes, the playwrights can, in the eyes of these critics, make more "elegant Entertainments." The adaptations singled out for specific praise, however, such as Garrick's *Romeo and Juliet*, were rarely lauded for their lack of bombast or metaphor. William Kenrick praises Hawkins's *Cymbeline* for just the opposite quality: "the language and images of Shakespeare are throughout the whole admirably preserved." Indicative of adaptation's weakening position was the sudden need for critics and playwrights to defend it. Before 1710, when the majority of all adaptations were written, the propriety of adaptation was rarely questioned, and consequently not defended. By mid-century, however, this security had eroded.

68. Thomas Wilkes, *A General View of the Stage* (1759), 31.

69. Richardson, "Postscript" to *Clarissa Harlowe* (1748), VII, 428n.

70. Frances Brooke, *Old Maid*, no. 18 (13 March 1756).

71. Arthur Sherbo, *Samuel Johnson, Editor of Shakespeare, Illinois Studies in Language and Literature*, vol. 42 (Urbana: Univ. of Illinois Press, 1956), 60. Sherbo's work deals more with Johnson the editor than Johnson the critic and contains only a brief chapter on the "Preface." For a more in-depth study of Johnson's "Preface," particularly in relation to early nineteenth-century literary theory, see G.F. Parker, *Johnson's Shakespeare* (Oxford: Clarendon, 1989). Other works examining the "Preface" within the context of Johnson's literary criticism are: L. Damrosch, *Samuel Johnson and the Tragic Sense* (Princeton: Princeton Univ. Press, 1972), Jean Hagstrum, *Samuel Johnson's Literary Criticism* (Chicago: Univ. of Chicago Press, 1952), and R.D. Stock, *Samuel Johnson and Neoclassical Dramatic Theory* (Lincoln: Univ. of Nebraska Press, 1973). Edward Tomarken examines Johnson's response to specific Shakespearean

plays, *Samuel Johnson on Shakespeare: the Discipline of Criticism* (Athens: Univ. of Georgia Press, 1991). Peter Seary discusses Johnson's attitudes toward previous editors in "The Early Editors of Shakespeare and the Judgements of Johnson" in *Johnson After Two Hundred Years*, ed. Paul J. Korshin (Philadelphia: Univ. of Pennsylvania Press, 1986), 175–86.

72. Johnson explicitly rejects quotation as a means of examining Shakespeare: "his real power is not shewn in the splendour of particular passages, but by the progress of his fable, and the tenour of his dialogue; and he that tries to recommend him by select quotations, will succeed like the pedant in Hierocles, who, when he offered his house to sale, carried a brick in his pocket as a specimen" (*Johnson on Shakespeare*, 62).

73. In this his response is markedly different from that of Samuel Richardson who dismisses poetic justice and substitutes the vaguer, more flexible concept of "Christian justice," citing the Tate adaptation as an example of the perverse modern taste for poetic justice. In Richardson's eyes, the Shakespearean original provided moral enough without the intercession of Tate ("Postscript" to *Clarissa Harlowe*).

5. THE SEARCH FOR A GENUINE TEXT

1. Numerous works have examined Garrick's Shakespeare Jubilee. Two recent books which incorporate the Jubilee into a study of Shakespeare reception are Bate, *Shakespearean Constitutions*, and Dobson, *Making of the National Poet*. For a full-length account of the Jubilee see Christian Deeland, *The Great Shakespeare Jubilee* (New York: Viking, 1964).

2. The exceptions are few: Tate's *King Lear* (or revisions of Tate's version), Cibber's *Richard III*, the dirge and tomb scene from Garrick's *Romeo and Juliet*, and Garrick's *Catherine and Petruchio*.

3. The one exception is William Kenrick, who was determined to dislike every aspect of Johnson's "Preface." The major reviews of Johnson's edition were all written by notable critics: George Colman, *St. James's Chronicle* (Oct. 1765), 8–10, 10–12, 12–15; William Kenrick, *Monthly Review* 33 (Oct., Nov. 1765): 285–301, 374–89; and William Guthrie, *Critical Review* 20 (Nov., Dec. 1765): 321–32, 401–11, and 21 (Jan., Feb. 1766): 13–26, 81–88.

4. In *Johnson's Shakespeare*, Parker places Johnson's edition within the context of eighteenth- and especially early nineteenth-century discussions of Shakespeare. For a discussion of the response to Johnson's edition, see pp. 4–6 of Parker.

5. Guthrie, *Critical Review* 20 (Nov. 1765): 329.

6. Anonymous, *Annual Register*, 1765, pp. 312–13.

7. Johnson's remarks on Shakespeare's "labour" at tragedy are dismissed as untrue and unproved. See Kenrick, *Monthly Review* 33 (Oct. 1765): 294. Kenrick also complains that Johnson did not quote particular passages, another example of a change in critical style.

8. Ibid., 293.

9. Colman, *St. James Chronicle* (Oct. 1765).

10. Kenrick, *Monthly Review* (Oct. 1765): 293n.

11. Kenrick, *Monthly Review* (Oct. 1765): 295. For most reviewers Johnson's rebuttal of Rymer, Dennis, and Voltaire is seen as unnecessary; those once major fig-

ures have dwindled in significance until their attacks on Shakespeare can be ignored or laughed away.

12. Ibid., 291.

13. Guthrie, *Critical Review* (Oct. 1765): 324. Guthrie's statement is largely incorrect. As seen in earlier chapters, Shakespeare's plots were frequently praised during the Restoration and early eighteenth century.

14. Colman, *St. James Chronicle* (Oct. 1765). Although Colman argues that there is such an important distinction between "drawing nature" and "painting life," he never makes the distinction clear. Presumably, Shakespeare paints life rather than drawing nature.

15. Guthrie, *Critical Review* (Oct. 1765): 328.

16. Boswell notes that "Johnson was at first angry that Kenrick's attack should have the credit of an answer. But afterwards, considering the young man's intention, he kindly noticed him, and probably would have done more, had not the young man died." *Boswell's Life of Johnson*, ed. George Birkbeck Hill (Oxford: Clarendon, 1934), I, 498.

17. Guthrie, *Critical Review*, (Jan. 1766): 13.

18. See Edmond Malone's comments in the endnote to his edition of *Venus and Adonis*, in *The Plays and Poems of William Shakespeare* (London, 1790), x, 72–3.

19. Martin Sherlock, *A Fragment on Shakespeare. Extracted from Advice to a Young Poet* (1786), 14.

20. Johnson could only find grains of instruction in Shakespeare's works: "From his writings indeed a system of social duty may be selected, for he that thinks reasonably must think morally; but his precepts and axioms drop casually from him; he makes no just distribution of good or evil, nor is always careful to shew in the virtuous a disapprobation of the wicked; he carries his persons indifferently through right and wrong, and at the close dismisses them without further care, and leaves their examples to operate by chance" (*Johnson on Shakespeare*, 71).

21. Elizabeth Griffith, "Preface" to *The Morality of Shakespeare's Drama* (1775), xii.

22. Ibid., 524.

23. *Hic et Ubique*, *St. James Chronicle*, no. 1716 (February 18/20, 1772). This column attributed to Steevens by Charles H. Gray in *Theatrical Criticism in London to 1795* (New York: Columbia Univ. Press, 1931).

24. John Stedman, *Laelius and Hortensia, or, Thoughts on the Nature and Objects of Taste and Genius* (Edinburgh, 1782), 157.

25. Garrick's *Hamlet* in particular came in for hearty abuse, abuse which decorously (and rather uncourageously) waited for publication until Garrick's death in 1779. While a few critics praised Garrick for "restoring" passages of *Hamlet* which had long been cut from productions (see for example Frederick Pilon, *An Essay on the Character of Hamlet as performed by Mr. Henderson*, 21–22), most others attacked its changes, especially the disappearance of the grave-diggers.

26. David Erskine Baker, *Biographia Dramatica. A New Edition Carefully Corrected, Greatly Enlarged, and Continued from 1764–1782* [by Isaac Reed] (1782), I, 443. Baker writes of Tate's *King Lear*: "Yet whatever by this means he may gain with respect to poetic justice, he certainly loses to pathos, nor can I think this piece as it is now altered, is on the whole equal to what it was in the original form," II, 186.

27. See Brian Vickers, "The Emergence of Character Criticism, 1774–1800," *Shakespeare Survey* 34 (1981): 11–21.

28. An essay on the faults of Shakespeare was also added to this selection of essays.

29. Richardson, "On the Character of Hamlet," in *A Philosophical Analysis and Illustration of some of Shakespeare's remarkable Characters* (Edinburgh, 1774), 130–31.

30. Richardson, "On the Character of Imogen" in *A Philosophical Analysis of Shakespeare's Characters* (1774), 195.

31. Richardson, "On the Character of Melancholy Jaques," in *A Philosophical Analysis of Shakespeare's Characters* (1774), 177.

32. Richardson, "Additional Observations on Shakespeare's Dramatic Character of Hamlet" in *Essays on Shakespeare's Dramatic Characters* (1784), 158–59.

33. Richardson, "On the Character of Melancholy Jaques," 155, 156.

34. Richardson provides a similar extrapolation in his discussion of Richard III and Lady Anne. Groping for a way to explain Anne's shift from profound grief to acceptance of Richard's blandishments, Richardson provides Anne with mental characteristics not observable in Shakespeare's text. He argues that Anne possesses "a mind altogether frivolous; incapable of deep affection; guided by no steady principles or virtues . . . the prey of vanity, which is her ruling passion," thus creating a cognitive pattern not traceable in Shakespeare. "On the Dramatic Character of King Richard the Third" in *Essays on Shakespeare's Dramatic Characters* (1784), 18–19. Richardson's extravagances here foreshadow the criticism attacked by L.C. Knights in his famous essay *How Many Children had Lady Macbeth?*, (Cambridge: Minority Press, 1933).

35. Thomas Whately, *Remarks on Some of the Characters of Shakespeare* (1784), 2. All further references will be to this text.

36. Maurice Morgann, "An Essay on the Dramatic Character of Sir John Falstaff" in *Maurice Morgann: Shakespearian Criticism*, ed. Daniel A. Fineman (Oxford: Clarendon, 1972), 146–47. All further references will be to this text.

37. See Rose, "The Author as Proprietor"; Woodmansee, "Genius and the Copyright," 425–48.

38. Addison, *Spectator* no. 409 (19 June 1712). Hume and Shaftsbury made similar arguments. See Hume, "Of the Standard of Taste" in *Four Dissertations*, 1757, and Shaftsbury, *Characteristics*, Treatise III, "*Soliloquy* or Advice to An Author," 1711.

39. Alexander Gerard, *An Essay on Genius* (1774), 301. All further references will be made to this text.

40. Wolstenholme Parr, *The Story of the Moor of Venice. Translated from the Italian. With Two Essays on Shakespeare, and Preliminary Observations* (1795), 79.

41. Steevens, "Dramatic Strictures" a column in the *St. James Chronicle*, no. 1716 (18/20 February 1772).

42. Edward Burnaby Greene, *Critical Essays*, I. "Observations on the Sublime of Longinus. With Examples of Modern Writers, As of the Holy Scriptures, To illustrate the several Figures remarked throughout the Work" (1770), 65.

43. Edmond Malone, "Preface" to *The Plays and Poems of Shakespeare* (1790), I, part 1, xi. For a discussion of editors and their evaluation of Shakespeare, see de Grazia, *Shakespeare Verbatim*.

44. William Duff finds that such imagery ruins the emotional effect of tragedy: Images . . . ought never to be introduced in tragedy when the affections are wrought up to a high pitch or motion; for then they have a bad effect by contributing to break or at least to divert the tide of passion" ("Of Shakespeare" in *Critical Observations on the Writings of the Most Celebrated Original Geniuses in Poetry* [1770], 145–46). William Cooke admits that there are times when figurative language is appropriate, for example, in "light and frivolous scenes," but he disapproves of such language for any composition "which pretends to any degree of elevation." He cites as an example Queen Elizabeth's lament for her murdered children in *Richard III* (IV.iv.9–14) where the "imagery and figurative expression are discordant in the highest degree with the agony of a mother who is deprived of two hopeful sons by a brutal murder" (*The Elements of Dramatic Composition* [1775], 76). Known primarily for his scientific work, Joseph Priestley predictably uses a similar appeal to logic in his consideration of figurative language in Shakespeare, arguing that the value of metaphor lies in its appropriateness to the action (Priestley's example of improper figurative language is the death of King John, who, though in his death throes, puns and quibbles in a most "improbable" manner (*A Course of Lectures on Oratory and Criticism* [1777], 189).

45. Gerard frowns upon some passages as inappropriate to the mental state of the speaker, such as Helena's string of similes in *A Midsummer Night's Dream*:

        So we grew together
Like to a double cherry, seeming parted
But yet a union in partition,
Two lovely berries moulded on one stem;
So with two seeming bodies, but one heart,
Two of the first, like coats in heraldry,
Due but to one, and crowned with one crest. [III.ii.208–14]

46. Walter Whiter, *A Specimen of a Commentary on Shakespeare* (1794), ed. Alan Over and completed by Mary Bell (London: Methuen, 1964), 59. All further references will be to this text.

47. The poet makes these connections, Whiter continues, "because they have been by accident combined under the same sound; and because certain words by which they are expressed, are sometimes found to be coincident in sense."

48.   *Jaq.*   O that I were a fool!
              I am ambitious for a motley coat.
    Duke. Thou shalt have one.
    Jaq.   It is my only suit —
              Provided that you weed your better judgments
              Of all opinion that grows rank in them
              That I am wise. [II.vii.42–47]

49. Besides, they are our outward consciences
And preachers to us all, admonishing
That we should dress us fairly for our end.
Thus may we gather honey from the weed,
And make a moral of the devil himself.

50. Whiter's *Specimen* was reviewed in only four journals: *Gentleman's Magazine* 44, pt. 2 (Oct. 1794), 928–30; *Critical Review* 13 (Jan. 1795), 99–101; *British*

Critic, V (March 1795), 280–90; and *Monthly Review* 25 (Apr. 1798), 400–405. Of these reviews, only the *Monthly Review* mixed its censure with praise—and apologies for the lateness of the review. In the introduction to Over and Bell's excellent edition (see pages xl-lxxi), Bell argues convincingly that there is no evidence that later romantic critics such as Coleridge and Hazlitt ever read Whiter's work, despite the many parallels between his essay and the romantic critics' writings on Shakespeare.

51. For more on the Ireland forgeries see Samuel Schoenbaum, *Shakespeare's Lives* (Oxford: Clarendon, 1970). The forgeries were a popular topic in cartoons of the time, such as John Dixon, *The Oaken Chest or the Gold Mines of Ireland: A Farce* (1796), (reproduced in Schoenbaum and in Bate *Shakespearean Constitutions*).

CONCLUSION

1. "On the Tragedies of Shakespeare" (1811). Lamb spends much of his essay denigrating theatrical practices, in particular the use of Shakespeare adaptations on the stage. Speaking of Garrick, Lamb declares that no "true lover of [Shakespeare's excellencies would] have admitted into his matchless scenes such ribald trash as Tate and Cibber, and the rest of them, that 'With their darkness durst affront his light.' "

2. William Hazlitt, "On Shakespeare and Milton," from *Lectures on the English Poets* (1818).

3. Arnold's criticism, both literary and social, focuses extensively on specific words as representative of larger issues. In "The Function of Criticism at the Present Time" (*Essays in Criticism*, 1865), for example, he makes a fetish of the name "Wragg" seeing in that monosyllable the underlying "grossness" of English society.

4. In *The Family Shakespeare*, first published in 1818, the Reverend Bowdler explains his aim as: "it certainly is my wish, and it has been my study, to exclude from this publication whatever is unfit to be read aloud by a gentleman to a company of ladies" (x).

5. A case could be made for twentieth-century filmed versions of Shakespeare. While Kurosawa uses Shakespeare as the inspiration for films such as "Throne of Blood" (1957) and "Ran" (1985), other directors, notably Welles ("Chimes at Midnight," 1967) and Olivier ("Henry V," 1945, "Hamlet," 1948, and "Richard III," 1956), have made significant changes, usually cutting large sections of the text.

6. This reverence for all parts of Shakespeare's text indicates once again the gap between the scholar and the stage. Theater managers and directors even today have found it necessary to reduce the playing time of Shakespeare's longer plays (especially works such as *Hamlet* and *Troilus and Cressida*) in order to please audiences with short attention spans.

7. Johnson, "Preface to Shakespeare" in Sherbo, ed., *Johnson on Shakespeare*, VII, 62.

8. William Guthrie, *Critical Review* 20 (1765), 330.

9. Nahum Tate, "Dedication" to *The History of King Lear* (1681).

10. Johnson, "Preface," 84.

11. Richard Cumberland, "Advertisement" to *Timon of Athens* (1771).

12. Dryden, "Preface" to *Fables, Ancient and Modern* (1700), in Watson, II, 288.

Index

actresses, 162n 27; impact of, 13, 16, 30; impact on drama, 40
adaptation, 13, 77–78, 128, 150, 151, 181n 67; abbreviated plays, 79–86; attacks on, 120–22, 135; as bad taste, 7; and critical theory, 6, 67; definition of, 7–8; of female characters, 25, 30, 32–34, 85, 87, 90, 96, 98–99; of language, 16–24, 75, 77, 94, 101–2; of male characters, 83, 84, 90, 97; and nationalism, 29, 101; and politics, 40–46, 93; and sentimentality, 83, 84, 85–86, 87, 90, 91, 93, 95, 96, 98–99, 100
Addison, Joseph, 51, 63, 64, 66, 111, 142, 167n 19, 179n 38; attack on Tate's *King Lear*, 120, 121
Adventurer, 106
Allestree, Richard, 31, 33
ancients, 54, 59, 111, 179n 73
Annual Register, 129
Aristotle, 48, 64, 65, 112, 142, 178n 31
Arnold, Matthew, 151, 186n 3
Ashley-Cooper, Anthony. *See* Shaftsbury
association of ideas, 140, 144–48
author, concept of, 4–5, 113–14, 122–23, 147

Babcock, Richard Witbeck, 2, 157n 8
Bacon, Sir Francis 133; *The New Organon*, 20
Baker, David Erskine, 135, 183
Balfe, Michael William, 172n 18
Barry, Spranger, 91, 94, 174n 40
Barthes, Roland, 157n 5
Bate, Jonathan, 176n 59, 178n 23, 178n 26, 182n 1, 186n 51
Bate, W. Jackson, 53
Beaumont, Francis, and John Fletcher, 2, 13, 52, 56, 58, 105, 160n 1
beauties and faults, 49, 53, 69, 107, 108, 123, 129
Bell, John, 160n 24

Bell, Mary, 185n 50
Bell's Shakespeare, 7, 91–92, 170n 1
Bishop, Sir Henry, 172n 18
Bloom, Harold, 53
Boileau, Nicolas, 48
Boswell, James, 149, 183n 16
Bowdler, Thomas, 8, 151, 186n 4
Branam, George, 80, 158n 13, 166n 2, 174n 35
Brown, Laura, 30, 38, 163n 33, 164n 52, 164n 56
Burke, Edmund, 179n 39
Burnaby, William, 163n 31, 170n 2

Capell, Edward, 68, 144, 170n 1
Caroline, Queen, 102, 176n 59
censorship, 41, 45
character analysis, 112, 132, 135–40, 145
Charles I, King, 45
Charles II, King, 40, 41, 44, 45
Cibber, Colley, 1, 37, 48, 165n 69; adapts *King John* as *Papal Tyranny in the Reign of King John*, 45, 86, 166n 70, 171n 7; adapts *Richard III*, 1, 21, 22, 45, 75, 78, 86, 162n 16, 182n 2; use of quotation marks, 86
Cibber, Jennie, 101
Cibber, Susannah, 90, 173n 26
Cibber, Theophilus, 76, 121, 181n 66; rivalry with Garrick, 89, 121, 181n 66; as Romeo, 100; adapts *Romeo and Juliet*, 76, 86, 87, 88–89, 90, 100, 173n 31, 173n 32, 174n 34; *A Serio-Comic Apology for Part of the Life of Mr. Theophilus Cibber*, 100
Clark, Alice, 162n 30, 163n 32
Clive, Kitty, 173n 26
Cohen, Michael, 179n 40
Coleridge, Samuel Taylor, 162n 20, 185n 50
Colley, Linda, 176n 58
Colman, George, 106–7; comments on previous adaptations, 77, 158n 12; as manager

of Covent Garden, 92; response to Johnson, 130, 131, 132, 182n 3, 183n 14; adapts *King Lear*, 77, 86, 87, 92, 93–95, 175n 50, 175n 51; adapts *A Midsummer Night's Dream* as *A Fairy Tale*, 80; adapts *The Winter's Tale* as *The Sheep-Shearing*, 78, 171n 9, 172n 25
conduct literature, 30–32, 35, 38, 163n 40, 173n 29
Connoly, L.W., 170n 4
Cooke, William, 174n 39, 185n 44
Copeland, Nancy, 174n 35
copyright, 4, 5, 141
Corneille, Pierre, 179n 37
Craft, Catherine A., 158n 13
cross dressing: in adaptations, 30
Crowne, John: adapts *1 Henry VI*, 42; adapts *2 Henry VI* as *The Misery of Civil War*, 30, 42, 43
Cumberland, Richard, 154; adapts *Timon of Athens*, 77, 86, 95–98, 99, 176n 58
Cushman, Charlotte, 157n 3, 175n 42

Damrosch, Leopold, 181n 71
D'Avenant, Sir William, 17, 18, 23, 34, 79, 160n 1, 160n 3; adapts *Macbeth*, 17–18, 24, 25–26, 33, 160n 3; adapts *Measure for Measure* and *Much Ado About Nothing* as *The Law Against Lovers*, 34, 79; adapts *The Tempest* (with Dryden), 15, 34, 38, 160n 3;
de Grazia, Margreta, 160n 25, 162n 19, 169n 41, 179n 33, 184n 43
Davies, Thomas, 84, 175n 50
Deelman, Christian, 182n 1
Dennis, John, 48, 50, 53, 55–56, 58, 108, 166n 3, 169n 40; attack on Collier, 55; adapts *Coriolanus*, 34, 55, 170n 2; attack on Mr. Law, 55; adapts *The Merry Wives of Windsor*, 55, 170n 2; on poetic justice, 65–67, 123, 124, 169n 3; on rules, 53, 55, 166n 3; on Shakespeare, 50, 52, 53, 55, 65, 66, 112, 168n 25; Works: *The Comical Gallant*, 55, 170n 2; "The Decay and Defects of Dramatic Poetry," 55; "On the Genius and Writings of Shakespeare," 49–50, 52, 55; "The Impartial Critic," 59; *The Invader of His Country*, 34, 55, 170n 2
Dickens, Charles, 157n 4
Dixon, John, 186n 51
Dobson, Michael, 158n 13, 161n 8, 166n 70, 169n 40, 170n 2, 171n 8, 173n 30, 182n 1
Dodd, William, 106, 119–20, 124, 181n 64

Doran, John, 174n 41
Downes, John, 160n 3, 162n 28
Dreher, Diane Elizabeth, 98
Dryden, John, 2, 48, 53, 103, 104, 106, 123, 124, 142, 166n 3; assessment of *Antony and Cleopatra*, 67; and French, 50–51; on language, 2, 62–63, 64–65, 120, 154; letter to Dennis, 58; response to Rymer, 56–57, 58–59; on Shakespeare, 34, 52, 53, 58–59, 61, 62–63, 64–65; adapts *The Tempest* (with D'Avenant) 15, 34, 38; adapts *Troilus and Cressida*, 36–37, 39, 63, 164n 48, 165n 61, 165n 67, 169n 39; Works: *All For Love*, 8, 32–33, 78; "Preface" to *All for Love*, 61; "The Defense of the Epilogue," 61, 168n 24; "Epistle to Lord Radcliff," 58; *Essay of Dramatick Poesy*, 5, 49, 52, 160n 2; "Preface" to *Fables*, 2; "The Grounds of Criticism in Tragedy," 62–63, 168n 32; "Heads of an Answer to Rymer," 56–57; *The Tempest* (with D'Avenant), 15, 34, 38; *Troilus and Cressida, Or Truth Found Too Late*, 36–37, 39, 63, 164n 48, 164n 61, 165n 67, 169n 39;
Duff, William, 145, 185n 44
D'Urfey, Thomas, 107; adapts *Cymbeline* as *The Injured Princess: Or, the Fatal Wager*, 19, 28, 33, 35, 36, 39, 162n 21, 164n 61, 173n 30

Eagleton, Terry, 159n 17, 176n 2
Ellis, Frank H., 173n 29
English language: evolution of, 17, 61; development of, 116
Etherege, Sir George, 107
Examen of the Historical play of Edward the Black Prince, An, 178n 17
Exclusion Crisis, 40–41

family, 82–83, 85, 96; as focus of drama, 86, 88, 93, 98; ideology of, 82, 83, 85, 86, 96, 99, 100
Feather, John, 159n 20
figurative language, 14, 16, 18–19, 46, 62–64, 115, 118–19, 124–25, 128, 143–44, 145, 180n 60, 180n 62; metaphor, 63–64, 145, 147, 168n 30, 180n 62, 181n 67; omitted from plays, 16, 18–19, 46
Fitzpatrick, Thady, 117
Flecknoe, Richard, 54, 167n 12
Fletcher, John. *See* Beaumont, Francis
Foote, Samuel, 108–9

Index

Fordyce, James, 173n 29, 176n 57
Foucault, Michel, 4, 149, 157n 5, 179n 36
Freehafer, John, 160n 1
French: anti-French sentiment, 50–51, 54, 106, 107, 109, 176n 58; French influences, 47
Fry, Paul H., 179n 40

Garrick, David, 3, 75, 76–77, 87, 127, 152, 175n 46, 186n 1; as actor, 117; attacks on, 117, 121; adapts *Hamlet*, 171n 10, 183n 25; adapts *King Lear*, 77, 86, 91, 92, 94, 175n 44, 175n 45, 175n 50; as Lear, 93; as Leontes, 83–84, 173n 26; adapts *Midsummer Night's Dream*, 80, 99; as Romeo, 90–91, 174n 40; adapts *Romeo and Juliet*, 1, 77, 89–91, 173n 32, 174n 36, 174n 37, 175n 42, 181n 67, 182n 2; Shakespeare Jubilee, 3, 127, 182n 1; adapts *Taming of the Shrew*, 1, 77, 78, 80, 81–83, 100, 157n 3, 172n 23, 182n 2; adapts *The Tempest*, 87; adapts *The Winter's Tale*, 77, 83–86, 181n 66; adapts Wycherley's *The Country Wife*, 158n 9; Works: *Catharine and Petruchio*, 1, 77, 78, 80, 81–83, 100, 157n 3, 172n 23, 182n 2; *The Country Girl*, 158n 9; *The Fairies*, 80, 99; *Florizel and Perdita*, 77, 83–86, 181n 66; *King Lear*, 77, 86, 91, 92, 94, 175n 44, 175n 45, 175n 50; *Romeo and Juliet*, 1, 77, 89–91, 173n 32, 174n 36, 174n 37, 175n 42, 181n 67, 182n 2
Gentleman, Francis, 90, 133, 174n 40
George III, King, 102, 176n 59
George IV, King, 102
Gerard, Alexander: concept of innate taste, 141, 142; on poetic language, 119, 145, 185n 45; on rules, 108, 109; on Shakespeare, 144–45, 146
Gifford, Henry, 171n 6
Gildon, Charles, 62, 166n 3; adapts *Measure for Measure*, 48; attacks Rymer, 59–60
gothic, 115
Gould, Robert, 50, 52
Granville, George (Lord Lansdowne), 22–23, 24–25, 30, 35, 75
Greene, Edward Burnaby, 143, 145
Gregory, John: *A Father's Legacy to his Daughters*, 86, 173n 29
Griffith, Elizabeth, 133
Guthrie, William, 109, 113, 114, 125, 142, 179n 37, 183n 13; review of Johnson's "Preface," 129, 131–32, 182n 3, 183n 13

Habermas, Jurgen, 159n 17, 177n 3
Hagstrum, Jean, 181n 71
Halifax, George Savile, Marquis of: *The Lady's New-Years Gift*, 31, 36
Halliday, F.E., 159n 23
Hanmer, Sir Thomas, 68, 170n 1, 179n 44
Harris, Arthur John, 175n 46
Hawkes, Terence, 158n 10
Hawkins, William, 173n 30, 181n 67
Haywood, Eliza, 181n 67
Hazlitt, William, 150, 186n 2
Heath, Benjamin, 117
Henrietta Maria, Queen, 162n 29
Hertz, Neil, 179n 40
Hill, Aaron: adapts *Henry V*, 30, 37, 45, 161n 7, 162n 18, 164n 50, 164n 51, 170n 2
Hobbes, Thomas, 21, 63, 168n 30; *Leviathan*, 21, 63
Hogan, Charles Beecher, 175n 46
Holderness, Graham, 78
Holt, John, 180n 58
Home, Henry. *See* Kames
Hooker, Edward N., 166n 2
Horace, 48, 104, 133
Howard, James, 162n 28
Howard, Sir Robert, 48, 54, 103
Hull, Thomas, 171n 10, 175n 52
Hume, David, 179n 40, 184n 38
Hume, Robert D., 162n 30, 164n 54, 166n 2, 167n 18
Hurd, Sir Richard, 104, 115, 119, 124, 177n 7, 177n 16, 180n 61

Ireland, William Henry, 148

Jauss, Hans Robert, 2, 158n 10
Johnson, Charles, 163n 31, 170n 2
Johnson, Jeffrey Lawson Laurence, 171n 10
Johnson, Samuel, 104, 133, 139, 153, 154, 183n 16; *Dictionary*, 116; edition of Shakespeare, 68, 103, 122, 170n 1, 179n 44; "Preface" to *Shakespeare*, 54, 122–26, 128, 153, 154, 182n 72, 182n 73, 182n 7, 183n 20; reviews of edition, 127, 128–32; on Tate's *King Lear*, 91, 121
Jonson, Benjamin, 2, 52, 166n 72, 177n 16

Kames, Henry Home, Lord, 113–14, 120, 125, 142, 179n 37
Kean, Edmund, 171
Keats, John, 113, 150
Kemble, John Philip, 7, 171n 16

Kenrick, William, 130–31, 132, 181n 67, 182n 3, 182n 7
Kielmansegge, Count Frederick, 174n 37
Kilbourne, Frederick, 158n 13
King Leir, 162n 26
Korshin, Paul, 176n 2
Knight, G. Wilson, 162n 23
Kroll, Richard, 161n 10
Kurosawa, Akira, 186n 5

Ladies Dictionary, The, 34
Lamb, Charles, 118, 150, 180n 54, 186n 1
Lampe, Frederic, 80, 172n 19
Langbaine, Gerald, 168n 25
Lansdowne, Lord. *See* Granville
Leveridge, Richard, 172n 19
Licensing Act, 14, 45, 170n 4
Lillo, George, 170n 3, 170n 5
Lloyd, Robert, 111, 113
Locke, John, 140, 148; association of ideas, 140, 146; *Essay Concerning Human Understanding*, 21, 63; on language, 21, 63–64, 168n 31
Longinus, 114

Macready, William, 171n 17
Maguire, Nancy Klein, 161n 8, 162n 27, 165n 68
Malone, Edmond, 144, 149, 167n 18; edition of Shakespeare, 3, 8, 68
Markley, Robert, 161n 13, 168n 25
McClellan, Kenneth, 158n 14
McKerrow, Ronald B., 169n 41
metaphor. *See* figurative language
Miles, Rosalind, 166n 72
Miller, James, 170n 3
Monk, Samuel Holt, 179n 40
Morgan, MacNamara, 83
Morgann, Maurice, 138–41, 144, 145
Munns, Jessica, 165n 63
Murphy, Arthur, 103, 104, 107–8, 112, 116, 178n 31, 180n 53

national character, 49, 50–51, 109, 110, 176n 58
nationalism, 49–50, 54, 101, 110, 116; *See also* adaptation; Shakespeare
Newman, Gerald, 176n 58

Oates, Titus, 40, 42
Odell, George, 171n 16, 173n 26, 175n 46
Olivier, Sir Laurence, 1, 186n 5
Ong, Walter J., 159n 20
opera, 78, 80, 99, 151, 157n 2, 172n 18

Otway, Thomas, 88, 89, 91, 163n 42; adapts *Romeo and Juliet* as *The History and Fall of Caius Marius*, 42, 43, 86, 87, 89, 163n 42, 174n 34

Parker, G. F., 181n 71, 182n 4
Parr, Wolstenholme, 143
pathetic play, 30, 32, 33, 35, 38, 40; Tate's *Lear* as, 26
pathos, 30, 32, 35, 36, 37, 38, 98; and rape, 38–40; and sentimentality, 87, 96, 98
Pedicord, Harry William, 172n 25, 175n 44
periodicals, 103
Philips, Ambrose, 170n 2
Pilon, Frederick, 183n 25
poetic justice, 14, 15, 28, 29, 65, 66–67, 129, 130, 133, 134, 151; in dramatic practice, 14, 15, 28–29, 151; political ramifications of, 15, 29, 66–67; as theory, 65–67, 122, 123–24, 129–30, 133, 134
poetic language, 61, 62, 134
Pope, Alexander, 3, 104, 108, 170n 1, 178n 19; attacked by Theobald, 70; *Dunciad*, 70; edition of Shakespeare, 3, 68, 69, 105, 174n 34
Popish Plot, 15, 40, 42
Priestley, Joseph, 185n 44
print culture, 5–6, 75, 103, 118, 127, 159n 20
Pritchard, Hannah, 91
Purcell, Henry, 172n 18
Purney, Thomas, 55, 167n 14

Ralli, Augustus, 159n 23
Ravenscroft, Edward, 41, 42, 65
Reed, Isaac, 68
Richardson, Samuel, 122, 182n 73; attacks Tate's *Lear*, 122
Richardson, William, 135–36, 137, 141, 142, 145, 184n 28, 184n 34
Rivers, Isabel, 159n 20
Rogers, Deborah D., 159n 20, 176n 2
Rose, Mark, 159n 19, 184n 37
Rowe, Nicholas, 54, 68–69, 70, 106; edition of Shakespeare, 24, 68, 161n 9; "Some Account of the Life, &c. of Mr. William Shakespeare," 52, 111
rules of drama, 6, 48, 53–54, 57, 60, 67, 108–9, 112, 134; attacks on, 54–55, 108; and decorum, 56, 57, 61
ruling passion, 136; *See also* character analysis
Rymer, Thomas, 48, 53, 56–60, 61, 167n 19; *Edgar*, 56, 167n 19; response to,

Index

56–60; *A Short View of Tragedy*, 57–58, 162n 25; *The Tragedies of the Last Age Consider'd*, 56, 65

Savile, George. *See* Halifax, Marquis of
Schoenbaum, Samuel, 186n 51
Scouten, Arthur H., 164n 54, 173n 31
Seary, Peter, 169n 41, 169n 46, 182n 31
sentimental drama, 86, 95, 96, 98, 100, 173n 29; *See also* adaptation
Seward, Thomas, 104–5, 181n 65
Shadwell, Thomas, 48, 175n 52; adapts *The Tempest* (with D'Avenant and Dryden), 78, 87; adapts *Timon of Athens*, 27, 42, 43–44, 95, 96, 97, 98, 162n 24
Shaftsbury, Anthony Ashley-Cooper, Earl of: *Characteristics*, 61, 168n 23, 184n 38
Shakespeare, William: adaptation of, 1, 157n 1, 181n 67; as ancient, 104, 152; as Author, 101; canonization of, 2–3, 46, 150; characters, 112, 114, 135–41, 177n 5, 179n 37; daughters in, 98; editing of, 3, 68, 70, 71, 104, 116–17; as English Homer, 7, 52, 60, 104, 151; female characters, 32, 34, 85; language, 13, 16–24, 61, 62, 63, 64, 101, 115–16, 117, 118–20, 124–25, 143, 145, 154, 168n 23, 168n 25, 180n 61, 181n 67, 185n 44; and learning, 52, 110, 111, 177n 7; as magician, 134, 143; morality, 65, 66, 106, 115, 123, 132–34, 183n 20; as a national hero, 50, 51, 102, 103, 104; and nationalism, 49–50, 58, 60, 76, 101, 109, 110, 116; as poet of nature, 52, 123, 131–32, 183; revival of, 76, 170n 3; and the rules, 53–55, 108–9, 178n 17; and sincerity, 113–14, 179n 37; and the sublime, 114–15, 119–20; versus French, 51
Shakespeare, William (collected editions, chronologically): *Third Folio*, 24; *Fourth Folio*, 24; Rowe's edition, 24, 68; Pope's edition, 3, 68, 69, 70, 105, 170n 1; Theobald's edition 3, 68, 70, 71, 105; Hanmer's edition, 68, 170n 1; Warburton's edition, 68, 170n 1; Johnson's edition, 68, 128, 170n 1; Steevens's edition, 170n 1; Capell's edition, 68, 144, 170n 1; Bell's edition, 7, 91–92, 170n 1; Malone's edition 3, 8, 68, 144; Bowdler's edition, 8, 151, 186n 4
Shakespeare, William (individual plays): *Antony and Cleopatra*, 67, 78, 147; *As You Like It*, 30, 135, 136, 137, 163n 31, 185n 48, 185n 49, ——— adapted by Charles Johnson as *Love in a Forest*, 170n 2, ——— adapted by James Miller as *The Universal Passion*, 170n 3; *The Comedy of Errors*, 164n 53, ——— adapted by Thomas Hull as *The Twins*, 171n 10; *Coriolanus*, 66, 173n 30, ——— adapted by Nahum Tate as *The Ingratitude of a Common-Wealth*, 18–19, 28, 34, 39, 42, 160n 4, ——— adapted by John Dennis as *The Invader of His Country*, 55, 170n 2; *Cymbeline*, 102, 135, 136, 164n 57, ——— adapted by Thomas D'Urfey as *The Injured Princess; Or, the Fatal Wager*, 19, 28, 39, 162n 21, 164n 61, ——— adapted by William Hawkins, 173n 30, 181n 67; *Hamlet*, 21, 63, 64, 133, 134, 135–6, 143, 157n 1, 161n 14, 186n 5, 186n 6, ——— adapted by David Garrick, 171n 10, 183n 25; *1 Henry IV*, 21, 138–41, 157n 1; *2 Henry IV*, 138–41, 157n 1; *Henry V*, 37, 135, 164n 51, 186n 5, ——— adapted by Aaron Hill, 30, 37, 45, 161n 7, 162n18, 164n 50, 164n 51; *1 Henry VI*, adapted by John Crowne 42; *2 Henry VI*, adapted by John Crowne as *The Misery of Civil War*, 30, 42, 43, ——— adapted by Ambrose Philips as *Humfrey, Duke of Gloster*, 170n 2; *3 Henry VI* adapted by Theophilus Cibber as *An Historical Tragedy of the Civil Wars in the Reign of King Henry VI*, 170n 2; *Henry VIII*, 157n1, 160n 3; *Julius Caesar*, 66, 69, 157n 1; *King John*, 185n 44, ——— adapted by Colley Cibber as *Papal Tyranny in the Reign of King John*, 45, 86, 166n 70; *King Lear*, 35, 38, 66, 78, 91, 102, 121, 124, 135, 136, 149, 162n 20, 162n 21, 171n 17, 175n 50, 176n 59, ——— adapted by George Colman, 86, 87, 92–95, 158n 12, 175n 51 ——— adapted by David Garrick, 86, 91–95, 100, 175n 44, 175n 45 ——— adapted by Nahum Tate, 1, 20, 26, 28, 29, 35, 36, 37, 38, 39, 42, 78, 91–94, 120–2, 165n 68, 167n 19, 182n 73, 183n 26; *Macbeth*, 17, 63, 136, 138, ——— adapted by Sir William D'Avenant, 17–18, 24, 25–26, 33, 160n 3; *Measure for Measure* adapted by Sir William D'Avenant as *The Law Against Lovers*, 34, 79; *Merchant of Venice*, 23, ——— adapted by George Granville as *The Jew of Venice*, 22–23, 24, 25, 35; *The Merry Wives of Windsor*, 164n 53, ——— adapted by John Dennis as *The Comical Gallant*, 55, 170n 2; *A Mid-*

summer Night's Dream, 79, 164n 53, 185n 45,——adapted by David Garrick as *The Fairies*, 80, 99, 172n 21, ——adapted by George Colman as *A Fairy Tale*, 80, adapted by John Frederic Lampe as *Pyramus and Thisbe*, 80, 172n 19, ——adapted by Richard Leveridge as *Pyramus and Thisbe*, 172n 19; *Much Ado About Nothing*, 79, —— adapted by Sir William D'Avenant as *The Law Against Lovers*, 34; *Othello*, 57–58, 59–60, 61, 133, 143; *Pericles*, 164n 57, —— adapted by George Lillo as *Marina*, 170n 3; *Richard II*, 34, 44–45, 63, —— adapted by Lewis Theobald, 170n 2, —— adapted by Nahum Tate as *The Sicilian Usurper*, 45; *Richard III*, 135, 138, 157n 7, 184n 34, 185n 44, 186n 5, —— adapted by Colley Cibber, 1, 21, 22, 45, 78, 86, 162n 16, 165n 69, 182n 2; *Romeo and Juliet*, 87, 157n 3, 162n 28, 174n 39, —— adapted by Theophilus Cibber, 86, 87–91, 100, 173n 31, 174n 34, —— adapted by David Garrick, 1, 89–91, 174n 36, 174n 37, 175n 42, 181n 67, 182n 2, —— adapted by James Howard, 162n 28, —— adapted by Thomas Otway as *The History and Fall of Caius Marius*, 4, 43, 86, 87–90, 163n 42; *The Taming of the Shrew*, 80, 157n 3, 172n 22, 172n 23, —— adapted by David Garrick as *Catharine and Petruchio*, 1, 78, 81–82, 86, 100, 157n 3, 182n 2; *The Tempest*, 178n 17, 180n 55, 180n 58, —— adapted by D'Avenant and Dryden, 15, 34, 38, 160n 3, —— adapted by D'Avenant, Dryden, and Shadwell, 78, 87; *Timon of Athens*, 95, 135, 136, 162n 23, —— adapted by Richard Cumberland, 86, 95–99, 100, 176n 58, —— adapted by Thomas Hull, 175n 52, —— adapted by Thomas Shadwell as *Timon of Athens, The Man-Hater*, 27, 43–44, 95–98, 162n 24; *Titus Andronicus*, 164n 57, —— adapted by Edward Ravenscroft, 42, 65; *Troilus and Cressida*, 66, 186n 6, —— adapted by John Dryden as *Troilus and Cressida, Or, Truth Found Too Late*, 36, 37, 39, 63, 164n 61, 165n 67; *Twelfth Night*, 30, 163n 31, 164n 53, —— adapted by William Burnaby as *Love Betray'd; Or, the Agreable Disapointment*, 170n 2; *Two Gentlemen of Verona*, 171n 10; *The Winter's Tale*, 79, 83, 173n 26, —— adapted by David Garrick as *Florizel and Perdita*, 77, 83–86, —— adapted by MacNamara Morgan as *Florizel and Perdita*, 83, —— adapted by George Colman as *The Sheep-Shearing*, 172n 25

Shakespeare revival, 76, 176n 58
Shakespeare Ladies Club, 76, 170n 5
Shakespeare Jubilee, 3, 127, 182n 1
Sherbo, Arthur, 158n 11, 159n 23, 181n 71
Sherlock, Martin, 133
Sheridan, Richard Brinsley, 99
Sheridan, Thomas, 173n 30
sincerity, 113, 114
Smart, Christopher, 177n 7
Smith, Adam, 175n 47
Smith, William, 114
Smollett, Tobias, 103, 180n 60, 181n 65
Sorelius, Gunnar, 158n 9
Spectator, 103, 105
Spencer, Christopher, 158n 13, 162n 16, 165n 65
Spencer, Hazleton, 158n 13
Spencer, Jane, 38
Sprat, Thomas, 21, 29
Stanford, Charles Villiers, 172n 18
Staves, Susan, 164n 60
Stedman, John, 134
Steevens, George, 68, 117, 134, 145, 170n 1
Stock, R. D., 181n 71
Stone, George Winchester, Jr., 158n 13, 171n 10, 172n 20, 175n 46
Stone, Lawrence, 82, 163n 32
Stratford-upon-Avon, 3, 127
sublime, 111, 114, 115, 119, 120, 142–43, 179n 38, 179n 39, 179n 40

taste, 51, 141, 142
Tate, Nahum, 1, 18–19, 33, 48, 77, 124, 135, 154, 159n 22; adapts *Coriolanus* as *The Ingratitude of a Common-Wealth*, 18–19, 28, 34, 39, 41, 42, 160n 4; adapts *King Lear*, 1, 20, 26, 28–29, 35–36, 39, 42, 43, 67, 78, 91, 92, 93, 124, 135, 182n 73; adapts *Richard II*, 44–45; adapts *Richard II* as *The Sicilian Usurper*, 45; Tate's *King Lear*, attacks on, 120, 121, 122; Tate's *King Lear* praised, 37
Tatler, 103
Taylor, Gary, 160n 25, 169n 41
Theobald, Lewis, 3, 54, 66, 71, 179n 44; attacked by Pope, 70; edition of Shakespeare, 3, 68, 70, 105; adapts *Richard II*, 170n 2; *Shakespeare Restored*, 70, 105

Index

Thomson, James, 8, 173n 30
Thornton, Bonnell, 113
Tomarken, Edward, 181n 71
Tonson, Jacob, 24, 68, 167n 18

unities. *See* rules of drama
Upton, John, 105, 115, 120–21, 180n 59
Verdi, Guiseppe, 157n 2, 172n 18
Vertuous Wife is the Glory of her Husband, The, 31
Vickers, Brian, 159n 21, 166n 5, 184n 27
Victor, Benjamin, 171n 10

Wallace, John M., 158n 13
Walpole, Horace, 104, 177n 5
Warton, Joseph, 111, 178n 17, 180n 55
Warburton, William, 68, 170n 1, 179n 44
Watson, Nicola, 160n 25
Webb, Daniel, 119, 180n 62
Weiskel, Thomas, 179n 40
Welles, Orson, 186n 5

Wells, Stanley, 169n 41
Welsted, Leonard, 114
Whalley, Peter, 109, 177n 7
Whately, Thomas, 137–38, 139
Wheeler, David, 158n 13, 170n 2
White, Eric Walter, 172n 18
Whiter, Walter, 128; *A Specimen of Shakespeare Commentary*, 8, 146–48, 149, 150, 185n 47, 185n 50
Wikander, Matthew H., 158n 13, 161n 8, 163n 42, 165n 65
Williams, Raymond, 5, 161n 6
Wollstonecraft, Mary, 173n 29
Woodmansee, Martha, 159n 19, 184n 37
Woods, Leigh, 175n 44
Worsdale, James, 80, 172n 22
Wycherley, William, 107

Young, Edward, 110, 111

Zimansky, Curt A., 56, 166n 2

www.ingramcontent.com/pod-product-compliance
Lightning Source LLC
Chambersburg PA
CBHW032044150426
43194CB00006B/415